double
burden

YANICK ST. JEAN

JOE R. FEAGIN

double
burden

BLACK

WOMEN

AND

EVERYDAY

RACISM

M.E. Sharpe ARMONK, NEW YORK
LONDON, ENGLAND

Library of Congress Cataloging-in-Publication Data

St. Jean, Yanick, 1945
Double burden : Black women and everyday racism \ Yanick St. Jean and Joe R. Feagin
p. cm.
Includes bibliographical references and index.
ISBN 1–56324–944–8 (hardcover : alk. paper)
1. Afro-American women—Social conditions. 2. Race discrimination—United States.
3. Racism—United States. 4. United States—Race relations. I. Feagin, Joe R. II. Title.
E185.86.S695 1997
305.48'896073—dc21
97–16069
CIP

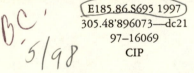

Printed in the United States of America

The paper used in this publication meets the minimum requirements of the
American National Standard for Information Sciences—
Permanence of Paper for Printed Library Materials,
ANSI Z 39.48-1984.

♾

BM (c)   10   9   8   7   6   5   4   3   2   1

To Zeta Sikes, and all the other unsung African American women who have striven heroically from 1619 to the present, including our respondents.

Contents

Preface

One of the famous books of the twentieth century, John F. Kennedy's *Profiles in Courage,* celebrates the heroic actions of five individuals.[1] All those celebrated are white men. In our book we celebrate those who are among the nation's most forgotten heroes: black women.

Why are these women heroes? What is it like to be a black woman in the United States? "It's tough! It's very tough!" says one of the African American women with whom we talked. Another woman finds it "very exciting. I find being a black woman today, in today's environment, just so invigorating, just so exciting. I mean it is tough, I think it is tough, but I don't know anybody who doesn't have it tough for any reasons whatsoever. We all have it tough. But, for me, that tough is just a part of being a human being. And certainly a part of the black woman's experience. That's what [we do] . . . ; we do tough!"

For an African American woman it takes great strength and courage to "do tough" in the face of discrimination and of misrepresentations, misconceptions, and distortions of black women at the hands of white Americans. These distorted views continue to prevail in U.S. society because those who write, tell, teach, and institutionalize them run most institutions. They predominate because they are part of the status quo, the white tradition. They have roots in the collective memory of white Americans, and they are embedded in many historical writings of prominent white Americans.

It takes courage for anyone to defy these whitewashed versions of history because they are so hoary and so set. It also takes courage for anyone to challenge the current expressions of that white memory—the discriminatory habits and distorting practices that reflect and help preserve the sincere fictions held by most whites about racial matters. These habits and practices are such a central part of the dominant culture in the United States, so important to its coherence, that their existence and effects on people go mostly unrecognized, particularly by those whom they benefit. Serious difficulties face anyone defying the white memory and the everyday racist habits and practices that help to perpetuate it.

It takes even more courage for black women to challenge the white memory and associated practices because they have been misrepresented for so long, made invisible as real human beings, and misportrayed in the writings of most white commentators and scholars. Invisibility and misrepresentation mean that black women's own narratives, such as are presented in this book, offer rich illustrations and interpretations of black women's lives. They offer a different view, a black woman's view—whether the narratives be slave or contemporary. Many whites may dismiss these accounts as lacking in credibility because they tell a different story from what whites believe.

Yet, despite being aware of white doubts about their foremothers' brutalized experience of slavery and segregation, and despite the possibility that their accounts of contemporary racist experiences may also be suppressed or discredited, and despite the dangers presented by their daily acts of resistance to racism, the African American women in this book speak candidly about, and often challenge openly, the racist circumstances facing African Americans. As we will see, they rely heavily for strength on the "foremothers," on mothers and grandmothers, as well as on fathers, siblings, and other members of their extended families. They seek and receive much support from kin in order to fight racism in their everyday lives.

While their responses often seem individualized, targeting racist actions one at a time, they have deep collective roots. Black women's responses to racism and other social barriers are generally abstracted from a pool of extended family and community recollections and examples--the collective memory and knowledge that is ever present. This collective memory and knowledge is part of the "social mind" each African American carries. It is used to compare each racist action that they and their loved ones encounter with past accounts and responses. The reference memory becomes sharper and larger every time a new experience with racism forces recording and the inclusion of a new interpretation in the collective memory. Black women and men often relate a particular experience to that of another member of their family, of fictive kin, of a friend, or of black Americans historically, with racism in the United States.

The reader should remember that the experiences presented in this book are authentic and are lived by actual people every day of their lives. In this book we meet real women and men who are not only survivors but also distinguished achievers. They are successful in spite of the hard experiences they have had. This success may well be because they challenge the general culture using the accumulated collective knowledge of generations of African Americans. They challenge constantly the racist context in order to maintain their families and to achieve their sense of identity and self-esteem. This takes great courage, indeed.

Acknowledgments

We would like to thank Michelle Dunlap, Beverlyn Allen, Eileen O'Brien, Karyn McKinney, Terry Mills, Dan Duarte, Debra Van Ausdale, Anita Haynes, Louise Allen, Juanita Fain, and Melvin Sikes for their comments and suggestions on various versions of the chapters for this manuscript. We would like to thank Tiffany Hogan for letting us quote from her unpublished manuscript on black and white women.

We would like to give special thanks to the many women and men who have provided the time for the interviews that made this study possible. They are our heroes as well.

double
burden

Chapter 1

The Lives of Black Women: Introduction and Overview

Few white Americans are in tune with what African American women have faced in North America. In this book we seek to have readers seriously consider how black women live, dream, suffer, succeed, and prosper in a still racist United States. Examining a large number of individual and focus-group interviews with African American women and men, most of whom are middle class, we explore their experiences in creating lives and communities in environments of continuing racial hostility and discrimination. We examine the impact of this persisting racism on African American individuals, families, and communities.

In these interviews we observe not only the racial trials and tribulations of African Americans but also their hopes, dreams, aspirations, successes, and achievements. Drawing on strong collective traditions and memories, most work hard to build and maintain their immediate families, extended kin networks, local organizations, and communities. In this book we examine black women's daily experiences using an intensive bottom-up approach. We give the participants the space to voice their own explanations of events and issues in the context of describing their own daily lives.

In the chapters that follow we examine how African American women are physically, morally, and spiritually stigmatized by a dominant culture determined to preserve for white men and women most that is of great value: the affluent life, the "highest" morals, the "beautiful" people, the power and privilege. Our analysis exposes the seamy side of a whitewashed society that labels black women as deviants and misfits. We show how the stigmatization of black women has many ramifications, including individual and family costs. We illustrate what the patterns of discrimination are for African Americans seeking to achieve the American dream.

In addition, we show how they view the larger issues around being black in a white society and how they and their families fight and contend with the constant acid rain of racism that pervades their daily lives. We do not concentrate only on problems and barriers, for we show how black Americans fight back, how they contend and cope with racial obstacles put in their path by white Americans, and how they create psyches, families, and communities that are home, places of meaning and memory that give one a respite from the presence and machinations of white Americans. We show how imposed situations of discrimination shape mightily a group's heritage and create the need for an oppositional culture, for an effective means of survival, resistance, and community creation.

One pioneering researcher, Philomena Essed, interviewed black women in Holland and the United States and noted that these women's accounts of racial discrimination (including "gendered racism") entailed distinctive systems of knowledge that are critical for fighting against and coping with racism in their daily rounds.[1] In their commentaries our respondents demonstrate a major store of knowledge about U.S. society, one rarely drawn on or recognized by the surrounding white society. In the chapters that follow the black reader will see much that is familiar and reinforcing. There may be few surprises. In contrast, the nonblack reader is offered a window into a brave and new world, a world with different and perplexing experiences, deep racial interpretations, profound understandings, and much creative genius.

In this chapter we provide an introduction to issues covered in detail in later chapters. We assess the character of harsh representations of black women, then examine briefly the character of the racial-sexual harassment and discrimination faced every day by black women. After taking into account the consequences of this racism for black children and families, we look at racism in the workplace and its impact. After noting the character of female beauty in this white-dominated society, we assess briefly the role of collective memories and legacies in the ways that African American women contend with the racial oppression that intrudes on their lives.

4

Harsh Representations of Black Women

Social Science Literature

As a group middle-class black women are well educated. They are likely to be engaged in a white-collar occupation. They are attorneys, physicians, dentists, journalists, corporate executives, college professors, private and public administrators, engineers, lawyers and judges, architects, business owners, school counselors, executive secretaries, social workers, and computer and other scientists.[2] They are likely to be wives and mothers, and they are probably active in church and community groups. In sum, they are achievers and are role models and reference figures for others, including young people.

Surprisingly, in-depth social scientific studies dealing centrally and thoroughly with the voices and experiences of these heroic women are still relatively few. Most assessments seem to be relatively short analyses placed in journal articles or in edited anthologies, or they take the form of personal memoirs or general essays. Some field research studies of black women focus on the poor or those dealing with the social welfare system. Rare are contemporary studies of middle-class African American women, those whose persisting experiences with discrimination, despite their educational and occupational achievements, provide strong evidence of the central play of discrimination in the lives of contemporary African Americans. A few studies are exploratory and helpful but offer only a beginning to understanding the lives of African American women. For example, Essed's pioneering analysis in the early 1980s involved a comparison of the lives of fourteen Surinamese Dutch women and eleven African American women; she examined some of their experiences with racism.[3] A mid-1980s study of five black women by sociologist Kesho Yvonne Scott explored in interesting detail some of their important "habits of surviving."[4] Given this relative neglect in social science scholarship, it is not surprising that contemporary black women are often misrepresented, mischaracterized, and misrecognized in public and private discourse. Indeed, they are burdened with a negative reputation shaped in part by social science publications since at least the early nineteenth century. The negative characterization of black women as domineering matriarchs or exotic sexual objects was created, and is still perpetuated, by white (usually white male) social scientists, and even by a few black male social scientists trained by them. These include John Dollard, E. Franklin Frazier, Daniel P. Moynihan, and Charles Murray, to mention only a few. In his still controversial 1950s book, *Black Bourgeoisie,* sociologist E. Franklin Frazier asserted:

> In the South the middle-class Negro male is not only prevented from playing a masculine role, but generally he must let Negro women assume leadership in any show of militancy. This reacts upon his status in the home where the tradition of female dominance, which is widely established among Negroes, has tended to assign a subordinate role to the male. In fact, in middle-class families, especially if the husband has risen in social status through his own efforts and married a member of an "old" family or a "society" woman, the husband is likely to play a pitiful role. . . . Yet the conservative and conventional middle-class husband presents a pathetic picture. He often sits at home alone, impotent physically and socially, and complains that his wife has gone crazy about poker and "society" and constantly demands money for gambling and expenditures which he can not afford.[5]

Frazier, an African American, continues in this negative vein, attributing the black woman's obsession with gambling to poor character and fascination with matters of the flesh.[6]

Citing Frazier's work, the prominent white social scientist (and U.S. senator) Daniel Patrick Moynihan has periodically pointed to the black woman as key player in a "tangle of pathology" in the black community. This is an excerpt from his famous report *The Negro Family:* "In essence, the Negro community has been forced into a matriarchal structure which, because it is so out of line with the rest of the American society, seriously retards the progress of the group as a whole, and imposes a crushing burden on the Negro male, and, in consequence, on a great many Negro women as well."[7] This long tradition of scholarship is in effect a strong assault on the character and lives of black women and men. In discussing African American families, then or more recently in the 1990s, Moynihan makes little mention of the reality of racial discrimination. From his and similar analyses African American families have mostly themselves to blame for their circumstances. There is no in-depth analysis of the impact of nearly four hundred years of white oppression—including persisting and large-scale discrimination—on African Americans and their families. By white racism we mean the socially organized set of attitudes, ideas, and practices that deny African Americans (and other people of color) many of the opportunities, freedoms, and rewards that U.S. society has to offer white Americans.

Recently, a lecture by a white male scholar at a historically white university revealed how the academic tradition of negativism in regard to the character of black Americans in general, and black women in particular, still prevails, though often in subtle ways evident only to a careful observer. This lecturer was critical of Richard Herrnstein and Charles Murray's *The Bell Curve* and of the so-called IQ tests used to label African Americans and other people of color as unintelligent. However, this lecturer apparently had difficulty coming up with an example of African American intelligence. The lecturer cited only the example of Josephine Baker, a light-skinned African American woman, whom he praised for her brilliant use of an alternative intelligence as manifested in her creative and provocative dancing. The lecturer emphasized that Baker had once saluted hanging portraits of white men, one by one, using a lower-body movement, and he demonstrated Baker's style by thrusting his lower body forward to give the audience the flavor of Baker's "genius." In this example a black woman's intelligence was linked to her sexuality. The image of blackness as sexual and primitive was, doubtless unintentionally, probably reinforced in the minds of the mostly white audience.

Grotesque White Stereotypes: "Jezebel" and "Sapphire"

In both the scholarly literature and in public and media discussion, images of hypersexuality and overbearingness often merge to symbolize the black woman. Sociologist Patricia Hill Collins, in her pioneering book *Black Feminist Thought,* delineated the historical images of African American women. One common portrayal is that of the domineering matriarch ("Sapphire"), an emasculator who is strong, unfeminine, and rebellious. In this distorted imagery the matriarch is disliked by black men who refuse or hesitate to marry her. But when chance is such that she weds, she rules so rigorously that her husband finally moves out. He condemns her to a life alone and, where there are children, transforms her into a displaced and destitute single head of household. Another common portrayal is the hot, exotic, and insatiable sexual player ("Jezebel") who is especially attracted to white men.[8]

These are very old images. Kim Marie Vaz has shown how these negative stereotypes had first developed in Spain by the sixteenth century and were exported to the Americas by seafarers and colonists.[9] In *The Myth of Aunt Jemima,* Diane Roberts notes how blackness has long been "loaded with sexuality." In the 1700s and 1800s African women and men were depicted by Europeans, in books and on maps, as naked and with exaggerated sexual organs. "The white world drew the black woman's body as excessive and flagrantly sexual, quite different from the emerging ideology of purity and modesty which defined the white woman's body," says Roberts.[10] Moreover, several scholars have recently tracked these negative myths in U.S. literature and mass media. Elizabeth Freydberg has shown how in the twentieth century the immoral-sexual (Jezebel) and dominant-matriarch (Sapphire) stereotypes of African American women moved from white-authored novels and other literature to many films.[11] Mary Young has made the point that these stereotypes of black women are recycled and revamped periodically by the mass media, as in the recurring portraits of black female Sapphires on television.[12]

Recent movies continue this tradition. In a review of a film about black women, *Waiting to Exhale,* the humanities scholar bell hooks has noted that the film is "so simplistic and denigrating to black women that we should be outraged to be told that it is 'for us.' "[13] In the film several black women are viewed as friends linked in an important network, yet they are mostly portrayed as centered in their sexuality or in female dominance. All but one of the black men in the movie is negatively portrayed. This film was produced by a white studio and based on a novel by Terry McMillan, a black female author. The white producers did not choose from novels by black writers that are more accurate and complex in their presentations of black women. It seems likely that this studio would *not* have made a similar movie centered principally on harsh and narrow stereotypes of white women.

Though on the surface somewhat inconsistent, the Jezebel and Sapphire images of black women frequently coexist in the same white minds. In some white accounts, allegedly ignored by black men and desperate for male satisfaction, the black female turns to white men

8

for companionship denied to her by black men. Some whites assume that associating with white men enhances a black woman's racial-gender position, because socially devalued black-woman attributes are counterbalanced or positively reduced by the addition of the more valued white-man attributes.

An example of this Jezebel image can be seen in the comment of one male writer about the inclusion of African American women in a men's magazine: "So, Black women have been elevated from the status of whore to 'Playmate.' Now white boys can put them in *Playboy* without damaging the magazine's respectability too much."[14] Jezebel was attractive but "voluptuary, with all the tawdry arts of a wanton woman."[15] In early Christian writings she is described as overbearing, with a powerful character, a plotter, lascivious wife, and lover of personal adornment. Sinful, amoral, proud, and unashamed—in sum, a detested woman, she was thrown out of a window and devoured by dogs. Hers was a harsh but merited punishment.[16] One can see how, particularly in a society whose white leaders often claim it is Christian, the representing of black women as Jezebels affects popular racial-gender thinking in ways that can justify very harsh treatment.

At other times, the black woman is represented as Sapphira (Sapphire), a Hebrew name meaning jewel.[17] In European and Euro-American thinking the cultural devaluation of a black woman's beauty as "ugly," usually accompanied by glorification of a white woman's beauty, appears inconsistent with this ancient name of Sapphira. Nonetheless, scrutiny of the modern whitewashed image of a black Sapphire as a matriarchal, domineering character suggests the dominant group's racist thinking. Though she may or may not be physically attractive, the black Sapphire, like the black Jezebel, is for whites a distinctive "sinner." Rather than exotic beauty, however, it is Sapphire's matriarchal dominance that is the white concern.[18]

Sapphire and Jezebel, stereotypes commonly associated with black women, trigger for many whites images of immorality, divine outrage, and earned punishment. Especially with their biblical names, these anti-black-female symbols are powerful, for they depict African American women as violators of things moral in a society of morally upright whites. Their representations suggest it is the women's own behavior that inspires dominant perceptions and actions toward them. For this reason, these negative representations are useful for the white definers. Sapphire and Jezebel provide the definers with a justification for unfavorable treatment of black women. Association with "sin" contributes to black female inferiorization, and this in turn supports restrictive mechanisms limiting African American mobility in many white institutions. Racial-gender stereotypes defend discriminatory practices. Black women are undeserving pariahs and offenders before whites and even the Almighty. Moreover, strong images can have consequences. In a recent article, Dr. Carolyn West, a mental health professional, has examined some of the noxious clinical effects of these images on black women, including such reactions as overeating and overworking to prove themselves to a white society.[19]

Fictions Created by Whites

The domineering matriarch and exotic sexual player images are productions of the dominant group's fertile imagination. These biting notions are old but lasting—brilliant masterpieces of racism that capture only the top-down viewpoint on the racial-gender reality. Other versions of that reality are silenced or ignored, with little or nothing said about the black woman's own point of view. Judging from historical and mass media evidence, as well as opinion polls, few whites care who she really is, what she likes and dislikes, or what her goals are. Indeed, few whites care to know about her actual family life, relationships with black men, experiences with racial or gender discrimination, or survival and fighting skills in a racist society. There is little concern with how her experiences resemble those of African American women in the racialized past or about her own or her group's interpretation of that past. Rather than a snapshot as faithful as possible to a racial-gender reality, or a montage of differing perspectives, prevailing societal representations of black women are an evasion in which they are marked by invisibility or imaginative racist renderings.

These portrayals of African American women commonly go unquestioned despite their fictitious nature and their grotesque stereotyping. They tell us far more about the white mind than they do about African Americans. Joe R. Feagin and Hernán Vera have argued that these white racist notions encompass more than how white Americans see African Americans. They also include overt or hidden images of whiteness.[20] Racial stereotyping and prejudices reveal how whites see themselves, as well as how they see the "others." Whites hold to a complex array of "sincere fictions"—socially constructed myths held individually and collectively. As we noted above, these sincere fictions define white men and women as morally superior to black men and women, and as "good people" even when they act in racist ways. The explicit or implicit privileging of whiteness is often done at the unconscious and half-conscious level, as Ruth Frankenberg noted in her research on white women in California; whiteness is even "difficult for white people to name. . . . Those who are securely housed within its borders usually do not examine it."[21] Long ago the brilliant African American leader Frederick Douglass noted these white fictions: "For wherever men oppress their fellows, wherever they enslave them, they will endeavor to find the needed apology for such enslavement and oppression in the character of the people oppressed and enslaved."[22]

Racial Oppression and Stigmatization of Black Women

Racial oppression by whites, and black responses to that oppression, are key elements in our discussion of the life-worlds of African American women in the United States. Today, as in the past, this racial oppression is multifaceted, with a number of important dimensions. These include the weighing down of a target group with "heavy burdens," the literal meaning of "oppression." These burdens include harshly applied white-power plays that take the form of racial domination, discrimination, exploitation, and cultural devaluation. In addition to the burdens and barriers of racial oppression, there are also the privileges and power that come to whites from this system of oppression. As Robert Blauner put it, "all forms of social oppression, whatever their motivation, confer certain privileges on the individuals and groups that oppress and are able to benefit from the resultant inequalities."[23] We will demonstrate in the chapters that follow not only the burdens on black women and men that are integral to racial oppression but also the white group privileges that underlie the oppression of all people of color in this nation.

One key aspect of racial oppression is the "misrecognition" of the full humanity and experiences of African Americans and other people of color by white Americans. At many points in this book, the reported black experiences with white Americans will underscore the comments made at the beginning of Ralph Ellison's famous book *Invisible Man* by a black protagonist: "I am an invisible man. No, I am not a spook like those who haunted Edgar Allan Poe; nor am I one of your Hollywood-movie ectoplasms. I am a man of substance, of flesh and bone, fiber and liquids—and I might even be said to possess a mind. I am invisible, understand, simply because people refuse to see me."[24] In a racist system black women and men are frequently not recognized for what they really are. Their bones, fiber, and minds are invisible to the many whites who do not see them as full human beings with distinctive talents, accomplishments, virtues, and burdens.

This process of creating invisibility is a process of misrecognition that denies the humanity of its black targets. "The failure to recognize someone else indicates a serious lack of respect. It implies, for the mis-recognized, a 'loss of face,' and a denial of a place in the social world."[25] In her work on human interaction Jessica Benjamin proposes that recognition is the "response from the other which makes meaningful the feelings, intentions and actions of the self."[26] The black women we interviewed often noted that they do not get full recognition and respect from many of the whites with whom they deal in the workplace and a variety of other institutional settings, both those that are relatively public and those that are private. White misrecognition of black women and men is very threatening and damaging, for it signals out-of-place-ness and self-worthlessness to its targets. Repeated indicators of recognition and misrecognition in everyday interactions in many places in the society generate mental blueprints for both the white perpetrators and the black recipients. These mental blueprints include the fictions of whites as superior (misrecognition of whites) and antiblack prejudices and imagery (misrecognition of blacks).[27]

The African American psychiatrists William H. Grier and Price M. Cobbs have suggested that to understand the social construction of "beautiful" and "ugly" for African American women we should "slip for a moment into the soul of a black girl whose womanhood is so blighted, not because she is ugly, but because she is black and by definition all blacks are ugly."[28] Following their suggestion, in this book we examine the harsh fictions that whites create, hold, and propagate about black women, those who are at the opposite end of the continuum of what white society generally considers feminine, attractive, and valuable. We refer here to the process of white-controlled, culturally ingrained stigmatization that presupposes beauty to be absent in black women, its presence to be threatening. It is the technique of motivated devaluers of the racial other to develop ideal and constantly reinforced conceptions of the lack of beauty in the racial others. White-generated stigmatization of black women as "ugly" entails a social misrecognition process that is independent of the true nature of those who are vilified.

Reflecting on the cultural defining of what is "beautiful" and "ugly," Stanley Diamond has noted that "one is struck not by the distinction between the beautiful and the ugly, but by their fundamental similarity; in a certain sense, their identity. . . . At the same time, disharmonies in one period may be the harmonies of another, so even here, one must be exceedingly careful about drawing too sharply the fine line between the beautiful and the ugly."[29] Like skin colors, such as black and white, the concepts of white beauty and black ugliness do not exist in actuality. They exist only in the ethnocentric constructions and definitions of the white cultural artists who control much of the social portrayal of beauty.

In the United States, as in other parts of the globe, the egregiously false representations of black women are usually somatic, moral, or spiritual—or all three simultaneously. Somatic devaluing, which is implemented and maintained by many whites in many arenas, is based on biased physical standards of beauty, the black women's deviations from a culturally preferred, glorified white female physical model. Ironically, many white women also do not meet this model, although the society at least allows them the possibility of trying to meet it. Indeed, this devaluation of black women is not done without attitudinal and behavioral inconsistencies on the part of many whites. Indeed, many white women seek out the perfect tan, and some get chemical injections to make their lips full, much like the image they hold of black women.

The white attack on black women has a "moral" dimension. It is frequently expressed in common white images of a black Jezebel or Sapphire, which involve assumptions about alleged departures from certain standards of purity. Alone or in combination, these types of negative imagining have a powerful impact on how black women are viewed and treated by the dominant society, and they can shape when and if black women are included in the distribution of critical societal rewards.

Beauty and ugliness are ethnocentric images, subjective evaluations relative to a point in time and a particular social milieu.[30] The stigmatization of African American women is a social and collective process controlled by whites. It is the consequence of a dominant-group artist's use of white cultural materials to create the most negative portrait possible, consistent with the dominant imagination. This is about fabricated effigies, not about black female realities. For instance, even as a middle-class African American woman displays great poise, dignity, and beauty, these traits will often go unnoticed by many dominant-group members because of their commitment to her stigmatization and their sureness about the moral superiority of whiteness. Poise, dignity, and beauty—particularly beauty that is not in line with a conventional white model—are positive characteristics too far beyond the reach of many white imaginations to be considered as accurate portrayals of black women. These positive images are inconsistent with cultural messages about black women as domineering Sapphires and animalistic Jezebels. The eyes of the white cultural artist or beholder may be so fixed upon ethnocentric notions that a black woman's somatic, moral, and spiritual beauty goes unnoticed.

This stigmatization of African American women becomes thought and practice for each new generation of white Americans. Unfavorable images of black women, like other tainted racial images in the typical white mind, are significant for the survival of the dominant ideology. There is a story that must be told, told well and believed by most white men, women, and children for the meaning of whiteness and of the United States as a "white republic" to be sustained. In light of that significance, we would expect major efforts to be made by the dominant group to protect that story and the centrality of white identity. Efforts to preserve white ideology include silencing the voices and stories of African Americans despite evidence of their authenticity.

One way to preserve the dominant ideology is through the societal and global transmission by whites of false images of the devalued other, especially to younger generations. We emphasize the role of younger generations in racial-gender ideological retention because they represent the future. In theory, younger generations of Americans should have a choice about which ideologies are retained, and passed to yet unborn generations, or questioned and rejected. However, left to themselves and without exposure to dominant propaganda, the younger generations might well take an unpredictable turn or, worse yet, a turn too humane and tolerant for most white adults or elites. The possibility of deviation from existing beliefs by these younger segments is alarming, so younger white generations become targets for indoctrination into negative fictions about subjugated groups. Not only are these younger generations socialized into an ignorance of the oppression of the racialized past, but through blatant and subtle strategies they are also encouraged to perpetuate the fictions and myths about black women and men.[31]

The dominant white society has the means to activate inferiorization in everyday practices. Negative representations of black women are commonly and effectively circulated by many white agents of socialization—the mainstream mass media, the schools, journalistic and certain social scientific writers, peers, and elite role models. The encounters of African American students with racism at the hands of numerous white students and teachers at various grade levels is well documented.[32] Also documented is the role of the mass media in the negative depictions and self-perceptions of young African Americans.[33] The white-controlled television networks regularly offer unflattering portrayals of black women, black men, and their families, which swiftly reach the younger generations. This misrecognition, which often seems intentional, indicates a serious lack of respect for those different from white Americans and suggests for the misrecognized a denial of a place in the "human" world. The often criminalized image of black men is a clear example. When TV news programs report a crime, they almost always note if the perpetrator is "black." If the perpetrator is white, that fact is often not mentioned, and some general notation like "suspect" may be used. Unlike textbooks and other educational writings that also have a powerful impact on the racial socialization of children and adolescents, but usually target school populations, television stories reach a mass audience at home. Misrepresentations are rapidly diffused in every U.S. household.[34]

Practicing Gendered Discrimination

The negative images targeting black women reflect the white culture's common portrayal of African Americans. For black women and men the white cultural logic includes much more than a set of negative images and attitudes. It involves a broad range of cultural practices, of everyday discrimination, that are sometimes termed "gendered racism."

This gendered racism involves negative white reactions, individual and institutionalized, to black female characteristics. In the everyday lives of black women there are distinctive combinations of racial and gender factors. They face not only the "double-jeopardy" condition of having to deal with both racism and sexism but also the commonplace condition of unique combinations of the two. Because racial and gender characteristics are often blended, they may trigger individual and collective reactions by whites that are also fused. This real-world blending often makes it difficult to know the separate contributions of each element in particular situations that involve both racial and gender barriers to social mobility and personal achievement.

The complexity or blending of racial and gender factors can be seen in many places in this society. Take the example of a white-black marriage. One member, say a white husband, is part of a racially privileged group, while the other, a black wife, is part of the group defamed by many whites. White reactions to each of the two in the mix will likely vary depending on whether each is alone or accompanied by the other. Walking alone, and not known to be associated with the black other, the husband receives privileges by virtue of his racial caste position, while walking alone the female racial other may be treated according to another code of etiquette. When both the white husband and the black wife are present and observable to whites, there may be yet a third reaction, different and perhaps more difficult to grasp because it is more complex. Does the presence of the racially privileged person have a negative or positive influence on white reactions to the couple? Does the proximity of the privileged person have more effect on the outcome than the presence of the racial other? How much influence does each component have? Such questions are not easily answered for such a combination is ordinarily clothed with intricacies obscuring the reciprocal effects of the elements. Prior research on racial relations in the United States, not surprisingly, indicates that negative images of racial others will probably be actively at work in most white assessments of mixed couples.

White responses to the racial-gender blend that characterizes black women may be conceptualized similarly. Separately, racial and gender elements may produce reactions that are different from reactions to a mix of such elements. However, the racial-gender blend is different and perhaps more complicated than the mixed-marriage analogue, because the element of *racial group* and the element of *gender* taken alone can produce negative reactions.

Gendered racism separates the experiences of black women from black men. Its female expression is encountered only by black women, and its male expression is experienced only by black men. As we will see in later chapters, there are many complexities to be considered. For example, in most cases black women interpret their blended racial-gender experiences with more emphasis on racial factors than on gender factors, thereby maintaining their connection to the situations faced by black men. Less often, they accent the gender factors and connect their conditions to those of white women. For example, black women do report sexual harassment from white men, as can be seen in our narratives, but such reports are rare. Other researchers and reporters have also found that black women tend not to report encounters with sexual harassment.[35] Moreover, a black woman's experience of sexual harassment by a white man may not be just because of her gender but rather may be linked to her racial-gender blend. The white male's motivation may be different from that influencing the harassment of a white woman. Except in cases where the sexual harassment of a black woman originates from a black man, which may also be linked to the gendered racism taught so pervasively to all in schools and by the media, sexual harassment may link black women to, rather than separate them from, black men.

In addition, racialized sexual harassment is not just a problem for women. Because of their racial-gender characteristics black men sometimes encounter harassment in the form of white representations of their allegedly distinctive sexuality. Accepting conventional racist stereotyping, some white women may assume that black men are easily accessible and exotic sex partners. Moreover, white fictions about black male sexuality and sexual aggression have led many whites, including many in law enforcement, to see black men as especially likely to be rapists, especially of white women. As a result, black men are frequently reacted to in unnecessary ways by many whites, such as avoidance or even unjustified arrest, just because of racial-gender fictions in the white mind.

While we will show the ways in which racism is gendered, we will also demonstrate that gendered racism is but part of a larger set of racial codes most whites use. In this society most whites use a complex and nuanced racial-gender discourse to buttress racist practice. The gendered racism of white practice in this society is an effective way to inferiorize the whole black group. Women, who are at the center of black families, play significant roles as wives and as mothers in the socialization of younger generations. If the black women's images are tarnished, they will be less effective as nurturers, socializers, and role models for black children. African American women are not seen as exemplars of the idealized conception of womanhood; white misrecognition takes the form of representations that transform black women into negative points of reference. Racist caricatures, which are the common portraits of black women offered in the mainstream media, may generate tensions between black men and black women, as well as family conflicts involving younger generations. Ultimately, they work to destroy positive self-recognition and self-esteem. The cultural devaluing of black women is an effective way racism hurts the entire black group.

Gendered racism such as sexual harassment assaults black women by misrecognizing or ignoring, among other attributes, their humanity and spirituality. Consequently, the more extensive a woman's experience with gendered racism, the more harmful the cultural devaluing. The more harmful that outcome, the less is the stigmatized black woman's value to family and society, the greater her exclusion from societal rewards, and the more convincing the white justification for her exclusion. Finally, the more successful the attempt to make black women "ugly," the greater the appearance value of white women and men in society. Perception of the dominant group's "beauty" and "purity" is enhanced by the black woman's devaluation. The mental blueprints of racism include not only the negative characterizations of black Americans but also the fictions of white superiority, which again entails a misrecognition of white attributes.

Outside the family, the negative imaginings of black women are seen daily in how these women are treated in the workplace. There stigmatization as an indispensable cultural imagery is actively produced, again with serious implications for the development and prosperity of black families and communities.

Racism at Work

Always Workers Facing Racial Barriers

Historically, African American women have participated more actively in the labor force than white women. As a group, African

18

American women have always had to work, well before the feminist revolution of the 1960s.[36] Yet in today's workplace the fabricated negative images influence black women's treatment by both white men and white women and, consequently, black women's relationships with both groups. Some distortions of the character of African American women are specific to the workplace, but these images are usually informed by the characterizations of the larger society. For example, the erroneous definition by whites of a black female employee as incompetent may sometimes reflect the image of a Jezebel in the white mind. The image of a Jezebel "explains" the alleged inadequacy because it does not seem possible that one could be productive while being obsessed with sexuality or personal adornment.

According to our respondents African American women are often not credited with being competent workers. Because of this, they face more difficulties than whites in the hiring and promotion process, as well as in everyday performance on the job. In a recent focus group a computer scientist who was looking for work described how she became the object of unwanted curiosity:

> When I first moved to this western city, which was five years ago coming out of a northeastern environment [where] I built computers and have done many things there—being a programmer, specialist [in] design—I applied at a high-level, so-called high-level computer company here. Over the telephone things went very well. . . . When I showed up, it was almost like I was on display. First of all, I was greeted by saying "*You* are Francine Rogers?" "Yes," [I said], "I want to apply for a systems analyst position as advertised." And, as I am completing the application, at least 10 people, all white, came out of the office, to look. They could not believe that, one, I was black, and two, I would have had the nerve to say I am . . . a systems analyst.

The respondent reads the surprised reactions of whites to mean that her applying for the position was unexpected, even audacious. These reactions seem to be in line with lingering white beliefs that competence and ability are not equally distributed across human populations, that somehow white Americans have a greater share than black Americans.

Despite common representations of African American women as less competent, well-educated black women have reportedly been hired more often than male counterparts in the 1990s.[37] Several of our respondents observed that a white employer who has a choice between hiring or promoting a black woman and a black man will often select the black woman. One reason offered for this is that the black woman is somehow more acceptable to white men in authority. Often but by no means always, she is seen as less physically threatening than the black man, as a black woman journalist explained in one of our interviews:

> The corporate world says, "Well, OK, we got to have *some* black folks in here. So what are we going to do? We'll find women. We'll find women. Because a woman is not a threat." A woman they perceive is not going to be as ambitious, she is not going to want to crawl to the top, and on a baser level she is not going to be coming into our situation and perhaps disturb white women ... I mean I still think that white men are on a lot of levels, especially sexually, are terrified of black men.[38]

In such cases the employment of the black woman is motivated by white fears. Note here the form that gendered sexism takes for black men. Apparently, in the white mind the allegedly aggressive and hypersexual black men would be working side by side with white women, posing serious threats to the latter.

Besides alleviating the fear of racial mixing, there are other reasons for preferring the employment of black women. Black women are hired, suggested one high school counselor, because they are

> twofers ... [a] double minority. We are female and we are black, so they [white employers] can bring that in.... It's just a fact of life. If I have to hire ... if it's a principal of a school, or if it's a president of a corporation and they [are] being told, "You have to hire a minority, you have to hire more minorities," well if they hired me they have a black, they also have a female. That cuts down [on] the number that they have to bring in, doesn't it? So everything is engineered. And as far as engineering, if anything was engineered to break up the black family, isn't it easier to set the black woman up where she is more successful against the black man. Even though it's not ... maybe it's not foremost in their

minds but they have been doing it for years. What better way to create tension?

Apparently, in some white thinking, if a black person must be hired, a black woman is the safer choice, the lesser of two evils. Recent research on black female faculty members in higher education has shown this same thinking among well-educated whites.[39] In effect, by the use of "twofers"[40] whites in authority can perpetuate white dominance by controlling the parameters of a supposedly integrated workplace. "Diversity" becomes what whites wish it to be.

Even when the hiring process goes well, and black women are successful in securing a position, racial discrimination continues to haunt them inside the workplace. This takes many forms, including a questioning of supervisory authority. One corporate executive explained:

> There are some whites who are unable to take supervision from a black woman, white males who are unable to accept supervision or being in a subordinate role. They are having a problem with it, I am not. . . . A concrete example is when someone who reports to you says, "I am going to the other department." They are not asking permission to go to the other department; they just come out and make a blatant statement to you, "I am going to another department." And when this occurred, I said, "I need you on the desk right now, so please wait until the other [employee comes in]." "Well," she said, "I am going anyway because you don't need me." She left. And her comment was, "As soon as you black people get a little authority, it goes to your head." I had to have her disciplined.

This executive is not respected, and this lack of respect stems from the people whose support she must rely on to perform well. This again suggests that whites do not see black female employees to be as knowledgeable or competent as whites.

Workplace Discrimination and Black Families

If white male employers, consciously or unconsciously, select or promote black women over black men, they give black women greater numerical strength in certain workplaces and sharpen the image of black women as surpassing in success their male counterparts. The

21

reputation black women have acquired in some sectors for taking jobs from black men can feed into the cultural representation of them as uniquely controlling matriarchs. White-created differentials favoring black women not only feed popular images of strong black women and weak black men but also can affect gender roles in black communities, producing friction between men and women. This can discourage marriage and encourage divorce.[41] Indeed, some social science research has found a positive correlation between dissatisfaction at work and dissatisfaction at home.[42]

When workplace choices play out this way, great pressures are experienced by black men, women, and families. These pressures stem from multiple sources, but primarily from a contrast between the dominant society's expectations for husbands and wives generally and the different realities for many black husbands and wives. Pressures are intensified by created status differences between black men and women. One woman, a journalist that we interviewed, underscored this problem:

> It just makes it real hard, because you don't want to be punished for achieving. You would like a man you can go home to, and you can relate to . . . who has the same interests. . . . Sometimes you might not just get that. If you are married, or if you are dating a guy perhaps of a different social class, you might be given like, "Now, well, here she is with her little middle-class BS and all this, and I can't [relate]."

Conditions of work are often beyond the control of black women and men, and these conditions can have family consequences. Home is where black women are expected, in the dominant group's stereotyped imagery, to act out the socially devalued role of a domineering matriarch and where black female stigmatization is disseminated to younger generations of black Americans.

Recognizing the employment dilemma forced on black women and men, one female entrepreneur in a recent focus group expressed her view of the general community situation in these strong terms:

> The situation that black women find themselves in is kind of a problem. Because, on the one hand, we are accomplishing things without accomplishing as much as the white woman. But we are ac-

complishing a lot more . . . than the black male, which creates a problem for the two of us, for the black male and the black female, because we seem to be getting more than he. We are going to college, he is going to jail, we are getting jobs, he is getting some jobs, but maybe not the jobs he should be able to get. We are getting better jobs in many instances than he is. . . . So we are doing a *lot,* but I think that sometimes we are sort of on a plane by ourselves, and why should we hold ourselves back because someone else isn't accomplishing what we are? Why should we not be viewed as valuable as women of other races?

From this perspective, which examines the larger community and not just the middle class, black women are caught in a dilemma. They are not allowed, by a discriminating society, to succeed to the level of white women, yet they sometimes can do better in employment than the men in their lives. Whether it is accurate or not, an image prevails in some circles that for many successful black wives there are much less successful black men who live under the same roof with them. These black men thus do not conform to conventional expectations of bread-winner and leader, nor do these black women conform to common societal expectations about the ideal wife. Though concern about this lack of conformity represents patriarchalism, it is rooted in the dictates of the larger society, and even moderate violations of these dictates have real consequences. Moreover, in the case of many black women, what would generally be considered signs of personal success if they were white men can trigger or reinforce their cultural denigration.

The "Beauty" of Racism

Cultural misrecognition and stigmatization of black women are reflected in commonplace societal concepts of female beauty, the ethnocentric notions that neutralize or denigrate the attributes of black women. Biased notions of beauty are routinely disseminated like other white-generated myths, by a familiar, friendly, and ostensibly convincing media. The widely circulated beauty myths can have a significant, if unconscious, impact on the self-esteem and identities of African American women. Racially skewed notions of beauty can contribute to friction between black women and white women who, as a black psychologist explains, see each other as competition rather than allies.

I am very resentful of white women. . . . I have white friends, but I am very resentful of white women as a whole . . . in general, because, you know . . . , Ms. Anne was set up on a pedestal, and what not. I see an awful lot of black men who are very famous and wealthy and their first wife, they were black women, who worked alongside them, and helped them, Sidney Poitier, I mean I can think of a lot of them, Quincy Jones and all of them. But when they got that money and that power, they married a *white* woman [respondent claps when she says "white"]. Same thing with Montel Williams . . . but now he's got a white woman too, but she does not have to work. I feel like the *black* woman always has to work.

"Mrs. Anne" (or "Ms. Anne") is a term that has been applied by black women to white women in positions of authority, such as the wife of a male slaveholder on a plantation or a white woman who dominates her black female employee at home. Continuing with this discussion of white women, a black female business executive in the same focus group speaks about O.J. Simpson and his choice of ex-wife Nicole: "That is insulting to me! you know . . . isn't there a black woman out there that is together, they could not be his wife?" The choices a few prominent black men make come in for much criticism in this focus group. And there are other important points made about the importance of the white female beauty image. This executive continues with a complaint about the murder trial of Simpson. She suggests there would not have been a big trial if the murdered wife had been black, and adds, "She was blonde, she was white, she was Ms. Anne, and she was a waitress, and she was still more valuable in society's eyes than a black woman." This female manager is very critical of what she considers the dominant and stereotyped notions of female attractiveness. In her view such white-generated notions of what is and is not beautiful are responsible for some black men's distancing themselves from black women.

Continuing the focus-group discussion, she further amplifies her central point on societal beauty standards:

What does society tell us is beautiful? [All respondents say in unison: "Blonde, blue-eyed white women."] That's beauty by society's standards. We are bombarded with this every time they have a commercial [and] they want to show you something you should want.

There is a white female, even if she is not blonde, there is a white female selling a car, she is selling a cigarette, she is selling, she is selling whatever. You look in the magazines, what is it that you should desire? White women, OK?

Seen from the dominant culture's perspective, female beauty *is* white, if not blonde and blue-eyed. Circulated fictions about female comeliness are widely accepted by most members of this society, even some black men. One female business owner expressed her irritation about the persisting situation for black women this way:

And it ticks me off that these black women have to slave and help these men make it into positions, and as soon as they get into these positions and they are making good money, and the fame and what-not, all of a sudden they [black women] are not good enough, their children are not good enough. And this white woman gets to sit back. It really ticks me off. And as far as Nicole Simpson, O.J. supported that whole [white] family. And the one that's coming out against him about victims' rights and everything, he put her through U.S.C. and two other sisters through U.S.C. Do you know how much it costs to go to U.S.C.? . . . The thing is that he supported that whole family. He was a fool! He supported that whole family. So they [certain black men] don't want to be bothered with us [black women], unless we have some money, or there is something they can use. I just feel always being used. I think the black woman is being used. And it really ticks me off.

Looked on by a few successful black men as a stepping-stone to a more valuable white mate and greater status, some black women have the right to feel used. While she—society's stepchild, likely abandoned by a spouse—is working to support self and family, a white woman, favorite daughter of society and current wife of the now successful former spouse, is enjoying a leisurely life. "So, it's like the white girls have everything," continues the business owner. "They got the black male, they have the white male, oh, they have the Hispanic male, and they got the Asian male."

We observe in these comments in the focus-group discussion some imagery suggestive of slave plantation life, imagery that is still part of collective memories in African American communities. The respondent sees the white woman's superior position vis-à-vis the black woman as a continuation of plantation life in a modern guise.

> They [white women] have everything and they've always had every-
> thing. And when the [white] male did not want to tire out his Ms.
> Anne on her pedestal . . . he just went to the slave quarters and the
> beautiful black woman, so Ms. Anne could have a rest. And it re-
> ally has not changed, you see, she is still resting and we are still
> working! A lot of times, he liked the slaves better than Ms. Anne
> too! . . . And she got mad about it [and] she'd find a way to get
> you back, because you were [with] her husband more than she was.
> And if you look at it in different terms, we're still the same way.
> It has not really changed! It's probably more civilized, but it's the
> same mentality. My life is not worth the same as Nicole's. I got
> three times as much education.

There seems a visible, connecting link between past and present, between the white woman today and in the past, between the experience of the contemporary black woman and the black woman in the old plantation South. Changes do come in racial relations in the United States, but when they do occur it is often at a glacial pace.

The Racist Past and Its Contemporary Legacies

The slavery era devalued the black woman as a woman and a person, as it did the black man as man and person. That extremely brutal, near-genocidal past—still not confronted by most nonblack Americans in schools and public discussions—had at its ideological heart the cultural devaluing of African American women, one that affected virtually all enslaved mothers and their families. Narratives of African American women in slavery describe numerous encounters with extreme pain and humiliations that included beatings, rapes, other sexual attacks, and family separations. The brutality came from the hands of white male overseers and slaveholders, and even their wives, sons, and daughters.[43] White representations of slave women were usually crude and helped rationalize cruel exploitation. Dehumanizing characterizations made the appalling expropriation of life and labor often appear the result of the black women's own doing. In situation after situation black women's negative treatment by whites in authority over them was said by whites to be warranted by their transgressions as some imagined rebellious or immoral Jezebel. Severe punishments were given for alleged moral violations.

Racial categorization of a group is directly linked to the group's treatment; it is often a rationalization of oppression. Slaveholders' portrayals of black women negatively influenced their situations. Cultural degradation, including negative imagery, helped maintain the women's enslavement while absolving slaveholders of their own immorality. After slavery white segregationists adopted essentially the same racist ideology to legitimate and rationalize the semi-slavery of legal segregation in the South and de facto segregation in the North.

Contrasts Between Past and Present

Today, cultural degradation targeting black women continues to maintain oppressive conditions against which these women daily fight. The lives of enslaved African American author Linda Brent in the nineteenth century and, for example, the contemporary African American law professor Anita Hill, though removed in time, share certain similarities. Indeed, Kim Marie Vaz has noted how ancient negative stereotypes of black women reappeared in 1992 with the Anita Hill case.[44] Like Linda Brent, Anita Hill was construed by many in the larger society, and particularly in the white-controlled mass media, as a femme fatale, an apparent Jezebel whose account of events could not be trusted.[45] Clearly, doubts about the integrity of African American women today are often deeply rooted in racist images flowing from the past. Common white fictions about and misrecognition of black character are handed down like an esteemed heritage worth preserving. The hand-me-down is a deformed, defeminized figure presented as genuine by these white cultural traditions.

As we have noted, African American women report frequent encounters with blatant and subtle devaluations in everyday dealings with white men and women, at work and in many other places. At work, despite their often substantial educational and other achievements, African American women often perceive their conditions as lacking in equality and dignity—and sometimes as reminiscent of the old slave plantation life. They report not being treated fairly and not being respected, as still pursued by the old tainted white images.

Nonetheless, we can note some dissimilarities between past and present. During slavery and subsequent Jim Crow segregation, the cultural devaluing of black women was very clear, and racial attitudes and practices perpetuated coarse and grotesque images of black women. Whites were overt and obvious about this degrading of black women. There was little need for subtlety or deception because stratified racial-gender roles were legally caste-like in the South and were strictly segregated by law or custom in the North. Virtually everywhere rigid segregation prevailed in its institutionalized forms. Overt racist thinking and expressions combined with discriminatory practice. Strict laws and informal norms protected whites from having to hide or take personal responsibility for their racial attitudes. In most cases, the attitudes of whites conformed to broader racial requirements. Penalties were in place for normative violations.

By contrast, modern racial oppression often has a new or disguised countenance. It often hides behind kind-faced, generous looking, sophisticated masks that seem so refined that the roots in old racist habits are no longer recognizable. The success of modern camouflage is critical from the vantage point of a dominant group that claims to be "not racist" and moral. Yet white racism is rooted in a history of great immorality, with severe ramifications for black women and their families. Today as in the past, the dominant group seeks to dissemble its wrongs and to discourage the circulation of any proof or memories of past or present racial immorality. Examples include the denial of the severity and recency of the slave trade or the common denial among whites of the pervasiveness of racial discrimination targeting people of color today. For the most part, whites in power seek to silence attempts at protest by frustrated segments of society, since such words or actions can trigger the dominant group's memory of its immorality and force it to rethink its claim to the sole ownership of racial morality.

Effects of the Racial Masquerade

Because of the camouflage the lives of black women are decontextualized by whites, and their racial problems are detached from their historical anchor. While whites ignore past oppression or relegate it to a period they consider of little relevance to the present, they maintain that today a spirit of humanity is nurtured and that black Americans focus too much on racism; while whites make sophisticated arguments denying this racism, the old racist representations of black women and men linger on. The racial inequalities persist, many black families face great difficulties, and evidence and insights that could slow or reverse the effects of discrimination on individuals and families are ignored if not suppressed. In contrast, the diffusion and confrontation of past experiences, particularly when painful, can be healing and beneficial for both oppressors and oppressed.

Our respondents report that whites commonly push the brutal aspects of U.S. racial history into a very distant past. Slavery is said to be so long ago that it is not relevant to present-day racial relations. Legal segregation too is forgotten or pushed into the distant past, although it did not officially end until the 1968 civil rights act. Many African Americans have recent ancestors who were enslaved, and a very large number of African Americans were born when legal segregation was still intact or have parents who were born in the segregation period. White arguments concerning the no-big-deal irrelevance of this slavery and segregation past for the present are self-serving and can foster a collective attitude of no responsibility for these oppressive white actions of the past.

This neglect or rejection of the racist past deepens the roots of current tensions that underlie the interactions of blacks with whites, and indirectly blacks with other blacks. The dominant group benefits today from silence because the inferior circumstances for most black women are decontextualized and made to seem as though black women earned their devalued station in society. In this fashion the current problems of black women appear as the outcome only of their own inferior values and cultural practices, for they are only anchored in the here and now; they are black women's own doing and are not culturally engendered. The more decontextualized and removed from societal and historical roots is this cultural devaluing, the more subtle, disguised, insidious, unrecognizable, and dangerous it becomes, particularly for younger generations of black Americans. Recent surveys find that younger Americans know little of American history, and this lack of historical knowledge helps to protect the continuing dominance of white America.

Fighting Back: An Oppositional Culture

In spite of dominant-group efforts to separate present from past, most African Americans recognize how historically rooted present-day racism and gendered racism both are. The women and men that we interviewed, as the following chapters make clear, perceive that present manifestations of racism are tied to previous experiences with racial oppression and slave exploitation in all its forms. Capturing the sense of their lives must be preceded by a better appreciation for where the women stand and how they, themselves, interpret that past and assess its contributions to current situations.

Extended Kinship Networks and the Oppositional Culture

The sense of peoplehood among black women and men is undergirded by a strong collective memory and is reinforced with each instance of family interaction. "Collective memory" here refers to how people experience their present in light of the past. It's "what is left of the past in the lived experiences of groups, or what groups make of their past."[46] Collective and individual identities are shaped by collective memory. Parents, grandparents, and other relatives, as well as libraries, cemeteries, photographs, and postcards, are mediators and carriers of the past to the present. They are sites of collective memory and promoters of collective identity.

Memories of negative experiences with white Americans, accumulated and communicated by individuals, families, and communities, web together with memories of contending and resisting racial oppression. Beyond this collectively recorded experience are many family and other collective memories *not* associated with dealing with whites or white racism. All these collective memories and knowledge become a major buttress of African American culture and communities.

Collective memory is about centuries of remembered motherhood, fatherhood, sisterhood, brotherhood, and other kinship experiences. The collective memory of African Americans is grounded in extended family networks that women, men, and children require and utilize to live their daily lives, including lifetimes of contending against the damaging impacts of oppression. Field research has shown that extended family organizations play a central role among African Americans in coping with life's many difficulties.[47] Extended kinship networks have particular significance for the socialization of young African Americans. The physical presence and spirituality of relatives like grandparents, aunts, and uncles facilitate the development of a strong collective memory of the family. In turn, this nurtures a strong family identity. Where memory and identity might otherwise be weak, black youth benefit from identifying with the extended group of relatives. In this circle they can acquire a sense of belonging from which to draw strength and knowledge.

Rooted in extended family networks and their collective memories is an oppositional culture, a culture of resistance positioned against the threats of the dominant culture. Today, as in the past, the experiences of African Americans sum to much more than a litany of victimization. The cumulative experience, with its accumulated knowledge, goes well beyond simply being victims of white hostility and aggression. Over several centuries this African American experience has involved the development of ways of fighting back against oppression. When faced with this racial oppression, black women and men can draw on a strong cultural heritage, with its collective ties, extended families, and collective memories. This store of knowledge not only includes strategies for working against racism but also encompasses positive role models and happy family circumstances that buttress self-esteem and an ability to thrive under adversity. From the beginning of enslavement by European Americans, African American women have played a critical role in the development of a strong and lasting oppositional culture.[48]

Recent research indicates that African American women have been organized against racism and its effects for more than a century now. Indeed, even in periods thought to be "quiet" by mainstream historians, such as the 1950s, "various groups of Black women (not just elite, educated Black women) were far from passive or apolitical. . . . In their homes, communities, churches, and collectivist organizations, African American women actively engaged in protest against the oppression they encountered on a day-to-day basis."[49] Such group protest is rooted in family and individual commitments to common memories and a culture of resistance. One female business owner explains the symbolic community:

> Another reason that white men are threatened by black men and, I think, that white people are threatened by black people in general, is that if you consider all the things that have been done to us since we came here as slaves, all the things that have been done, all the laws that have been passed . . . all the doors that were slammed

in our face when people were smiling at us, in spite of all of that, we don't commit suicide as much as they do. We continue to grow, we continue to strive. . . . I own my own business right now. I was just telling [Mary] that, you know, it's growing and it's being successful and, you know, this is our fourth business, we continue against all those odds.

Constant and creative struggle, a certain toughness of mind, a spirituality, and strategies for survival and for success—against "all those odds"—are part of a culture of resistance developed over many generations by African Americans. African American women have been very important in the creation and maintenance of this oppositional culture and the networks in which it is embedded. In a recent doctoral dissertation Beverlyn Allen explores these issues and shows how "black women continued to develop networks for resistance from the post-bellum era to the present. The networks were established within several contexts, but particularly with the black family."[50]

We will see in later chapters how black women not only fight to create strong and viable families but also work to maintain strong collective values, and communities. Most must contend hard against misrecognition by white Americans in their everyday lives, and most do not give up. The question of suicide, cited in passing by the previous respondent, is of interest and importance. The differences in the suicide rates among racial and gender groups are striking. Recent data indicate a high suicide rate of 21.7 per 100,000 population for white men, but a much lower rate of 12.1 for black men. While white women also had a much lower suicide rate than white men (at 5.2), black women were by far the lowest of all, with a rate of just 1.9 suicides per 100,000, a figure not even 10 percent of that for white men.[51] These data are suggestive of how strong most African American women (and men) are in dealing with the trials and tribulations daily inflicted on them in a racist society. As we will see in later chapters, the underlying factors at work here are likely to be the important supportive networks and extended families of African Americans, which they are seldom given credit for in the larger society.

Throughout this book the reader will note our African American respondents' regular use of "we," "us," and "our." Everyday oppression is shared, as is the inherited repertoire of responses to that oppression. Even as the respondent above provides a personal example, she immediately ties that example to collective experience and collective response. "*We* continue against all those odds," she says. "We," of course, could refer to this businessperson and her spouse. Yet the context indicates that it is likely she is speaking of African Americans as a group and is including her current success in the pool of positive outcomes realized by that group in spite of racial and other barriers. The group's remembrance of old successes is kept alive by her experience and memory. One school counselor summed it up: "They [whites] have not been able to get rid of us!"

Collective Memory and Resistance

In a book on social memory Paul Connerton notes that "our experience of the present very largely depends upon our knowledge of the past. We experience our present world in a context which is causally connected with past events and objects."[52] Because of their experience with oppression most black women and men seem to intuitively understand the importance of reflection on past lives and distant and recent histories, both those of themselves and their families and communities. Drawing on their culture of resistance, they recognize that important links exist between racial situations today and yesterday. The past is inscribed deeply in their personal, familial, and communal memories. Indeed, the survival and success of the black community and of its oppositional culture are closely linked to the operation and strengths of this collective memory.

The narratives of our respondents, who are a diverse group in terms of residence, age, and occupations, manifest a general awareness of the present as an extension of the past. Evident throughout their discussions is the racist heritage that seems to supersede the differences between them. That heritage frames and guides our respondents' perceptions and explanations of everyday discriminatory situations, whether the actions of whites are blatant, covert, or subtle. Black women share with black men the group condition of oppression and a cognizance of that condition. The women carry a memory of racism that they see as gendered at times, but intended, ultimately, to keep them and their families in an inferior racial place.

What do black women gain from recapturing a deep sense of their past? That sense is part of a sisterhood that is far more than a reaction to the ravages of racism. Past memories flow into present memories, as past communities are the basis for present communities. In a 1950s play, poet Jean Brierre described two young Haitian girls reminiscing about their predecessors, the foremothers. A strong desire for closeness with predecessors takes these girls back in time as they daydream about their heroines and become reacquainted with their heroic feats. Because of this imaginary encounter, Brierre's characters feel positively not only about their past but also about themselves. These girls describe their ancestors as "century-old women who are like mothers that have long been lost and whom we miss."[53]

Contact in the mind with these historical figures is often fruitful if not critical for black women and men. With a common history reinforced and a common heritage renewed, Brierre's characters are linked in an extended family relationship. They are invigorated by a brief but special encounter with a shared past. They acquire a shared sense of unity and form a symbolic alliance with absent but similar others, precisely because of their reinspired connection with common, valued ancestors.

A similar and strong sense of group identity and a collective heritage can be observed clearly in our respondents' interviews. Like Brierre's characters, these women and men sometimes actively seek out the memory of specific foremothers or forefathers. In general, there is a clear, detectable sense of peoplehood and an identification with other African Americans. That identification springs in part from a common past and legacy. Despite their consciousness that the racial legacy is a nightmare—streams of injustice complete with false representations, coercive work conditions, gender-role pressures, marital separations, and much more—this legacy is part of history and an important source of bonding. Words to the effect that "again history repeats itself" recur periodically as comment and warning in our interviews with black women and men.[54]

Collective memories link and guide the women and men who speak out in this book. Awareness of a shared past and present connects black women with other black women, black men with other black men, and black men with black women. Shared events that structure the group memory include collective experiences with oppression and responses to it that intensify the sense of group presence and resources. When family members or friends share their experiences with discrimination, it revives the listener's own memory of racism experienced personally or by another friend or family member.[55]

The African American heritage includes horror stories of many oppressions, but there are also good, happy stories of individual, family, and community endurance. The memories that bind together black psyches, families, and communities encompass far more than memories of racism or gendered racism. These memories center on the loves, joys, sorrows, successes, and failures of everyday life, just as they do for other human groups. Black families and communities create their own spaces where whites and white racism are excluded for long periods, where the normal joys and tribulations of family life and community life are central to the moments of everyday existence. While it is true in one sense that racism created "black" Americans, in another sense black Americans, as *African Americans,* have created and re-created themselves as vital, vibrant human beings whose individual and collective realities are far more than some set of mandatory reactions to white malice and oppression.

A typical remembrance of the past combines horror stories of human violation with successful stories of rise from horror. Collective memory is not a dream. While dreams offer a way out of reality, African American memories do not. Rather, these memories keep the rememberers within boundaries of their generally racialized reality. The sense of belonging that runs through the respondents' discussions is rooted in remembered racial events, which are often transferred to each new generation through oral history, from parents to daughters and sons. In her interviews with black women, Scott demonstrates this transmission of their "habits of surviving."[56] This transfer takes place in the presence of daily repetitions of harsh racist realities appearing in various costumed guises. Each instance of present-day discrimination experienced by a member of the group revives the past and makes both the horror stories and stories of successful struggles more believable. Present is situated in past and past reflects present.

This may be one reason that attempts are made by whites to silence hard memories of the racial past and to foster a present-day orientation. Michel-Rolph Trouillot describes how historical narratives are unevenly produced in a society and how those with power can effectively silence the past. Silencing makes sense for many reasons, but most certainly because the remembrance of painful events by racially subjugated groups can serve as a catalyst for change.[57]

Voices of Black Women and Men

The women and men quoted in this book on matters related to the lives of African American women were interviewed in several field-research projects. One project was a national study of more than two hundred African Americans interviewed in more than a dozen cities across the nation in 1988–1990. Virtually all these respondents were middle class, had at least a few years of college education, and held white-collar, usually professional or managerial, positions in the workplace or were college students preparing for such positions. Most who were not students had above average family incomes.[58] In addition, we draw heavily on several recent focus-group interviews with fifty-five African Americans in research projects in the West, Midwest, and South; these were conducted in 1995–1996.[59] Most of the participants in these focus groups are also middle class, and most have college educations. For the most part they are employed in professional or managerial jobs. Most of those we interviewed were between twenty-one and sixty years of age. Selection of our respondents often involved snowball sampling of those known to be middle class. While our samples are not statistically random, we did use numerous different starting points in a variety of cities and regions in order to insure a diversity of respondents.[60]

Several of our respondents own businesses or are college students, but most are health care professionals, legal and other professionals, teachers, social service workers or administrators, other government workers or officials, college administrators, corporate managers or other business supervisors, mass media professionals, or sales professionals. Most of those we quote are "middle class" in the common usage of that term—that is, they have completed at least some college work, have good incomes, and hold white-collar jobs. There are debates about who is middle class in the United States, but for our purposes this general usage—generally higher levels of education, occupation, and income—is sufficient.

Contrary to arguments made by some social scientists and other analysts about the "declining significance" of racial discrimination in U.S. society,[61] "race" turns out to be a central and recurring problem in the lives of these African Americans. In spite of their educations and accomplishments, they live their lives in the midst of omnipresent white attempts to devalue and marginalize them. They struggle virtually every day against some intrusion of white racism. Moreover, most middle-class women and men with whom we talked face many problems with white Americans that are common to African Americans in other class or status groups, especially those who venture out into white business, commercial, and workplace worlds on a regular basis.

The situation of middle-class African Americans is of particular poignancy because they are frequently seen by white Americans as having "made it" in America, as having secured all the perquisites and privileges that go with the American dream of success. Indeed, some whites feel that these African Americans have achieved their status more or less unfairly, through affirmative action (often called by whites by the misnomer "reverse discrimination"), and that whites have suffered greatly in the process. Various mass media articles and popular books have featured the alleged success and full integration of the black middle class into U.S. society. These accounts speak of black middle-class achievements and of the "extraordinary integration of the races" in the United States.[62] In this distorted version of contemporary U.S. history the black middle class is said, like white ethnic groups who moved up before them in the cities, to have secured the American dream.

In both the one-on-one interviews and the focus-group interviews, we made use of open-ended questions about a range of personal, family, and societal issues—with a particular emphasis on family goals and society's racial barriers and the respondents' ways of dealing with the latter. We offered these women and men the time and opportunity to respond to our questions in their own language and with their particular interpretations and emphases. In discussing the difficult and challenging situations faced by African American women, our respondents speak articulately about histories and memories, often setting individual experiences in larger family and community contexts. As we will see, much of what they discuss is about recent experiences. For the most part, they are not speaking of some distant set of events or about theoretical abstractions, but rather they give dynamic and reflective accounts of everyday lives. Their accounts, narratives, and interpretations tell us much about current and past racial realities in this nation. These black women (and men) give us a group portrait of being black and female in contemporary America. They reflectively describe events, and responses to events, generally in a cumulative and collective framework. As we will see, what one respondent reports about daily experiences is often closely linked to or amplifies what another respondent has said. The experiences of these women and men provide much more than recurring accounts of mostly negative encounters with white Americans. Indeed, they become part of a much larger whole—the accumulating experiences and culture of resistance and success developed by African Americans over more than fifteen generations of residence in North America.

Conclusion

Our respondents go far beyond the interpretations of their lives often offered by white journalists, media pundits, and social scientists, accounts too often filled with blatant and subtle black caricatures. They know from actual experience, and it is they who voice their stories of racial horror, survival, success, and joy in life. We explore the character and meaning of their poignant and revealing stories and show how a collective African American memory connects past to present.

Despite the wishes of many in the dominant group, this relevant racial past cannot be relegated to the domain of faded memories but is kept too alive, day after day, by white actions and fabricated images, by subtle and blatant misrecognition and aggressive racist actions. African American women and men denounce white caricatures and challenge the hypnotized cultural artists among whites who misconstruct, hide, or camouflage persisting racism. They demand that the public and private messages transferred by whites be clarified, open, and honest—and that the messages take into full account African American experiences, perspectives and memories. They demand full human recognition for themselves, their families, and their communities.

Today, as in the past, this society is centered around ideas of the American dream with its accent on personal and family success. African Americans have taken the promises of that dream seriously, and the black middle class has certainly worked very hard, making many individual and collective sacrifices, to do what is thought required to meet the ostensible requirements for achieving the American dream, which is said to include a nice house, cars, good schools for children, full citizenship, and personal and family dignity. Yet they have not achieved this dream. They may have secured many of the material requirements, but they as yet, and this is a painful "as yet," have not secured full citizenship and full dignity as Americans. As we will see, the women and men we interviewed face this hard reality with courage and sacrifice, with perseverance and creativity. Most are paragons of diligent effort, hard work, and achievement. As a group, they probably match or exceed in intelligence and talent any randomly assembled group of white middle-class Americans. Yet these middle-class African Americans do not have the same opportunities and rewards for achievement that white middle-class Americans have and take for granted. W.E.B. Du Bois wrote perspicaciously around 1900 that the problem of the twentieth century is the problem of the color line.[63] As we approach the beginning of the third millennium, we can add that a central problem of the twenty-first century will *still* be that color line.

Chapter 2

Black Women at Work

Degradation of and discrimination against African American women inside and outside a variety of employment settings today remain important dimensions of the racial oppression noted in Chapter 1. Today, as in the past, the workplace is central to the lives of the majority of adult Americans. What goes on there not only shapes job tracks and careers but also affects the way in which individuals come to see themselves. In addition, what takes place in the work world has its impact on families and communities. Work can be trying whatever one's racial or gender background, but it is especially difficult for those who face everyday racism and sexism.

Discrimination in its many forms literally weighs down the everyday lives of black women. In our interviews black women and men share their insights into racial-gender life in the workplace. They consider some ramifications of that life for the woman, the man, and the family. These accounts and commentaries are important because black women have practical, firsthand knowledge of their situations, thus qualifying them as much better judges than outside, nonblack observers. Black men too offer unique insights from their stance, not only into the women's situations but into their own.

A succession of black women mostly engaged in white-collar occupations relate some highlights of their everyday encounters with whites. Each describes some aspect of workplace difficulties and associated implications for their lives and those of their spouses and families. Each struggles and fights against the racial barriers they face. Each looks for meaning in the dilemmas of everyday racism. Likewise, a few black male respondents share insights into racial barriers as they affect women and men in traditionally white-dominated organizational environments.

Racial Discrimination at Work

Discrimination against African American women is widespread in workplaces and other organizational settings, as a few field-research reports are beginning to make clear.[1] Occupational ceilings are common; mobility is often confined only to certain levels and organizational positions. Popular perceptions among white employers and colleagues target black women as not very competent. These workers face stereotyping, excessive demands, an absence of mentoring, exclusions from work cliques, and being ignored and harassed. Frequently defined as workplace "twofers," black women may carry the stigma of affirmative action hiring, whether they were hired under those circumstances or not. In this racialized order, generally assumed to be fine by the white oppressors, black women have their "place," and they must "know their place" if they are to survive.[2]

The hiring process frequently presents a complex and difficult set of racial barriers for African American women. A respondent who has strong computer skills gave an account of how she was denied a position for which she was well qualified:

> I applied for a position at [names company]. . . . It would start off paying about a thousand dollars more a year but once I was certified it would give five to six thousand extra to my paycheck—not a small amount of money. I went through the interview process. I was number one throughout the entire testing process, number one, without a doubt, certified personnel records. Went through the interview. Still, number one. Went through the chief's interview. Walked out feeling extremely comfortable. This job was mine. I was feeling extremely comfortable. I was qualified in every way, shape and form, no question. They had two positions—one they gave to someone in the office, one they gave to a friend of somebody else, none of which were of color I might add. And I am in the middle of a legal battle with it. I earned the job. The job was mine. The discrimination was blatant.

It is often said by whites that a lot of "unqualified minorities" have been hired in business workplaces. However, judging from this respondent's report, it is the black woman who is better qualified than the whites who were in fact hired. This may in fact be the more common occurrence.

Once one is past the hiring barrier, discrimination within the workplace has many more faces. The question of the black woman's ability may be raised again and again in the stereotyping minds of white employers, clients, or colleagues. A school counselor illustrates this point:

> What I resent is, a lot of times, that if I do something and do it well, it's like "Oh my God," like they are so surprised. "Oh, you write really well. You speak really well. . . ." Last year, I conducted a workshop at my school—we have one of those career in-service days and whatnot—and you'd be surprised some of the whites, so many of the whites, would come up to me and say, "Oh my God, you did such a good job, you speak so well," or this and that, and they thought they were complimenting me. But, actually, I was a little offended. They might have complimented someone else, but I got the feeling it was like, "Oh, my God, you are black and I did not know you could really talk like that!"

Her show of everyday competence was apparently thought by some whites to be out of the ordinary and deserving special praise. Yet, she sees it differently, as normal job performance. The gap separating these evaluations may again be explained by the erroneous view of many whites that blacks generally trail whites in a range of abilities.

This questioning appears in many different types of employment settings. A corporate executive recently gave a parallel account of some white assumptions about her abilities:

> Initially, when you first become involved with a group that you are working with, you become a part of the team, their initial thing is they think you are stupid. They don't give you credit for what you know. So they are all testing you. . . . They talk to you as if you are stupid. "Show me how to work the computer, OK?" And then when you get on it, and then you show them that you've been doing this for 20 years, back when there were no lights on them [laughs], they become intimidated because you have skills.

And a journalist recently offered a review of a similar set of experiences in yet another type of workplace:

> It was just you being made to feel stupid, because you have holes
> in your story, and here is my editor saying, ". . . You do this, you
> do that," and I never saw him do it to other people. I mean I have
> a friend who is a Chinese-Vietnamese woman who actually did
> worse than I did. . . . they ran her down but never to the same as-
> pect. They just said, "Your reporting is incomplete." I mean, some
> minor stuff. Like, let's say I have explained a point in my story,
> and they just, the way they reacted, the ugliness, the cutting re-
> marks, they just made me feel stupid.

Here the pain and anger caused by apparent white stereotyping and discriminatory actions are evident. In all these respondents' accounts the U.S. workplace is replete with differential treatment that places the negative image of what African American women are, or can be, behind the white actions. Conscious or not, many whites seem to hold the belief that talents are unequally distributed across racial groups and that whites will in practice be more competent and successful than blacks.

Another problem in many historically white workplaces may be that there are no, or few, other African American workers even in those racialized places that white society reserves for people of color. Basic to racial oppression in many a workplace is the intentional isolation of black employees and the failure to hire more than one black person in a department or other employment unit. Some type of social isolation is an experience commonly reported by black women. A college-educated administrative assistant makes this clear in her reply to a question about whether she ever felt racially or socially isolated in the workplace, a question presented to her in a recent focus group.

> *Five days a week.* I am the only minority. I mean, you are isolated. . . .
> I'm so used to it, I forget sometimes. I went to a rural county, we
> were invited to a Christmas dinner just this past December. This
> was a government function, all of our employees were invited. . . . I
> kept wondering, "Why are these ladies staring at me?" There was
> not another minority. And when I say minority, I'm not just talking
> black, I mean I didn't see Hispanic, Spanish, in the whole room. . . .
> Everybody was like "Where did she come from?" [laughter and agree-

ment from others] And I was sitting there trying to eat my food. I got such indigestion. I could not eat because it was like all eyes were upon me. I almost felt like they had never seen a black and especially to be sitting and eating with one! It was like, do I have the plague?!

Social isolation has consequences beyond the fact of the exclusion itself. These effects include the pyramiding stress and physical reactions that must be daily endured. Other black women in this particular focus group add that they too have faced similar situations in white gatherings. A senior planner adds:

I'm always conscious of, you know, when I go to meetings, I always look around the room, because I want to see someone who looks like me, and [another female voice: "You don't!"] . . . If there is another black person there, it's a woman, I hardly ever see black men. They're all white men and women. And I'm like, there have to be some qualified black people out here who can do what these people are doing. I know there are. . . . It's the same everywhere, really. And we used to have these statewide conferences, and every year . . . I would go to these conferences. The first year I went, and everybody who is making a presentation is white, you know? And they were talking about an array of subjects, from health care, to human services, to industrial development, everybody's white! And then the next year I go, everybody is white! And I asked someone who was heading up the conference, "Are there no black people in the state who are experts that can be [at the] conference?"

Being the "only one" is sometimes a topic of conversation in groups of black workers. This condition of isolation and exclusion was supposed to be a target for societal change during the late 1960s and most of the 1970s, but in recent years few white employers in the public or private sectors seem to care that their "token" black female workers often find themselves alone or marginalized in the workplace. As this professional woman notes, this is not a natural condition but stems from a lack of commitment to real multiracial diversity in the workplace.

The reason for the token representation of African American women and men in many corporate settings is the preferential hiring of those who fit a certain white or white male model. In a recent focus group a female supervisor describes this condition:

> I think we all suffer . . . and everyday you wake up and look in the mirror, you say "I'm black." If you walk out, you know it. . . . I went to apply for a job, and a friend of mine said, "[Why] are you applying for that job?" And it was a black guy, he said, "because a blue-eyed blonde is gonna get it." And normally that's what happens, and . . . I went and told someone else. I was like "I was gonna apply for that job." But I just felt like a white person was going to get it because it was, it was a sales job for [names major corporation]. And it was in this area. And, people, just let's face it, people are not receptive to blacks with that corporation. I mean, because when, if you think of them, you think of a corporate Fortune 500 [firm], you see a white man! A white woman!

A certain type of white female beauty image is more than hinted at here. For some jobs employers have a certain type of occupant in mind, one who is expected to fit a conventional white model of "good looks." (We will return to this issue in Chapter 3.) Indeed, many public and private organizations, including some large employers, seem to exhibit a white image, a white face, to the general community. This may be subtle or it may be blatant, but it is seldom missed by African American observers.

Yet another problem for African Americans in many school and employment settings is that they are expected by whites to be spokespersons or actors for their racial group. Some whites seem to think that black women, despite their broad knowledge and experiences, are primarily interested in issues directly concerning African Americans or African American women. Commenting on this white practice, a school counselor elaborates:

> That really bothers me. This happens all the time. Something will come into the school that refers to black people or minorities, something of that nature. Now we have eight counselors where I work. The . . . person in charge of activities will bring it to me. And I just have to tell them because I am an outspoken person: "Why are you bringing this to me? Because it deals with . . . black people? Are they looking for a minority? White counselors can look [out] for minorities, and white counselors can choose kids just like I have

to choose all kinds of kids when I deal with it. Why do you ab-
solve them from having to do that?" And the Hispanic male counselor there feels the same way. Anything Hispanic that comes
across, they want to shove it on him. And we have gotten together,
we have told them, "Stop doing that, let the white counselors do
some of that. Don't see it as the black counselor's [job alone]."

What she describes might be viewed as a form of professional segregation where competence has its place and color. Similarly, black
female and male students at historically white colleges and universities have often reported to us that they are singled out, whether they
wish to be or not, by white professors or white students for comments
when issues of racial relations or African Americans come up in class
discussions.

The Costs of Discrimination

As we have seen, racial discrimination and hostility can involve subtle,
covert, or blatant actions. Whatever its level of subtlety, however, it
usually has serious personal and health effects on its targets. Recent
personal commentaries by African American women, including some
university professors, have made the costliness of discrimination increasingly clear, as can be seen in the accounts in the recent collection,
Spirit, Space, and Survival.[3]

Those with whom we have talked also describe a range of costs
stemming directly or indirectly from workplace discrimination. In a
recent focus group in the Midwest the moderator asked the participants how they know their poor treatment by a white male employer
or manager is "because of discrimination and racism." Two of the
women in the group respond in a direct way. First, a nurse speaks
about picking up the signals of discrimination.

Well, you can feel the tension. You can feel the humiliation. You
can feel the downgrading. . . . It pours out of them. And you as a
human, you know basically just through human instinct. . . . And no
matter how subtle it tries to be, or how covered up they try to do
it, you know. Their actions can't be totally hidden. You know when
someone doesn't care—is trying to make you miserable and trying to
enrage you.

This downgrading at work entails a type of misrecognition, and it can carry with it much human misery. As we noted previously, it is common for our respondents to speak about this lack of full human recognition from whites and its often painful consequences. Another woman in the group then tells of some blatant signals of discrimination from her white male supervisor: "He would just tell the rest of the people and then they would just tell me, 'Well, I don't like women. They're stupid. I don't like blacks. They're ignorant.' " There is more than a cognitive dimension to this manager's strong racial comments. Stereotyped notions, we see clearly in cases like this, can be emotionally loaded. White employers and managers can indicate their negative feelings about African American women in both subtle and direct ways.

In one focus group an administrative assistant noted how some racial comments and incidents involving whites are often swept under the rug:

> And I think it was mainly because I didn't file the complaint. I told, I told the chief judge, "If I filed a complaint for every time I heard a racial comment, there would be no rain forest because there would be no trees." [other voices: "Umm-hmm," laughter] Because black folks just deal with it every day. There is not a week goes by that I am not reminded. One other incident, very briefly, I had a judge call, rural county, "Which one of you black females is that down there, I know there's two of y'all. Which one are you?"

For most African Americans, women and men, these insulting remarks and serious racial incidents do not take place once every year or so. For those who spend large amounts of time in predominantly white workplaces and similar settings, these incidents are commonplace. A black male printer, now retired, recently estimated for us how many racial incidents of a significant sort crash into his life each year. His estimate was "about 250 times" a year. Making regular and formal protests of serious racial incidents, as the woman above notes, would indeed have a negative impact on the world's forests. Note too that in many cases the whites making racially insensitive remarks or taking racist action are well-educated professionals.

A male professor underscores the varying racial realities for both black women and men in the workplace:

> Oh, well, some of these [work] relationships are very good; some-
> times they work out very well. If you find a white person that sup-
> ports you, likes you, you find instances where they will become
> your mentor. And they will do anything they can for you. But most
> of the relationships are not that way. White men tend to feel as
> though most blacks are there because of affirmative action programs,
> they are there just so there is a black, and they need a black to sat-
> isfy those requirements. And, therefore, they don't have as much re-
> spect for their black co-workers as they should.

The downgrading of black abilities includes those cases where whites
hide their old-fashioned stereotypes of black intelligence and abilities
in the new racism of comments like "you are only here because of
affirmative action." Being encouraged to do so by white leaders, officials, and media commentators, many whites—even those in well-inte-
grated settings—view the black female presence as having more to do
with affirmative action than with merit. This is true not only for workplaces but for educational settings across the nation. For example, in an
interview at the University of California, Berkeley, a white student was
quite candid: "Every time I see a Black person, not an Asian, but any
other person of color walk by, I think, 'Affirmative Action.' It's like
that's your first instinct."[4]

What is particularly ironic about the commonplace white criticism
of contemporary programs of affirmative action—many of which are
today no longer operative—is the white use of a blatantly non-meritocratic system to promote white interests from the early 1600s to the
late 1960s. Some aspects of this pro-white system are still in place.
How this privileging works is recognized by our respondents. In a
focus group a black female supervisor notes the operation of this non-
meritocratic system: "And this white person can come in there [to a
major corporation] with no experience, but her daddy is such-and-so,
whoever. And he says, 'Give her that job.' She's got it, and you've
been there twenty years, and you won't get it. So yeah, that's painful,
it's painful because it's like you know that's not fair. And you can, you
can fight it and fight it, but it still stands. It's not fair."

One of the important aspects of the U.S. employment world is the
way in which certain white privileges are frequently transmuted into
what is called "merit." The United States has long been structured so
that whites are privileged in many areas. Often, inherited white privi-

leges, such as having parents who can afford to send a child to an expensive Ivy League university or getting hired because of father's connections, become translated into "merit." Whites who benefit from these non-meritocratic advantages, many of which are secured in part or in whole because of a historical legacy from slavery and segregation, may soon forget that they made it through this ancient affirmative action program for whites. It is often these beneficiaries of white privilege who complain about the much more modest affirmative action programs for people of color, most of which were phased down or out after only a few years of operation.

Fighting Back in the Workplace

As we noted in Chapter 1, dealing with racism is far more than a matter of being the victim of an oppressive racial system. It is also about developing ways of fighting back against the color barriers constantly imposed by white society. When faced with racial hostility and discrimination from white employers or co-workers, black women and men often draw heavily on their cultural heritage and collective knowledge about contending and coping strategies that work, as well as on knowledge about how white society works. Long ago African Americans developed an oppositional culture out of the cultural tools brought from Africa and those they developed as they dealt with their new oppressive circumstances. Today, the racial burdens of the workplace are countered and resisted by drawing on this developed culture of resistance.

In many cases black female employees, like their male counterparts, risk jobs and careers by actively resisting the racist actions of whites inside and outside the workplace. They speak up or make official complaints about poor treatment in hiring or employment conditions. Indeed, many white employers and managers are confronted by black women who are not afraid to protest the discrimination they encounter on a daily basis, as can be seen in this report of a female respondent's encounter with her white male supervisor.

> I think he felt that he was better than everybody, whites and blacks.... There was him. Then there were white males, then there were females, then there was a black female, then there was a Latino

guy—I think that he might have been below me. . . . Even though I
had done my job for a long time and was competent at it he was
constantly finding little things like, "If you are doing this, I want
you to do something different." And then the way that I dealt with
it. I told him that I couldn't stand it and that he made me sick to
my stomach. ["You actually confronted him?"] Yeah. Sure. Yeah.
Then I called his supervisor and told him that I didn't like the way
he was treating me. . . . So, then I called his supervisor and said
that my supervisor discriminates. He does not like females. He does
not like minorities, and he definitely [does not] like females and minorities with big mouths.

As a group, African American women are well down the employment
hierarchy, and this can make their protests over discrimination all the
harder to bear for their white supervisors. They often take action and
stand up for fairness at work. Even in taking such action, however,
black women may have an advantage over black male employees who
protest discrimination because many white male employers do not view
their black female employees as threatening to their authority or mas-
culinity. Indeed, the white male response to a black woman who speaks
out may be a patronizing arm around her shoulder and a "now, now,
honey, don't get upset."

A number of our respondents speak about giving up on government
redress agencies and taking action to secure their rights in the workplace and in other places that are supposed to be integrated or egalitarian in practice. They periodically refer to "getting our rights," or
similar ideas, as they develop strategies for dealing with hostile or
inhospitable whites in a variety of institutional settings.[5] A basic part
of the oppositional culture of African Americans is this deep respect for
civil rights and for the laws enforcing them. Over a long history black
protest strategies against racism have included not only the legal strategies cited by our respondents but also legal demonstrations and non-
violent civil disobedience.

In a recent focus-group conversation about racial incidents, one administrator comments on the impact of her assertiveness about fairness
on white men where she works:

I think, I'm a double whammy for them. [laughter; other voice:
"Yes you are."] I mean, I'm a black person, and I'm a woman. And,

many of these men are in this "good ole boys" school. . . . And they have a way of thinking. So they bring that way of thinking to the business place also. And I make a lot of assignments for my boss. . . . And sometimes you make the phone calls, and people don't call you back in a day or two. You're not sure whether it's because you're a woman, because you're black, whether you guess that they don't have time or whatever. But when it happens repeatedly, there is this red light that comes on, that something is wrong. And I started thinking about ways to deal with people like that, I mean, [when] people don't call me back. I do, and I start writing stuff down, start documenting stuff. . . . And many of them I have developed work, a working relationship with them. But I don't fool myself into thinking that it's any more than something superficial. Because it doesn't go really deep, and I know I don't fit their mold of "colored girl." And I'm serious. I mean, they have this idea of black females, and what we should be doing as opposed to what we are doing.

Racism clearly breeds distrust. Many African Americans will speak about the "perceptiveness" or "second sight" that the experience with white Americans gives them—the ability to pick up on being targeted by whites for hostility or discrimination, whether blatant or subtle. This perceptiveness comes from years of experience.

After discussing how some whites try to "buddy up" to her at work, one woman tells the focus group how she explained her cool response to her supervisor:

"I don't want them in my circle," . . . and I told him, "because I think they're racists. And they may cloak it well, but I still think that they're racists, and those are not people that I want close to me. Because you can't trust people like that." And that's really how I go about the daily work, and, as I said, I see it done to other people, and I see it done, I mean, even directed at me. And it's not an easy environment to work in, when you're constantly having that to deal with in addition to trying to do the work that you are paid to do. Because you're dealing with all of that extraneous stuff.

The accumulation of racist incidents at work, both blatant and subtle, makes it difficult if not impossible for real trust to build between black and white employees. Extraneous white actions destroy the basis for real communication, and racial barriers are thereby reinforced, usually on a daily basis. As this woman explains, she and others in similar situations are not interested in pseudobuddy relationships. Because of this the employment situation becomes a harder place to be, and one may develop a "just get the job done" attitude in the face of the disturbing and distracting incidents that cross one's path every day.

White Manipulation: Using Black Women

In the United States the historically white work world can be, as we have seen, hostile, perplexing, and painful for black workers. White employers and co-workers make the place of employment a center for recurring racial trials and troubles. The actions taken can vary in subtlety and degree of manipulation. As we noted briefly in Chapter 1, a subtle racial aspect of some workplaces lies in the very presence of a black woman there, for her presence may be construed by many whites as "a move toward diversity," even though it actually means that a black woman was intentionally preferred over a black man by whites for that position. To the extent that a black woman's achievement flows from the rejection or downgrading of one or more black men, her success also includes failure and dissatisfaction for the larger community. White hiring that favors black women generates stigmatization for black women and men and can have a negative impact on black families and communities.

In one interview a male university professor suggests this point in assessing the situation of black women in the workplace: "Black women seem to be able to get along much more easily with the work environment than does the black man. I don't know, it just seems that way." The capacity black women sometimes have for more successful adjustment to white settings is linked directly to white male responses to them. Dealing with white men in order to maintain their jobs, some black women may, intentionally or unintentionally, tailor their responses in gendered terms to facilitate interactions with white male peers and employers. However, gendered accommodations can in turn reinforce a negative image of these women workers in the white mind. Workplace intricacies so mark the situations of black women, noted a male university administrator, that they are often difficult to untangle: "I hear black women say, 'Well, I've got two strikes against me; I'm black and I'm a woman.' However, you also hear that white men get along with black women better than they do with black men because they're threatened by black men more than they are black women."

The last two comments reflect different aspects of the same workplace reality. Black women are often treated differently by whites, particularly white male employers and co-workers. They generally face two types of oppression—racial and gender oppression—that in interaction constitute gendered racism. Yet, despite the perpetuation of this oppressive gendered racism, black women are frequently more acceptable to white male managers, supervisors, and co-workers than their black male counterparts. Lying behind these white choices is the likely rationale that the black woman poses less of a "threat" to whites than the black man. If necessary, black women who get out of line, from a white male manager's point of view, can be controlled or exploited by virtue of their gender.

Starting from his view of the larger society's job conditions and its patriarchal role expectations, a university student explains some other nuances in the interpretation of this matter:

> Sexism provides a role of the man being the breadwinner. But oftentimes in the black community it's the woman who has the job. It's the woman who provides money for the family. So, oftentimes I think that's kind of destructive because they can't play out the role that society sets out as the, just the role that a man is supposed to play. His innate role. And I think that causes black males a lot of problems. . . . A lot of times I think that black males are oppressed because they represent power to white sexist males. I'm not saying that black males are not sexist. But as a white sexist male, I think that they would prefer having a woman working for them who doesn't provide, who doesn't project as much power.

This respondent seems to be applying his comment to women and men across several class or status levels, not just to the middle class. He recognizes that privileging men as "breadwinners" is part of sexism in the dominant system, but he also sees that black men who face unemployment cannot meet that proclaimed standard. This unemployment is aggravated by the preferences of some white employers for less threatening black women. The preference for black women facilitates a rendering of racism so that "more black females [are] getting ahead," to quote a business executive in a northern city who, at the time of his interview, was suing his employer for discrimination. As some respondents see it, the preferential hiring of black women is frequently woven into the business fabric. One woman noted that "the black female gets the position because her hiring presents fewer risks to white employers."

Why is this the case? What may be going on in the minds of white employers and supervisors? Several respondents suggest that black female workers are thought by many whites to be more easily managed, controlled, or manipulated than black male workers. For example, a government employee in a southwestern city puts it succinctly: "The people who make many decisions are frequently white men, and I think that white men are much less threatened by black females than they are by black men. I think they feel they can control a woman more than they can a man." White perceptions that somehow black women have pliant gender characteristics that soften their racial threat frequently earn women some priority over men. Again we discern how racial and gender issues are interrelated in the workplace. There is irony here in that the negative white stereotype of black women as domineering Sapphires seems to be conceived in reference to black men dealing with black women, but not necessarily in regard to white men dealing with black women. This is yet one more contradiction in the sincere fictions frequently held in the white mind about African Americans.

A business executive in a northern city underscores the way in which black women are used by white men in a variety of employment settings:

> To the extent that the people they are committing the racism upon can defend themselves, the next step is to take the easiest route. And the easiest route is—to the extent that they're giving the impression of being fair—to give that fairness to black females, and to do all they can to make sure that black males don't get to a point where they can seriously challenge the practices of racism and do things for them. So they can push off on that and say, "We're fair, because we have these blacks in place."

This respondent continues to describe the complex ways in which whites practice gendered versions of racism.

> And more and more, they're becoming females as against males. They're continuing to practice racism, but in a way in which it's less threatening to them.... The system tends to discourage their being able to act in a positive way. And so you have more functioning, available to work in the workplace, black females at that point than you have black males.... And those structural constraints extend into the corporate workplace and it extends into universities and colleges, where today there are more black females going to college than there are black males; the forces acting against [black males] are considerable.... You know, the white males have kind of said, "This is it. We're going to stop them, we're going to hold the ground at this point in time." And that's a formidable obstacle to confront black males, to look at that and say, "Where am I? What are the chances of my getting there?" ... I can tell you as a matter of fact that there will be all kinds of efforts taken to make *sure* you don't get there, or even close to there.

This executive interprets the deeper meaning of white society's practices that inferiorize black men—and, consequently, black women and black families. This degradation is sometimes achieved through the elevation of black women over black men. When directed at the more vulnerable or manipulable women, the old habit of racism endures, but in ways that seem less risky to whites. Perhaps, as white employers see it, these strategies are less likely to trigger strong reprisals from the black targets. Like much modern racism, this racial unfairness in the workplace is encapsulated in apparent fairness. "Inclusion" clearly loses its traditional meaning of real racial progress. Instead, it is transformed into a partiality that is exclusionary, however hidden and subtle the strategy may be.

Commonly, workplace unfairness triggers chain reactions, with consequences for many areas of life. Among the serious side effects are black men's resentment and problems in internal relations in black families. A woman counselor in a southern city explains: "I had been faced with black men when I first started working telling me to give up my job for black men, and I was quite angry about that. I don't think I should give up my job." This type of confrontation results in part from the awareness of black men that white society often prefers black women. Not surprisingly, many black men resent exclusion from the prerequisites for the traditional breadwinner and father roles. They may denounce this process of demasculinization, and black women can sometimes become targets for their resentment. If a black woman in turn reacts negatively to this male displeasure, there is potential for serious friction in her relationship with a black man.

White Fear of Black Men

There is complexity and nuance in black female interpretations of this matter. This female counselor, despite her initial chafing at such male comment, continues and makes it clear that she understands the racial structures and situations lying behind the black male resentment.

> I do think black men have it a lot tougher than we do. I see it in my own organization. There are not many black men in our organization. There are not many black men at the top. I could see them accepting a black woman faster. There is some hesitancy, or some fear, of black men. And I think it's unfounded, but I also think it's crazy. Because I do think that they fear us because they think we're violent. And of course, the black man is stronger and bigger, so, therefore, he can hurt them. And I didn't believe that until recently when I saw the fear in a white group when a black man came in. And it was like they were nervous. And I didn't understand at first. And I've watched it over the years at concerts and workshops. It's just that their body language changes when a black man comes in. . . . But black men are—I think white people are afraid of black men. And I don't think it's a founded fear, I think it's an irrational fear. And I don't even know, I think if you asked a white person that, I think they would deny it. . . . I'm very observant of body language of people, and I've watched over the years at seminars, workshops, meetings.

Black men commonly experience whites "seeing" them as taller and heavier than they really are. Lying behind size imagery is apparently the stereotype of black men as violent. Among white Americans the image of a threatening black man is an old racial dream (nightmare), yet somehow it has come to be real and shaping of everyday behavior in a large variety of organizational and public settings. White Americans hold the power to transform these irrational dreams into realities ranging from subtle body language to discriminatory practices, all of which do much harm. White reactions, including body language and avoidance, are stimulated or buttressed by entrenched white images and ideologies.

The exclusion of black men, by whatever means, from certain occupations and employment settings appears logical to many whites in a society where the distribution of most rewards is racially based and in light of white fears of the black man. An accountant adds his views about white fears of "the large black man":

> If there's a choice between a black woman and black male, all things being equal, the black woman will be given the benefit of the doubt, for a whole lot of subjective reasons. I'm not saying that black women are necessarily less aggressive, or anything like that, but it's sometimes too intimidating. Like . . . if you're six feet four inches, obviously you're going to be noticed. And a woman may be more easygoing and not as aggressive in some situations, and I don't always agree with that. But all things being equal, I think it's probably, corporate America would probably rather deal with a black woman than a black man.

In the black experience, whites exaggerate the size of black men or fear them regardless of size, presumably because of stereotyped notions of violent aggression. Still, there is the question why black women are seen as more controllable by white decision makers. One reason is their gender. If a black woman speaks up to her white male boss, she can be put down or controlled by a sexist action or remark, such as the "now, now, honey" and arm-round-the-shoulder routine. Such a response to assertiveness is not possible with a black male subordinate, who therefore may be more intimidating if he disagrees openly with his boss. A woman may be more easily controlled by white male bosses in these physical, sexual, and psychological terms.

We noted in Chapter 1 the importance of common white failures to recognize black men and women as they truly are. White misrecognition of black men—racist dreams and nightmares about fearsome and threatening black men—dates back at least to the first decades of

African enslavement in the American colonies.[6] From the 1600s to the end of the colonial wars white colonists generally portrayed Native Americans and Africans as "uncivilized" and "savages." One reason for this labeling was doubtless that it legitimated in the white mind the brutal oppression of these people of color. One historian of racist ideas, Winthrop Jordan, traces the negative image of African men to the irrational notions of early European colonizers that African men were especially virile and lusted after white women. This highly developed imagery was not rooted in fact but in irrational white fears and passions. As Jordan sees it, the racist images of black men lusting after white women ease white male guilt over white male lust for black women—with the latter the only lust likely to be carried out, in the rape of enslaved African or African American women.[7]

In the contemporary United States white fears of "black rapist monsters" persist and have serious consequences for black men, as in the case of "Willie" (not his actual name) Horton, a black male who was convicted of attacking a white woman. In a late 1980s presidential election campaign some Republican operatives working for George Bush circulated a photo of a bearded "Willie" Horton to the mass media in an attempt to scare fearful white voters. While there were several distortions in the advertising campaign, one stands out: Then as now, most of the men who rape white women are *not* black. Most are white men; yet not a single Republican ad portrayed these numerous white male rapists. Even more conspicuously, there were no ads anywhere in the political campaign about white male rapists who had attacked black women.[8] These common images of fearsome black men are frequently used by many whites, including politicians and presidents, to legitimate whites' continuing racist practices directed at African Americans. Hoary white nightmares about the character of black men and women are converted into harsh and hostile racial-gender discrimination, whose effects on the victims can linger on and, again and again, shape and reshape white prejudices.

Black Women as a Competitive Threat

Not all our respondents see the black woman getting advantages over the black man in the contemporary employment setting. The situation, a few made clear, is complex, variable, and depends on the circumstances. One respondent, a counselor at a western university, drew on her experience to suggest that black women are often not more accepted than black men. Her observations at first seem to diverge completely from previous comments: "I feel that black males in corporate America are for some reason more accepted than black females. And I have my own selfish feelings about that. I feel that in many cases across the board, black females seem to be a threat, because, not just because I'm a female, but I just feel that we're strong." This successful professional makes the important point that black women—having always worked, being familiar with white work settings, and having long experience as breadwinners under adversity—are in many work settings a more serious competitive threat to whites than are black men. The reason may lie in part in the demographic reality in many workplaces. One consequence of there being fewer black men than black women in many white-collar settings is that the women represent more of the black workers in such situations who actually compete with white workers, including the white men. In such employment situations an assertive or competitive black woman, like a competitive black man, may find whites considering her a particular employment threat. The feeling that black men are "more accepted" needs to be understood in this interpretive context.

Scholars such as Norma Burgess and Hayward Horton emphasize how, in order for African American women and their families to be fully understood, the work roles of black women need be placed in the relevant historical setting.[9] Writing about the Northwest, for example, Joan Cashin demonstrates how black women working in the nineteenth century developed creative and flexible gender roles in the black family. As she explains, "Once they arrived in the Northwest, black women faced challenges that distinguished them from most American mothers. Those who managed their households could not abide by white middle-class norms, of course, for domesticity and submissiveness required a husband in the house."[10] Later Cashin adds this about married women: "Domesticity also took on another meaning for these married black women, for most had to work for pay, either outside or within the home. . . . In striking reversal of white, middle class norms, 'good' women worked for a wage to bring their loved ones together."[11] Given their long history in the U.S. workplace, it would not be surprising if black women were sometimes viewed by whites as a greater economic threat than black men.

As we will see throughout this book, collective knowledge and collective memories are important for our respondents, and doubtless for most African Americans. The university counselor quoted above continued by noting the historical background of African American women being central to their families. First she mentioned that in the past women often worked when men could not, then adds this comment on what that means:

> And when I say that, I'm thinking about history and the old days.
> . . . And I'm not saying that they [black men] weren't strong. But I
> do feel that as a female, because we were mothers and workers and
> that person, that rock that could be relied upon when things were
> going bad, strengthened us, to the point of being determined to sur-
> vive at whatever cost. Now, with respect, but at whatever cost in
> terms of her family surviving, [she] became what might be said
> today as very forceful, very threatening. So that, on one hand I say
> that black males are accepted in the corporate field and have more
> of a chance in terms of being promoted, versus a black female being
> looked upon as a threat. Because she's going to speak her mind, and
> she is quite confident, she does know what she knows. And again, I
> don't want to say just because I'm a female, but this is the way
> that I see it.

This woman draws on her own work experience, in which her assertiveness has apparently been perceived as threatening by whites.
While her generalization about the greater acceptance of men does not
coincide with the view commonly expressed by most of our respondents, her concern for the history of black women as mothers and as
workers is shared, as is her sense that women have been the "rock" on
which black communities are built. As our respondents see it, black
women, like black men, are frequently viewed as an economic or racial
threat by white supervisors or peers. Neither black women nor black
men have come close to real equality with white male workers in most
of the major job sectors of this society.[12]

The Relevance of the Racist Past

For African Americans current racial difficulties are rooted very much
in the racist past of the United States. Through collective memory,
historical experiences become part of the present. The relevance of

history is underscored by a male college student at a southern university.

> I think that a black male represents more of a threat to the power
> structure in this country than does the black female. And I also be-
> lieve history will bear me out, in that black women historically had
> more access to the main household, than did men, slaves I mean.
> The ones I think who had access to the house were typically cas-
> trated or effeminate or whatever. And I think that might be a valid
> conclusion from that and from things that exist now.

This student sees a connection between the past of slavery and
the present of discrimination. In fact, some black women did apparently receive more "favors" from whites than did black men on
the slave plantations, although all enslaved women suffered cruel
oppression. The issue here is the favoring, such as it was, of black
women by white men and women, and clearly not one of black
choices in the matter.

The resemblance between the white plantation mentality and some
contemporary white thinking is suggested by a female business owner:

> I think as far as black women are concerned, I think it goes back
> to the slave mentality times, too, black women being easier to deal
> with, but yet more capable of being controlled. So, you know,
> there's a downside, too. And as a result then, I think the demise of
> black women is that the white, male, Anglo-Saxon power structure
> feels as though it can manipulate black women. And with black
> men it's better to castrate them at the beginning and not let them
> in as a player and that way you eliminate the competition.

Throughout our interviews and many other accounts from African Americans in other sources we see recurring references to the
history and legacies of more than two centuries of slave oppression
in the United States. While for most whites this slavery may be
part of a mostly forgotten past, for most African Americans it remains real and alive. The recurring allusions to slavery are important to the language of the respondents' accounts. In the last
commentary continuity with the historical past is seen in the white
image of the threatening black man.

A receptionist at a university underscores the historical roots of white attitudes in the present: "I can tell you that white men have been threatened by black men throughout history." She gives the example of whites who lynched black men "'to protect our women' and 'to protect ourselves' . . . there's a historical precedent for that type of attitude." Evident among many respondents is a strong sense of a very racialized American history, a shared interpretation of the past, a perception of a common cradle. One can note, for example, the thousands of lynchings of black men and women by whites. Lynchings were brutal killings, and they often involved ritualized torture and body dismemberment. They were representative of an almost genocidal mentality among many white Americans. This past violence has become, not surprisingly, indelibly imprinted on the African American mind, from one generation to the next over many decades of U.S. history. It is reinforced in the present by continuing white violence—for example, by white police officers. At the center of white violence and brutality was—and still is—the white male fear of the black man, who is imagined in the racially obsessed white mind to be a particular threat to whites, and especially white women. Some white men may also be reacting with violence because they fear, however subconsciously, that the black man may seek revenge for the horrible crimes done against him by whites.

Consequences of Racism at Work:
Black Families

Traditionally U.S. society has defined the male spouse as head of the family and, for that reason, has viewed men's employment as a prerequisite for that function.[13] In principle, a man's employment is still the avenue through which his family's support is supposed to be earned. This is true in spite of the fact that gender roles in the United States have become less traditional and that the jobs of many wives are critical to family income.[14] Through men's employment the traditional family structure is thought to be protected, and societal expectations preserved. In accenting men's job needs over women's this tradition is patriarchal and sexist.

Forced movement away from patriarchal norms can mean that black men, women, and families suffer confusion as well as the social blame that comes from white Americans asserting the priority of the patriarchal ideal.[15] This conflict and complexity in gender roles is not new. In an analysis of slave plantation households one researcher has noted the consequences of white oppression for black women: "Slavery forced upon them a double view of gender relations that exposed the artificial or problematic aspects of gender identification, for by stripping slave men of the social attributes of manhood in general and fatherhood in particular, it afforded women no satisfactory social definition of themselves as women."[16] Not surprisingly, after slavery a male-centered household image became important to black women and men, but with meanings that are sometimes different from those for white Americans.

This issue did not die with slavery or Reconstruction because whites have persisted in racist practices across all major U.S. institutions to the present day. The impact of the continuing, often slavelike oppression on black men and black families is still a matter of discussion not only among scholars but also in African American communities. Today, as in the past, regular employment in a decently paying job is a major key to building successful lives and families. To conform to the traditional family model, or to one that is more egalitarian, black men need a rate of employment at least equal to that of white men. However, black women, particularly those with a college or postgraduate education, generally hold better-paying jobs at a higher rate than black men. Many of these women, because of these economic and educational circumstances, become the primary breadwinners in their families. This is not a matter of personal choice. The white-racist society and economy long ago created and still maintains this oppressive situation through its direct and indirect discrimination targeting black men. White society's discriminatory practices mean for many black men that they must violate the larger society's prescriptions for a conventional, patriarchal family life centered around a man as the primary breadwinner. This discriminatory employment situation forces many African American parents and their children into what are in effect alternative lifestyles. Harsh social penalties, inflicted by white society, often accompany these lifestyles.

Our respondents report that the family situations forced on many black Americans by the racist realities of employment and the workplace can create much tension between black men and women. When a black man is not employed, or is severely underemployed, he may feel impotent and more or less withdraw from his family. In this regard, he is not unlike other American men who face recurring unemployment or underemployment. He is much more likely, however, to face these conditions than white men. In addition, even if fully employed, a black man is likely to face significant racial hostility and discrimination at his workplace, and this too can affect his relationships and his family.

Given the context of a patriarchal society, certain advantages accrue to black men and black families from the regular employment of black men. A strong male figure is not necessarily in the interest of white Americans, as a social worker explains:

> An intelligent black man is more of a threat to white America than an intelligent black woman. Because the black man heads the family, and if we get our black men on track, then white America would have some difficulty with that. I really believe that. On the other hand, black women struggle with "If I pursue this, does this mean that I'm interfering with a black man getting what he needs to get?" So there's a struggle and this tension all the time. And you don't, you don't want to deny your own self. And you know you have a self to actualize. But then what happens to the black men, what happens to the black man in the process? And I believe that whites pit us against one another, and they've done it very, very well, and done it very successfully. And if you just look at middle America in terms of the professions, there are many more black women than there are black men. So, I think that we as black women, those who have achieved, have a hard, like a reality that's sort of sad that you have to deal with. And I think America uses it against us very well. And I think our black men buy into it sometimes, and I think our black women buy into it, and we end up fighting with one another, and we forget who the real enemy is.

This perceptive woman again highlights the role of white society in "using" black Americans and in creating tensions and frictions between black men and black women. In several respondents' quotes we see references to a "divide and conquer" strategy that is sometimes tried by whites in workplaces and other settings to separate black women from black men and to reduce unity. This may or may not work, but it is tried. This respondent also notes the internal struggle that black women must go through. As she says, a black woman has "a self to actualize," yet she cannot achieve her maximum without being concerned for what happens to the black man. One of the heavy and significant costs of persisting racism lies in the many limitations on self-actualization for black women and men.

One detrimental consequence of the traditional role reversal forced on many black women and men by the machinations of a racist society, particularly the racialization of unemployment, is that many black women end up raising children alone or without much income coming in from the unemployed or underemployed spouse's job. A female business owner in a southwestern city explains: "The black woman is oftentimes left with children to raise on her own. So, even though she may get more breaks in the job market, which I think is probably true, she has got the extra burden of providing and caring for a family as well as herself. And unfortunately, in a lot of cases that's without any kind of financial help whatsoever from the father." The black woman may be somewhat better off in the job market than black men, but this has its negative impact. Thus, noted a male dentist, a black woman is burdened, playing the head of family, provider, and nurturer roles: "Well, black women have it hard, they have it very hard. They have the hardest job. Very seldom do we hear of a black female walking out on her children, her family. Husband walks out, but for the most part, the woman is stuck, and so they have to make the best of that situation." As a group, our respondents indicate great respect for the many hurdles that African American women must face and overcome. Women must cope with and juggle multiple and sometimes conflicting obligations and roles.

Role juggling can affect all women, whether they are single or married. In both cases black women are burdened by multiple roles that are legacies of the racialized past. One married woman, a professor in the health sciences, noted the complexity of her role: "You are the nurturer in the family, you're the mom, you're a breadwinner. And though you may be the powerful and high-powered businesswoman at work, somewhere on the freeway you change hats. And you walk in—my son calls me 'Doctor Mom.' I become the mother person." Not surprisingly, under these conditions many black women are not completely satisfied with their lives. While marriage is not necessarily the primary standard for happiness and satisfaction in their lives—they often have a broad view of their talents and abilities (see Chapter 3)—it is an important consideration for most black women.

In fact, some of them report that they have a hard time finding black mates. A female university student expresses the feeling shared by many:

> In looking at the personal lives of black men and women, I think
> black women experience a tougher time in that . . . there are certainly
> a lesser number of marriageable men, and there are more black women
> who stay single longer. And so, black women can say that they're not
> very satisfied in their lives. If they were to compare their lives to white
> women, there are more marriageable white men for white women, than
> there are black men for black women.

Marriage statistics support this assertion that black women have fewer potential mates.[17] We might note that these marriage statistics are central to some prominent discussions of problems in low-income sectors of black communities. William J. Wilson has shown that many low-income women cannot find marriageable black men, that is, those with decently-paying jobs, and thus must raise their children on their own.[18] The failure of policymakers to provide decently paid work for every person seeking employment is the major reason many women have difficulties in finding spouses who can fulfill the traditional role of primary breadwinner.

Forced into the role of primary breadwinner in a racist and patriarchal society that generally does not value that position for women, at least in its public statements and values, black women have fewer chances of developing traditional husband-wife relationships with black men. When black men are less able to provide for families, and view black women as generally more successful, marriage difficulties may be a logical outcome.

A counselor at a university expresses her concern over what she regards as a troubling trend:

> This is a very touchy subject for me. I feel that black women are re-
> ally . . . doing things, they're growing, but our black men are not.
> So, we're going to get a society of educated black women and unedu-
> cated black [men], which is going to throw off our whole family.
> We already have an unbalanced situation. . . . Oh, I'm going to step
> on toes now. I'm really a traditionalist. I'm old-fashioned. And I
> feel that the black man should be the head of the household. I feel
> that he should run that house. And the woman, we know that we're

the ones who are the backbone. But that man should be there, and he should not be intimidated. We should be there to help him, to help our families. But we should not be trying to supersede them and make them feel less than what they are. They are our black men and that's where they should stay. But we run into situations now where they are not up to par. There are very few who are thinking about what they really want to achieve in life. Or those who think that they want to achieve some things, but feel they're so burdened with other things . . . feel they can't accomplish these other goals.

Here is a strong commitment to black men having the traditional head-of-household position in a society that celebrates that type of family. Like the other respondents she understands from experience that black men and women often have to deviate from conventional patriarchal traditions. As a result, tensions and other negative ramifications develop. Despite its roots in a history of exclusion of black men from well-paying jobs in the economy, the role reversal is not seen in these terms by most white analysts, including some social scientists. Instead, the conflict with prevailing norms of marital life is interpreted in terms of black culture or values rather than white-generated oppression.

A different history can mean a different interpretation of what on the surface appear to be similar female experiences with traditional gender roles. As the black feminist and civil rights activist Barbara Omolade has recently put it, since the days of slavery African American women have come to see that "the very traditional experiences of motherhood and sex within marriage were not necessarily viewed as oppressive to black women, for they were the literal and symbolic weapons she could utilize to assure the biological and social reproduction of black people. Marriage and motherhood were humanizing experiences that gave her life meaning, purpose, and choices."[19] How one views marriage and motherhood can depend on where one is positioned in the society's class and racial hierarchies. The traditional family can provide more family members to interact with and thus more of a haven from a racist world not of one's choosing. The historical and contemporary experiences of African American women with family life as home and place of refuge often give them a different viewpoint on some family and work issues raised by white feminists in the United States. In recent decades the organized feminist movement has generally reflected the interests of white women, including wives and mothers who have found the male-dominated home anything but a haven.

Recent research has made it clear that the lack of employment at a decent wage is at the heart of other major problems for black men of all ages and in all regions of the United States. The common limitations on black men getting decent work are viewed by an administrative assistant in this way: "It's by design that black men can't get equal and fair and good employment. That they become frustrated, and they want to give up. It's a problem . . . all over America. That black men, that black youth unemployment is higher and double than anybody else's, you know. It's probably by design." This respondent, like several others, seems to be referring to the problems of black men in various class or status groups, from low-income youth to middle-class professionals. From this vantage point the male devaluing in the work world may be by white society's design. Black men are shaped by white-generated oppression outside the home, which seems intended to bring the racialized image of the chronically job-troubled black man to life. With this exploitation of black men, white imaginings of black men's responsibility for their own economic problems are perfected.

The periodic reversal of traditional family roles means that not only black women and men suffer but also children, families, and communities suffer. As we saw in the previous section, this view of the degrading of the black male is central to many black memories of the racial past. The remembered past includes the brutalizing of individuals and the cruelties to families under slavery, a recurring theme in our interviews. A male psychologist suggests that in situations other than the workplace whites play out this mode of degradation.

> To me, that's a historical technique of divide and conquer. . . . The other thing it [preferential hiring] does, it's another way to castrate the male. Historically, the black male has always been castrated, back in slavery time even, and after that the black female and the white male were the strongest people. The white female and the black male were nothing. In my own situation, when my parents were trying to buy a home in the Midwest, my father couldn't get the loan. My mother went down and got it the same day. What you get is a castrating kind of thing where the black male is con-

cerned. If they can pit male against female, black against black, then it's really destructive. These are the kinds of games I see being played constantly.

Not only does the black man face difficulties in securing a decent job and income for his family, he must also face discrimination as he tries to use that income to better his family's condition. The white demasculinization of the black man can be seen in many areas of life, including trying to put a roof over his family. Indeed, this attack on black men can occur wherever the white image of the black man comes into play.

Conclusion

Imagine for a moment a society with an absence of white stereotypes of black Americans, a true assessment of black character as human, and an inclusion of black men and women on an equal basis with whites in employment settings and positions of power. Think of a typical black man fulfilling his gender role as traditionally defined by the larger society, as primary breadwinner, husband, and father. Think, further, of the potential outcomes of this fulfillment for his spouse and his family. (Here we are not advocating a patriarchal standard for the black family, but rather emphasizing the double standard that guides white expectations about black and white families.) Many whites probably cannot conceive of such a societal condition, not only because they are unaware of current black attempts (often relatively successful) at such family structures even under conditions of oppression, but also because white society is directly implicated in creating the oppressive societal conditions facing African Americans. Even today, as recent research clearly shows,[20] a majority of whites are unwilling to squarely face the fact that they and their ancestors are directly implicated in nearly four hundred years of racist oppression, and thus are unable to support large-scale programs aimed at eradicating racial discrimination in the workplace and other organizational settings.

At business and government workplaces in every state of the union, the fictitious female characters of Jezebel and Sapphire still reign strongly, though frequently they are imaged in more subtle ways than in the past. Everywhere, these and other negative images linger and loiter in many a white mind. They seem to haunt and possess much of white America. The domineering black matriarch is often seen as determined to walk over black men at whatever cost, and she dominates and takes the best positions from these black men as a matter of personal choice. In a common white vision, the black woman typically leaves for work from a home shared only with children. Or if the black woman goes home to a black spouse—frequently assumed by many whites to be lazy or incompetent—she brandishes her superior status as a modern Sapphire.

The negative renderings of black women are frequently white-racist dreams. The white vision is self-fulfilling, often converted into discriminatory practices in the workplace and elsewhere—and thus into the white-desired social reality. Historically racial dreams still inspire many whites in their portrayals of the black woman as deformed, empty, and difficult to grasp. Rank-and-file whites are joined by many white scholars in their often consistently negative images of African American women. For example, the myopic view of social scientist and U.S. senator Daniel P. Moynihan popularized the idea of the typical black woman as a controlling head of household and matriarch. Writing about the black family in a section subtitled "Matriarchy," Moynihan specified: "A fundamental fact of Negro American family life is the often reversed roles of husband and wife. Robert O. Blood, Jr. and Donald M. Wolfe, in a study of Detroit families, note that 'Negro husbands have unusually low power,' and while this is a characteristic of all low income families, the pattern pervades the Negro social structure . . ."[21] Moynihan did hit on the reversed-roles issue that does face many African American families, but his extended analysis was much too crude and one-sided, if not stereotypical.[22] Nowhere in his report did Moynihan stress the fact that the majority of African American families did not fit what he called a disorganized ("female-headed") family pattern. This is particularly true for working-class and middle-class families, those above the low-income level. In addition, Moynihan apparently did not care to talk with mothers and fathers in African American families in order to better assess the meaning of his impersonal family statistics.

While we have seen that the partial or total reversal of gender roles is viewed by many of our respondents as a serious problem facing many African American families, they provide much more nuanced accounts of how this plays out in families pressured by the often oppressive employment and related economic conditions of U.S. society. Moynihan does not assess, much less stress, the historical and current role of whites in creating a discriminatory and oppressive racial situation that may force reversed gender roles. Moynihan may have told his side of the matriarchy story while possessed by old white memories of legendary Jezebels and Sapphires, for their silhouettes surface in his whitewashed report. Moreover, as we see clearly throughout this book (see especially Chapter 6), there is much to be said about the large number of African Americans who live in hardy immediate and extended families with strong husbands and wives.

Moynihan is not alone. Even where they seem irrelevant, the shadows of traditional images of black women can be recognized elsewhere in the unfavorable statements of whites about black working women. This was often seen in the 1991 senatorial hearings on Supreme Court nominee Clarence Thomas and the charges made against him by Anita Hill. For example, Charles A. Kothe, a white Oklahoma lawyer and former dean of Oral Roberts University, who worked with Professor Hill, dismissed her allegations by saying, "I find her references to the alleged sexual harassment not only unbelievable, but preposterous. I am convinced that such is the product of fantasy."[23]

Playing into white hands, even a few black men make use of these antifemale images, which historically have been drawn by white cultural artists. Consider the following statement by John N. Doggett, III, a black conservative who graduated from Yale Law School, attended Harvard Business School, worked as a management consultant in Austin, Texas, and was a witness at the nomination hearings.[24] To show sexual and other aggressiveness on the part of law professor Anita Hill, a trait consistent with the image of the Jezebel or controlling black woman, Doggett described for white senators her behavior at parties attended by colleagues: "I observed from a distance—and I am not a psychiatrist, I am not an expert, just a man—Anita Hill attempting to be friendly with men, engage them in conversation, initiate conversation, elongate conversations, and people talking with her and eventually going away."[25] The behavior might well be described simply as being sociable or amiable. However, in the case of Professor Hill, a black professional woman of many accomplishments, this portrait played into the hands of white male senators whose minds were likely conversant with traditional black-female stereotypes. Construed as aggressive and perhaps replete with immoral in-

71

tentions, Hill's behavior is rendered negatively by this black man acting as an ally of the white cultural artists.

In the hearings Hill was often portrayed as flawed, impure, and unacceptable. She was misrecognized as a stereotyped black woman. Countless references by members of the Senate committee, and others outside the committee, to Professor Hill's alleged sexual fantasies suggested that she embodied the traditional white image of the black woman. In the committee's eyes, which were all white male eyes, Hill seemed to personify a type of Jezebel. She fit the contemporary white artists' portrait and the historical image provided by their predecessors. Hill was portrayed in an evil-looking wrap that conformed to the old white design. Her portrait lingers today, preserving or intensifying her moral and spiritual degradation in a myriad of white racial libels.

Thus, as depicted by our respondents, the workplace is an important site of racial experiences where the cultural stigmatization of African American women is strongly shaped by white images and practices. Taken together, our respondents provide a comprehensive account of, and nuanced explanations for, racial barriers in the workplace and how those barriers affect several areas of black life. When directed at black women, gendered racism in the workplace is often dressed in a costume of a certain "female privilege." Far from being a real privilege, however, this costume is a historical legacy that continues the social denigration or emasculation of the black man and the parallel degradation of the black woman. This workplace destruction of black women and men leaves its imprint everywhere, on the black family and community, and ultimately on white America as well. Not surprisingly, the often coinciding explanations of current workplace events by our respondents point to the old, still lingering white habit of racism.

When it comes to the independence and strong performances at work of many black women, especially in historically white workplaces, the negative reactions of many white men also reflect lingering habits of sexism.[26] Negative white male reactions to black women who are too high-achieving or outspoken for their taste may signal white male fear of feminism. These African American women embody the independent, assertive, self-sufficient and successful woman. These same white men, it is likely, will not have a positive reaction to white women who adopt a similar level of assertiveness and independence.

Chapter 3

Black Beauty in a
Whitewashed World

Significantly, much Caribbean literature associates black women with the very best that each island has to offer. In the language of Émile Roumer, the black women there are "plus savoureuses que crabes en aubergine" (more delightful than eggplant stuffed with crabs) and "marabout de mon coeur" (high yellow of my heart).[1] Regardless of status or color, women of African descent are commonly celebrated as beautiful human beings. As another Caribbean writer proclaims, "Qu'elles soient mère, fille, épouse, amante, Qu'elles soient mulatresse, grimelle, négresse, chabine ... elles sont toujours une source d'inspiration" (Whether mother, daughter, spouse, lover, whether mulatresse, grimelle, négresse, chabine, ... they are always a source of inspiration.)[2] The terms *mulatresse, grimelle, négresse,* and *chabine* refer to different skin tones, from light to dark.

Associating women with nature, good food, and beautiful flowers is a type of sex typing. However, in the Caribbean context these associations are considered very positive and contrast sharply with common racist-sexist views of African American women among whites in the United States. In the Caribbean quiet strength, both physical and moral, is a valued feminine characteristic that, transformed by the cultural beholder into grace and beauty, inspires many a Caribbean writer.[3] Femininity as strength is evident, for example, in the Creole advice to women in difficulty: *"Mété fanm sou ou"* (literally, "put woman on you," that is, "wear your femininity"). A woman's "attractive smile" and "glowing eyes" (often read as the window of the soul) are recurring themes in Caribbean songs and writings; her internal strength radiates beauty and reveals her as a real person with broad talents, abilities, and ambitions. Even the strength seen in a woman's assertive attitude radiates beauty.[4]

While these representations are sex-typed and can be seen as sexist, one should keep in mind the social context. The black household in the Caribbean tends to be egalitarian, with the wife-mother having considerable power. In light of the data in this chapter we might take these representations to be relatively positive, in contrast to the Jezebel, Sapphire, and other misrecognition applied to black women in the United States. These racialized characters are unknown in the Caribbean. Of course, beauty is relative, and what is beautiful in one society may not be so in another. However, many experiences of African American women are brutalizing and tragic, for what is black female beauty at home is arbitrarily transformed by white Americans into black female "ugliness" in another setting. That white-defined lack of beauty is exploited to the benefit of the powerful, and glorified to the detriment of the African American women.

Stigmatizing Black Beauty

Beauty and power are intimately connected. Beauty is status. It is associated with triumphant goodness in fairy tales and adult literature.[5] Aristotle found beauty to be a "greater recommendation than any letter of introduction."[6] Yet beauty is also ethnocentric, resting in the eye of the cultural beholder, a battlefield where polarized groups struggle to capture an aesthetic image. To the extent that beauty is identified in the United States with white femininity and is differentially associated with access to rewards such as employment, income, and self-esteem, it moves beyond the surface-level reading and is momentous to women whose lives are particularly affected by the prevailing standards of female attractiveness.

During the nineteenth century, in the early years of the development of sciences such as medicine, biology, ethnography, and natural history the human body was of central interest. Among white European and American scientists the best body type was considered that of white Europeans, whose physical superiority was linked to "intellectual, aesthetic, and moral superiority . . . over all other types."[7]

Other types of bodies—of blacks, Jews, women, and homosexuals, among others—were considered ugly and identified with degeneracy and sexuality. These groups were often mixed in the white male mind: "Jews and homosexuals are called black and often depicted as black, and all degenerate males are said to be effeminate. Medical science occupies itself with classifying the bodily features of members of all these groups, dissecting their corpses, often with particular attention to their sexual parts."[8] The central ideal of beauty was one of manly virtue and the white male. And light-skinned, fair-haired, slender white women, who were clearly objectified and sexualized, were construed to be the standard of female beauty. At an early stage in Western science, as well as in Western thought more generally, white superiority took many forms, including the appropriation of what was beauty and the definition of what was ugly.

Today these deep structures of racist imaging persist in the United States. The scholar bell hooks has suggested that the rule of beauty is still consistent with the ideology of white superiority: the fairer, the better.[9] Thus, black women who depart from this standard and occupy inferior positions in the beauty hierarchy are penalized by means of fewer rewards. Given these costs, black women will likely consider the rules a burden, a means of racial-gender inferiorization and exclusion.

Honoring the request of Grier and Cobbs to "slip for a moment into the soul of a black girl whose womanhood is so blighted, not because she is ugly, but because she is black and by definition all blacks are ugly,"[10] we give heed to a black college student as she describes some of the heartrending effects of white beauty ideals on her life.

> Beauty, beauty standards in this country, a big thing with me. It's a big gripe, because I went through a lot of personal anguish over that, being black and being female, it's a real big thing with me, because it took a lot for me to find a sense of self . . . in this white-male-dominated society. And just how beauty standards are so warped because like my daddy always tells me, "white is right." The whiter you are, somehow the better you are, and if you look white, well hell, you've got your ticket, and anything you want, too.

Underneath this experience with white standards lies a young black woman's struggle to secure her racial-gender identity. Because the aesthetic is racialized, with the tastes of white men at its core, deviations from the norm that are not in any sense "ugly" are nonetheless inferiorized. The black woman's full humanity is not recognized by the larger society, and this misrecognition takes many forms and has serious consequences.

The student's comments suggest the problematical socialization of black teenage girls. With affection, this young woman recalls her father's wisdom about the harsh racial reality of "white is right," though she adds elsewhere in her interview that "at least they [whites] think it is." Moreover, later in the interview the student notes that her parents taught her to think of herself as beautiful. But the white societal signals of misrecognition are very strong.

Additional signs that the dominant white group is unfairly glamorized by prevailing standards of beauty are explicit in the selection—usually, or initially, by white selectors—of black women closest to the white look as the most attractive of their group. This can be seen in the case of black women who win the so-called beauty pageants—including the Miss America Pageant—that are judged mostly by whites: The lighter their skin, the straighter their hair, the more appealing to whites they are. Indeed, lighter-skinned African American women may be taken by whites to be Latinos or some ethnicity other than African American. In contrast, the more African or non-European their features, the less favorably black women are often viewed. A college student underscores this point: "Most white people, if you asked them on the street who is more beautiful, Jayne Kennedy or Cicely Tyson, . . . Cicely Tyson to me is one of the most beautiful black women I've ever seen, . . . they'd say Jayne Kennedy. Because she's got the nice long, straight, light hair, light features, angular, Anglo features. That's very racist because what you're saying is black people, their natural features are ugly. And that's very racist." In addition to skin color, she cites hair as an important component of white visions of female beauty. The old and symbolic meaning of female hair endures. Long, straight hair often seems to represent femininity and unrestrained sexuality, whereas short hair, perhaps seen as a symbol of inhibition, is less alluring and less feminine, particularly from the dominant male perspective.[11] The significance of hair in this society is evident in the economic success of the hair care industry. Tyson is further removed from the white aesthetic ideal than Kennedy, who, besides light skin, has other valued attributes such as flowing hair. Kennedy, the respondent predicts, will be defined by most whites as the more attractive of these two women. It is usually when black women advance in the direction of the white standard that they please most white beholders and their beauty may be acknowledged.

A black female hair designer in a southern city noted that she had been asked by whites the important question: "I know you [are] mixed with something, what kind of blood do you have, because you don't have those Negroid features." Given the associations of white with beauty, and black with what is not beautiful, if a black woman is seen as attractive by whites, she may be thought to be mixed with some measure of nonblack attributes. Moreover, because popular white thinking about racial matters often mixes in the idea of "blood," a woman's beauty is taken to be rooted in the very fountain of her life. On its face the black-mixed-with-white comment might seem positive, but it probably signifies aesthetic depreciation in the mind of a white person. In other words, a mixed black is an improved black, but she may also be considered a degraded white.

This question about physical features reveals that old ideas linking biology, "race," and beauty persist, surging into everyday discourse. In much popular white thinking, membership in the privileged white group requires the "right" blood, which in turn means the "right" appearance. While fallacious, such associations work well in confirming for whites that they own the beautiful. Beauty is stable and unchangeable rather than a mere social construct. These popular connections reaffirm that, for black women, equal access to beauty necessitates that they be whitened. The implications of these social-racial pressures were long ago noted by Frantz Fanon, who wrote, "For a black person there is only one destiny and it is white."[12]

Another black college student underscored how whiteness is an essential condition for beauty: "To be the perfect thing in America, you've got to be white—little pointy nose, and blonde hair and blue eyes. That's their standard." For almost all black women, of course, these ideals are an impossible quest, regardless of personal expense and effort. While appearing harsh, the social messages about dominant standards of beauty—which may even be conveyed to black children by some black parents—reflect the persisting racial reality in the United States.

The message about beauty is harsh because the underlying racial reality is harsh. A different version of that harsh story is also told daily—to men, women, and children—by dolls, magazines, films, and television.

The Meaning of Dolls

Most adults understand the significance of dolls for children, and especially for the socialization of girls. Some of today's dolls appear almost real; they can be groomed and have names, belly buttons, and birth certificates. Young girls playing with dolls learn early not only how to mother and nurture but also how to evaluate superficial traits like skin tones, hair texture, nose shape, eye color, and lip size. At an early age, children learn to differentiate between the good and the bad, the beautiful and the ugly. Some black children's white doll choices can reflect a sense of black not being beautiful that is innocent, oftentimes unconscious, yet consistent with society's and toymakers' direct and subtle messages about blackness. For others, the choices can reflect a yet uncontaminated child's thinking, simply based upon what doll aspects seem interesting at the moment, and are thus nonracial. The doll studies we cite below may sometimes misread black children's innocent choices.

During play children sometimes engage in self-evaluation, looking for contrasts or resemblances between themselves and the dolls. Depending on their judgments, they may relate or refuse to relate to the dolls and what they represent. To the extent that their learning through play is effective, black girls (and boys) can receive at an early age a cruel lesson about their place in the larger society, one that is painful and potentially damaging to their budding self-esteem and self-concept. One reflective mother, who has her own business, describes a daughter's experience playing with Barbie dolls:

> My daughter's going through a situation right now with black dolls and white dolls and it's very interesting. One of the things that I found out was that, the way that I found racism penetrating my daughter was that the black dolls' hair that they put on the Barbie dolls is harder to comb than the white dolls that are Barbie dolls. I started noticing why she was playing more with white dolls in the tub, because she could easily comb their hair. That was very disturbing to me.

The mother then suggests the logic behind her daughter's choice of the white dolls for play time:

> She says, "Well this one, her hair gets tangled up too much, and this one I can comb her hair." And it was very true. And it was like a silent racism that was occurring with my child, which really disturbed me.

Subtle racism, what the mother designates as silent racism, is generally hard to detect or prove. Other reasons could conceivably be offered for black Barbie's tangled hair, but, given her lifelong experience, this mother looks deeply into the matter. The incident illustrates subtle gendered racism for her because such dolls effectively carry to girls the makers' messages about black women. Such messages directly target girls, but they can also have an impact on boys who come into contact with the dolls. The episode with the Barbie doll is interesting for other reasons as well. It may be that the girl had prior exposure to associations of snarled hair with undesirability, which might explain her actions. However, even if she had experienced the difficulty of combing tangled hair firsthand and was using as a frame of reference her memories of such sessions, it seems likely that, not having been rejected herself, she would not have come to the conclusion the black doll is to be spurned because of tangled hair.

In another context psychiatrists William Grier and Price Cobbs have explained that for black Americans "the combing and plaiting of the hair, in whatever stylish manner the mother may adopt, results only in the child's being rendered 'acceptable.' . . . For the pain she goes through, she might well expect to be stopped on the street by strangers stunned by the beauty and the transformation wrought by the combing and the stylized plaits. Not so. She is simply considered to be of an acceptable appearance."[13] We suspect that the child's reaction to Barbie has little to do with a wish to avoid the type of hair combing described by Grier and Cobbs, but rather with the issue of appearance suggested here. It seems that the rejected Barbie doll conveyed some other message to the child, one that is powerful and negative and beyond the issue of some tangled hair.

Indeed, the black girl's reaction calls to mind the studies of psychologist Kenneth Clark some years ago. Clark found that, given a choice between a white and brown doll, many black children selected a white doll. According to Clark, "racial awareness is present in Negro children as young as three years old."[14] The girl's reaction is also consistent with Gordon Allport's suggestion that black children "almost uniformly prefer the white doll."[15] Harvard psychologist Gordon Allport once described a black boy's response "when shown two dolls and asked 'Which one is most like you when you were a baby?' Bobby's eyes move from brown to white; he hesitates, squirms, glances at us sidewise—and points to the white doll."[16] Repeating the Clark study more recently, Darlene and Derek Hopson found a positive correlation between knowledge of black contributions to history and children's choices of dolls. These researchers concluded that "*talk*—open acknowledgment of racial issues, positive modeling, and reinforcement of Blackness" was important in children's thinking about these matters.[17] These studies have been interpreted as indicating that the white aesthetic acculturation of black girls and boys begins early and that one can expect that many black children, particularly those who have not had much significant family discussion of blackness or African American history, will find the white doll more desirable, with some implications for later mate selection.

The important questions of how the rejected dolls looked or what image they projected to the children are generally not addressed in the early research studies on black children. We know from Kenneth Clark that, except for their skin color, his dolls were similar in every way. However, it may be that the black children thought the brown dolls offered to them were less desirable for reasons other than skin color. The refusal on the part of the children to identify with the darker dolls might be due to unidentified factors indicative of a healthy self-concept. Since brown and white dolls came from the same mold and were dressed alike, perhaps the clothes they were dressed in were a complement to white complexions but not to dark ones. The white dolls might have been dressed better. Or perhaps the brown dolls' skin color may have looked artificial, and not like real black children. Moreover, it is likely that most of these black children had no experience playing at home with such brown-colored dolls, since they did not become common until some years later.

It is also possible that preference for white dolls sometimes reflects young children's broader and more inclusive conception of beauty at an early stage of life, a conception that captures the human character in totality and is not yet deformed by a racist socialization. Even if these young children understood that they and the darker dolls actually shared skin color—and they might have been lighter or darker than the dolls—they might have dismissed the shallow skin resemblance as unimportant. Can a young child not be selective because he or she is black? To expect that a young black child will select a doll strictly because the doll seems to be black to an adult seems a stereotyped expectation. A child would have to repeatedly do so after being presented with a variety of truly black-looking dolls—which were rare at the time of the early studies—before such an explanation is reasonable. (Interestingly, some young white children at day care centers reportedly choose black dolls for nonracial reasons.[18])

A similar logic is applicable to the daughter of our respondent who refused to relate to Barbie with the hair not easily managed. Without knowing how that Barbie looked to that child and what it embodied, a conclusion about the girl's behavior is of course speculative. Still, it may be that she was making a judgment about blackness. Skilled toymakers are perpetrators of subliminal messages that may make perceptive children uncomfortable without their knowing why, or where adults see nothing beyond the ordinary. Our respondent noted black Barbie's tangled hair only after her daughter's action and remark. As we have noted, some social scientists have pointed to such selections as evidence of low self-esteem in young black children. Learning through play is a dynamic transmitter of values to girls and boys, who may infer that white beauty is real beauty, and that to be attractive and acceptable conformity to a white cultural icon is de rigueur. Such conclusions may be reached in the larger social context where these children come to understand they are restricted in their selection of friends and that skin color is important because it transcends other qualities such as inner beauty.

Even the experiences of some members in the black professional group may be in line with these social scientific studies. For example, one female psychologist expressed concern about a network's dismissal of what she considers meaningful behavior by a television personality—behavior that, if analyzed, could have been instructive to the viewing public:

> I think it was revealing . . . for Carole Simpson to say, when she
> talked about the black doll experiment, when she admitted that she
> chose the white doll. And here she is in a leadership role, admit-

ting that she chose the white doll, and none of the critics afterward, ever commented about what that image meant, to hear, for
black America, to hear this woman say, she chose the white doll.
And here she is in a leadership role, how scary!

Clearly, the choice of the white doll is read by this respondent as a
negative choice.

There are other aspects to the way in which toys like dolls communicate white images of beauty and social reality. Black parents are
aware that play sessions with whites transmit a group or family memory and teach children lessons about the character of everyday choices
by whites. One mother recounts her explanation to her child:

> I explained to her how her [white] friends that she goes down to
> play with, had she ever noticed that they had black dolls in their
> house? And she said, "No." And then I said, "Well you need to un-
> derstand why they don't have black dolls in their house. And you
> can't always go down there to play with them if they don't come
> to your house, because it's like the black doll and white doll situa-
> tion in the house."

Reciprocity in home visitations is missing, which is likely to be revealing of white attitudes toward the black home. Such recurring
situations serve as an important lesson about identity and attractiveness, profoundly affecting mother and child. The child is urged to
refrain from associating with certain white families who do not have
black dolls or who react to black children in a certain way. The
dilemma of play choices may be accentuated for children whose limited exposure to white society makes such irrational white behavior
confusing. Such incidents will likely be remembered for a lifetime
and perhaps be transmitted to the next generation of black children
by these youngsters as they become adults.

The toy culture of a society reflects and reinforces its dominant
cultural fictions and preferred racial images. In her interview the previous respondent also noted the ways in which toy manufacturers
reveal white stereotypes of African Americans. Commenting on a conversation with her daughter, she recounts a revealing incident about
her daughter buying white dolls.

And so I asked her, "When you went to the store with your daddy, why didn't you get a black family?" And she said, "Well, they didn't have one." And I said, "Well, that's real interesting." And so I got one for her. What was interesting was that, she ended up having, this particular day, a whole ... white family, and the white male was not separated in the toy store ... at that point there was no Ken available without another Barbie doll and a baby. And there was no black Ken available for her black Barbie doll. ... And she wanted her Barbie doll to have the Ken, and so that's why she ended up making her decision. And I told her, "You need to think about your decision, because you're spending a lot of money on these people that don't look like you, and you're spending a lot of money on people that don't spend money on buying dolls that look like you."

This is an important account of toys in the context of social meanings. It would seem that at least some white toymakers or distributors reflect, perhaps unintentionally, in their work and sales practices the misrecognition of black families as mostly female-headed or incomplete. At a minimum, they do not make great efforts to supply America's children with an array of multicultural choices for playtime. Since toys play a role in child socialization, the lack of appropriate toys has serious implications for the ways that children learn about racial matters across the towns and cities of the United States.

Images in Magazines

Negative messages about African American women filter into the minds of teenage girls as white, Barbie-type models in popular magazines project white society's ideal of female beauty. Some black teen audiences strive to fit the mold, despite parental cautions and praises for black beauty. An honors student at a historically white university reveals this point:

My parents tried to tell me one thing, they tried to instill in me that I was a beautiful person, that my blackness was a beautiful thing, that the fact that I braided my hair was fine, that I didn't have a perm was fine. But when you're like, nine, ten, eleven, you tend not to listen to your parents, and you tend to listen to everything else, which is white people. In my case white people, and all society, which is white, so we'll just say white people ... with *Teen*

magazine and *Seventeen* magazine flung in my face all the time,
Barbie dolls flung in my face all the time, soap operas with all
these white folks with blonde hair and blue eyes . . .

Drawing from collective memory, many black parents teach their children about the biased aesthetic realities of American life. They draw from other aesthetic standards, including perhaps images of African beauty (for example, African queens) and the collective memory of positive black female and family traits and expressions. The actions and feelings of their child revive this memory of family traits and expressions, helping to center the child as beautiful.

The task of black parents is daunting given the toy and magazine images the children constantly encounter. That black teenagers often listen to whites and the media instead of their parents about the meaning of beauty is telling. This partially explains why black parents may often not be effective in protecting the children from social harm. Black girls, as well as young black women, may prefer listening to white society's possessors of "the good life" even when they send warped messages conflicting with the messages of caring parents. This youthful response must be understood in the larger societal cultural context. The college student just cited recounts her dilemma:

> I mean, it came from all sides, you name it and I got it. And I
> used to anguish over why I couldn't be like that. I mean, I used to
> have my little subscription to *Teen* magazine, and I'd wait for it at
> the mailbox and breathlessly open it up, and compare myself. I
> didn't realize it, on a subconscious level, I would compare myself to
> these females. And did not understand for the life of me why I
> couldn't look like that, or why I didn't have all these boyfriends
> like my white friends had, or why I wasn't considered to be pretty.
> I didn't realize it was because there wasn't anything out there that
> looked anything like me, remotely like me.

What young children face with available toys, teenagers often face in the scarcity of positive role models in the mass media. In encounters with the media many teenagers ignore or forget what their parents tell them about the harsh racial realities outside their homes and communities. This forgetting can create an illusion that may temporarily protect a black person against painful truths.

Black girls' being troubled over the dominant image of beauty is not surprising given their constant exposure to white settings that depreciate blackness, to places where black women are under-represented or absent and where white Barbie look-alikes are constantly flung in their faces. The bodily image of most black girls and women contrasts with what white society prefers or promotes daily by means of powerful media organs in towns and cities across the nation. The white reaction to this imaging of African Americans should be considered as well. Media images can lead to white choices affecting black children. Black girls face misrecognition of their beauty and their abilities at every age. In a recent focus group in the South a nurse recounts an experience at her children's school:

> We are never good enough. I mean, my children go to a predomi-nantly white school. . . . They've been there all their lives and every-thing. We went to an academic bowl. And I sat in back of some of the boys. Those white kids, some of them were the worst spellers you could ever [see]. They were just horrible. And, when, there was a little black girl there who was excellent. She was an excellent speller. She was just knocking them all out. Those [white] boys sat there, from *our school,* and said to their teacher, "I'm going [to team up] with a white girl." Even though . . . this little black girl was knocking them out, and the white kids weren't doing anything, that's what they said. And I went back to their teacher, and I said, "If you want me to come and talk about racism, that overt, that in-stitutional racism . . ." But these [white children], they grow up with it.

The white boys probably had more antiblack stereotypes in their minds than just a negative image of the girl's physical characteris-tics, and they signaled an aversion to the intelligence and attractive-ness of a black child. As this mother suggests, negative images of black children and adults are taught to white children in many dif-ferent settings.

Other Media: Films and Television

Like magazines, mainstream films and television shows often celebrate those black women who conform to the white prototype. Many tal-ented black female actors have trouble breaking through this barrier. A black male student at a major university relates a comment by

Cicely Tyson about difficulties encountered in her career as an actress:

> I was watching an interview one time, with Cicely Tyson, and she
> was talking about being a black woman in the movie industry
> today. Now, that's really tough, because there aren't any parts,
> major roles, for black actresses, and there aren't any major parts for
> black women in those roles. So, she always thought it was tough
> for her to get by.

Providing support for Tyson's viewpoint, this student shares the observation that African American women are usually absent from serious roles at the cinema: "If you look at the movies right now, hardly any of the major actresses in those roles are by a black woman, they're all by white women. The major roles, those that are nominated for the Oscars, are white women." In our interviews black men as well as women recognized the operation of the white-image standard against black women. This relative absence of black actresses in leading parts in important movies is also true for movies and serious drama series on television.

Moreover, portrayals of femininity on television and in many movies tend to promote the tastes of the dominant group. Black women often are portrayed as clownlike, unattractive, or homely; they play roles that yet again suggest an inferior position in the beauty hierarchy. A television anchorperson in a southwestern city discusses several older television programs that centered on black characters in reply to a question about the portrayal of African Americans in the mainstream media.

> I think it's terrible. I watch *Good Times*, the only reason I watch it
> is for John Amos, but I can't believe I watch that show and enjoy
> it so much.... I think it's just the fascination of seeing black peo-
> ple on TV on a consistent basis, because I didn't know anybody
> like J.J. And my momma used to always say, where do they get
> these ugly black people to be on TV? Because you think about it, a
> lot of the black people who are on television are unattractive peo-
> ple; you never saw an ugly white person. Or if you did, she was
> making money, à la Phyllis Diller.... I mean, some of the charac-
> ters on *Sanford & Son* that would come through, even though I
> loved that show. Because Fred would talk about them being ugly.
> Aunt Esther, he told her that ... if they rolled [her] face in dough
> they could make gorilla cookies.

The awareness of white-generated misrecognition of black women is central in these perspicacious comments about a number of black figures in the media. On television white women are seldom seen as consistently ugly. Moreover, if a white woman—particularly a middle-class woman—does depart from the common white beauty model, she can pay for hair dye or even surgery in order to get closer to the white Barbie look. Or, if she is not close to the Barbie model, she is likely to be portrayed as otherwise able or successful. When white women have status or money, their physical appearance is frequently downplayed or overlooked.[19] In contrast, a television show like *Julia,* starring the fine black actress Diahann Carroll, is uncommon. A nurse whose military officer spouse died in Vietnam, Julia rears her son alone and well. Such a positive presentation of black women as attractive and intelligent is rarely seen on major television networks. Particularly rare are shows *starring* such a black woman.

The white beauty mystique entails fictitious depictions, misrecognized human realities that reproduce old historical images in popular memory today. Naomi Wolf writes, "An economy that depends on slavery needs to promote images of slaves that justify the institution of slavery."[20] A society that directly and indirectly accents white racial purity and glorifies stereotyped attributes of white women—who are key for preserving this racial purity—promotes a serious misrecognition of black women, thereby justifying their exclusion from many rewards and from social celebration.

A white beauty mystique necessitates stone-blindness to mahogany and ebony, to marabout, chabine, and négresse. One professor in the health sciences put it this way:

> The media tend to find the lightest of complexions to portray us at any level. . . . And they're very mindful of making us have primarily Anglo-American features, which is craziness, because we are of a race that goes from one extreme to the other . . . from the very broad to the very keen in features. And we should be portrayed like that by television realistically how we are in real life.

The lighter an African American actor or model is and the more Anglo-white her features, the greater her chances are of accessing certain societal rewards such as movie or other media exposure. For whites in the mainstream media in particular, African American women often appear to project an unattractive image and lack femininity as defined by the dominant culture. Darker African American women are made into societal misfits who are targeted for more devaluing than their lighter counterparts by the white cultural artists.

Contradictions and Consequences of Stigmatization

While the consequences of the cultural devaluing and misrecognition of black women are very serious, we should note that there are some contradictions in white attitudes and actions toward black women. We noted in a previous chapter that even though African American women are frequently the victims of white beauty ideals, some white women emulate them in hairstyles, by tanning or lip surgery. Moreover, some white men find black women alluring and may attend to them in a way that seems, at first examination, to be somewhat positive. A closer look at white male behavior, however, leads to a different verdict, as a male teacher and counselor notes: "White men have *always* loved our women. Always. You just ask any sister about how many times she's been harassed by white men. Constantly. It's a constant thing." Such attention from white men does not mean that the image of black women is a positive one. The term "loved" here is not meant in the sense of shared affection, but in terms of sexual pursuit taking the form of harassment. We will examine these issues in more detail in the next chapter.

This respondent further comments on racial integration in the larger society: "That's one other reason why I think this is a very interesting time. Because white people, if they wanted, have been involved to an extent with black people. But it's always been hush-hush." Observing that today white attitudes seem to be changing, this man remarks further on how some whites are openly expressing their appreciation for black actors, at least as sidekicks: "[Whites], I guess, [are] becoming more sloppy in their adoration for us because it's coming out more. It's become very evident in magazines and TV to a certain extent."

The dominant group's discourse can be so deceptive and difficult to unravel that white expressions or actions cannot be easily assessed. White signals may be the cause for deep reflection by African Americans. Take the following situation, in which a mature woman, a hair designer in a major city, is confused and cannot determine if a remark made by a white man is harassment or a genuine expression of approval. Though ambivalent at first, on reflection she takes the incident to be an assault on her womanhood. "I just couldn't believe [he said] 'cute little colored girl.' So I said now, 'I'm over forty and I don't think I look like a girl.' And why would I have to be, I could be cute, but why does the color have to come into it? Why couldn't I be just an attractive young lady? But 'a cute little colored girl' just hit my nerve." Expressing deep frustration, she adds, "If I could have spit in that man's face I would have." Was the man's remark meant as a compliment or a put-down? In reality, his intention matters little. What matters is that, rather than flattered or uplifted, the woman feels inferiorized, reduced to the level of a child, and stripped of her identity as a woman. She wants her beauty evaluated not on the basis of color, but in terms of a less particularistic aesthetic standard. Yet in spite of her angry response to this white man's remark, she seems ambivalent about the white aesthetic: "I should have been elated that this white man finds me attractive, I guess. Because usually they don't, they don't compliment, just walk up and compliment black women. They might look at you, but you have to have certain features in order for them to find you attractive." Apparently, this woman's "certain features," perhaps light skin color or fine features, place her close to the white model, thereby justifying the white man's attention to her physique. She reasons that she is an exception, for in her experience a white man's attraction to beauty other than white is rare.

Among some white men there is ambivalence, a desire for the black woman, perhaps for the decadence of an exotic femme fatale. Historical analyses suggest that many white men have long considered the biracial ("mulatto") woman a symbol of free sexuality. The preference of these white men is for lighter-skinned black women, those with a more desirable femininity than dark-skinned women. Indeed, bell hooks tells us that during slavery lighter-skinned African American women were "frequently bought at a higher price on the market or were easier to sell."[21] Moreover, in recent decades men's magazines designed for white men tend to use black models—if they are used at all—that are light-skinned. Indeed, in the United States it is difficult for dark-skinned black women to develop a career in modeling for mass circulation magazines generally.

We should note that in black communities there has been an ongoing debate about the preference for light skin, particularly in the case of women. This preference, whose strength has varied considerably over time, reflects a colonized vision of female beauty.[22] A successful entrepreneur describes how skin, hair, and looks have sometimes represented battlefields within black communities:

> I have always been aware of [color consciousness] because I came from a very southern town in . . . the Deep South, and . . . I would always used to have to be one to stop the fight. The dark-skinned ones didn't like the light-skinned ones, and the light-skinned ones didn't like the dark-skinned ones. And when it came down to something, it came down to that. . . . "You think you're better than them because you're yella, you know, high yella." And things like that. I mean that happened. That absolutely happened. Why? I still try to figure out why. I don't know today where that came from. All I can see is just self-hatred. We ourselves, it's just a form of self-hatred. But . . . when I look at people, I don't look at you in terms of your complexion, or your hair, or your eyes. I look at you as the context of your mind, and if we can communicate.

We learn from our respondents that in the United States the white beauty model has real consequences for African American individuals, families, and communities. African American women must struggle hard to have their own beauty recognized, sometimes even in their own communities. Their efforts often appear to be in vain because of the myopic conceptions of white aesthetics, the suppression of positive models of color, and the distorted characterizations of black women disseminated through the mainstream media and in the form of toys for children. One female college student confides:

> I went through a long, long time thinking I was like the ugliest thing on the earth. And, I think that is a way in which being a black person, and a black female comes together, the whole idea of your self-esteem as far as defining what a woman is, which I still haven't defined! [laughs] Because I mean it's not like there are a lot of role models out there to choose from. I mean, I guess if you ask a lot of black women . . . how they define themselves as a female, . . . they might say turn to their mothers, which to a large extent I do. But I just . . . don't see a lot out there representing . . . a black

female. It's very hard for me to get an identity as a woman, I'm still struggling with that right now.... I just want to be loved and appreciated, like every other black female, or female for that matter, for being a black woman. What is so difficult, what is so damn difficult? I don't understand. It's so hard to get a sense of self in this country, in this society, where you have every role of femininity, looks like a Barbie doll.

Again cultural misrecognition and whites making black women "ugly" is explicitly grappled with by a young black woman. This young woman is struggling hard to assert her black womanhood and indeed her very self. Even as she, and similar black women, young and old, might wish to dismiss the prevailing white beauty model as only skin-deep and frivolous, its constant use by the larger society as a criterion for keeping black women outside major reward systems accents issues of self-esteem and personal survival. For most white women, who are already in the eye of the white male cultural beholder (even if they are not blonde and blue-eyed), some version of the beauty model may be more easily attained. However, for white-devalued African American women the beauty model can create a battlefield where selves may be warped and countering strategies must ever be developed.

Fighting Back Successfully

The comments of our respondents suggest that the majority of black women, even in the face of negative societal images, somehow develop more or less successful strategies for fighting these images and for coming to respect themselves in positive terms. This is not an easy task, and it likely means a heavy dependence on collective knowledge and social networks. Interestingly, one exploratory research study indicates that by some measures black adolescent girls as a group have higher self-esteem than girls in other racial and ethnic groups. Examining groups of Asian American, Latino, white, and African American girls, researchers Sumru Erkut and Fern Marx found that most of the black adolescent girls they studied saw themselves as physically attractive, yet their self-worth was most highly associated with positive feelings about their social and scholastic abilities rather than physical appearance. Interestingly, among the white adolescent girls in this recent study personal self-worth was most highly associated with perceptions of physical appearance. The African American girls put a high value on personal characteristics other than physical appearance.[23]

Significantly, among these groups of adolescents the black girls were also the most likely to report having an adult female with whom they talked about their lives. As the researchers put it, "parents, especially mothers, are an important source of influence on future plans, show understanding, care about their feelings, value them and regard what they do as important."[24] These data suggest a collective passing on of ways to deal with society's attempts at degradation from one generation of black women to the next. Moreover, in her research in Holland and the United States, social psychologist Philomena Essed has found that black girls are often warned early about distorted societal notions of beauty and about the misrepresentations in black images in popular culture.[25]

In contending with a whitewashed society where beauty is literally skin-deep, black girls and women have come to understand that their own appearance is unlikely to win white society's approval. As a result, they may accent other aspects of themselves in developing self-esteem and in living their daily lives. Recently, a black woman who was raised in a white family described how she came to see herself.

> A lot of women do their utmost to be good rather than following their own fantasies. And especially for Black women that is a never ending race, because you are never good enough. You can look really beautiful, you can even be seen as sexually attractive, but the very next moment, someone may just spit in your face. And once you figure that out, you can decide to stop trying. Then your own imagination is the only thing that's left. I think my imagination has been my most important tool of survival; imagination and a certain amount of nerve.[26]

Nerve and imagination are the virtues this woman prizes, and these have been important for her in surviving and thriving in the larger society. One irony of the white beauty image is evident here. It seems that when African American women come to understand that their physical appearance is not highly valued, at least outside their families and communities, they may develop a greater recognition of and respect for their range of talents and assets beyond physical appearance. In this way, they may become more complete human beings than those white women whose self-esteem and self-concept are linked more centrally to emulating the almost anorexic models of white female beauty often celebrated in the mass media.[27]

Beauty Standards and Black Men

As we have seen, Americans live in a society in which the standards of those at the top of the racial-ethnic hierarchy greatly shape the beauty model of the society generally. This takes place through everyday socialization in families and schools and through advertising and the mass media. The case of black men and this white beauty standard is important to note here. Particularly since the O.J. Simpson trials in the mid-1990s, we have seen comments in the mainstream media, as well as in black-oriented magazines like *Jet* and *Ebony,* that "prominent black men prefer white women" for dates and mates. The typical argument cites black male celebrities and suggests that they are seeking to build up their own social status by seeking out white women who have higher racial status in this society.

A number of scholars have grappled with data indicating that African American women are more likely to remain single, to marry later, and, if they marry, to divorce and be less likely to remarry than their white counterparts.[28] These marital conditions are linked to many factors, including the unemployment and violence that black men frequently face in this white-racist society, as well as to the decisions of black women in the face of trying economic and housing conditions. However, the cultural rendering of African American women may be an overlooked factor in this situation. Some black men come to desire women in the image of the ever-present white cultural model. The dominant group's power over media and schools effectively maintains the cultural denigration of black women, with ramifications for black families. Given these multiple economic and cultural factors, the decreased chances for black women to maintain stable marital relationships mean decreased chances for black children to enjoy the apparent benefits of a two-parent family.[29]

While there does seem to be evidence that some black men are inclined to the white cultural model, and while it is clear that most black men are bombarded with this white model throughout their lives, we suspect that the majority of black men are not like white men when it comes to the dominant beauty model. There seems to be no research on this issue, but we would like to suggest that the views of the majority of African American men on female beauty are probably more reflective and diverse than has often been perceived. In a recent interview we explored some of these issues with a black man, a former administrator, who spent much of his early life with white young people.

> What is beauty, who is beautiful? I have been thinking and rethinking this question for most of my life. I can remember specific periods in my life when it was necessary, very important to think about what it meant to me. It was important because what I felt about beauty said a lot about me and what I thought about myself. . . . When I started school there were only two black families (seven persons) in nine grades. Two of them [were] females. . . . Most of the girls that I thought were pretty were the same ones that my white classmates thought [were pretty]. Every place that I went to there was nothing but white people around; even in church everything was white. I was even an avid fan of the British invasion and didn't listen to the Motown sound unless it was fashionable and my white friends listened to it.

In his early life, then, he was bombarded with white cultural styles and images of beauty. Over time, however, his view of female beauty expanded considerably.

> I find myself taking that second look at black women all the time, while a white women can walk by unnoticed. The image of beauty that was being sold and I bought into was one of sameness, the extraction of anything that she was until there was nothing left but parts and those parts didn't differentiate one from the other. Beauty consists of substance, most of which comes from within. I believe that the most beautiful women are black but it doesn't have to do with race but character—a quality that is not easy to define or put your finger on. I was at the post office the other day and one of the postal workers was a black female. She was a very interesting-looking woman. Since I don't know her, I can't say that she is beautiful, but she was somebody that appeared to be worth knowing. She did not conform to any of the prescribed notions of beauty, but she had all the grace that could be contained in one place.

In a later comment he added that he thought that African American men as a group had a broader view of what constituted female beauty than white men as a group. For many black men, especially those who do not spend most of their early years in a white world, it seems that personality and style are more important than the physical beauty model.

Interestingly, two white social scientists who read portions of this chapter, both of whom have dated or been friends with numerous black and white men, contrasted the black men and white men they had known in ways that suggested the latter are more limited in the type of woman they seek as a mate than are black men. One white woman described her experience in these terms:

> White men seem to be extremely picky about finding a woman who fits the 34–24–34 hourglass, Barbie-doll figure as closely as possible. They are often quick to reject a woman on the grounds that she is "fat" when she is even slightly overweight. Perhaps this is why so many white women starve themselves and go through plastic surgery to be more appealing to men than—it seems to me—do African American women. African American men that I knew and that I dated in college, on the other hand, seemed to appreciate women of a wide spectrum of varying shapes, heights, weights, and sizes. I had several friends who were African American males, and would often listen to them comment on women they saw in the media or around campus. It was difficult to find similarities between the women that any one man found attractive, except just that he thought she was "fine," or "cute," or had "style." The same man might find a five foot six inch, thin woman with long hair beautiful, and also comment on the beauty of a five foot two inch, 135-pound woman with short hair. The men I knew did not automatically reject a woman based on her being a few pounds overweight. . . . What seemed most important to the African American men I knew was that a woman have her own personal style, be self-confident, and be able to be witty and hold her own in conversations.

The second white woman who read our manuscript generally agreed with this probing assessment. As these women see it, many, perhaps most, black men seem to have a greater appreciation for different types of female beauty, including that beyond skin-deep, than white men.

Despite the negative somatic images of the black woman in U.S. society, it is clear that female beauty is relative. What is considered beautiful in an earlier period may become an embarrassment for people later, and what is beautiful in one part of the society may not be in another part. Indeed, the alleged beauty of the near-anorexic white female model would not be appreciated among the people of East Africa, where chubbiness is a desirable feminine attribute.[30] It would appear that many African American men in the United States seem to have a similar viewpoint. While we can only speculate on the basis of the limited evidence given above, apparently many black men develop a standard of female beauty that goes well beyond the dominant white beauty model offered in conventional advertising and the mass media.

Conclusion

There are social settings where black women are celebrated for what they are and what they can be. These are mostly in African American communities. Outside such settings, the white beauty standard remains central and dominant. This reality has serious consequences for the present and future not only of African Americans but also for the society as a whole. A social worker in a northern city sums up the problem of imagery: "A white woman with blue eyes and blonde hair is still the perfect woman. And that's projected, and it's inbred and everybody's supposed to want that. Well, what if you're black with a big nose and big lips. . . ? What happens to you? What happens to our little girls and little boys when they look at television?" All body imaging is culturally bound to a huge degree, a matter of values and choices about what are usually small differences and nuances in bodily character. As mentioned in Chapter 1, Stanley Diamond has expanded on this issue.

> Suppressing the cultural issue—i.e., the specificity of cultures—for a moment one is struck not by the distinction between the beautiful and the ugly, but by their fundamental similarity; in a certain sense, their identity. . . . If beauty can be defined as the pleasing harmony of parts—so that what is beautiful has the character of a mechanical, a superficial integrity—then what is ugly can be defined as disharmonious totality: a nose too large

for its face; protruding teeth ... a character notably deficient in certain respects. ... At the same time, disharmonies in one period may be the harmonies of another, so even here, one must be exceedingly careful about drawing too sharply the fine line between the beautiful and the ugly.[31]

The dominant concepts of beauty and ugliness are socially constructed, mostly by those with the power to do so. The celebrated concepts of beauty discussed in this chapter are for the most part created and perpetuated by white ethnocentric definitions and delineations. One likely purpose of these prevailing standards of beauty seems to be the reproduction of white men's taste for women most like themselves. This process distances black women from white men and helps insure the "racial purity" apparently desired by many white Americans.[32]

Changes in these ethnocentric constructions will likely come only with changes in those who have the power to define, and thus with organized protest against these constructions. Murray Webster and James E. Driskell have noted: "While discrimination because of race or sex may decline because of changes in laws and educational practice, discrimination based on attractiveness evidences no comparable movement."[33]

The misrecognition and degradation of African American women by white Americans is extremely costly, not only for African American women, but also for the larger society. How much extra time do these women spend in front of the mirror at home? How much money do they spend at beauty shops trying to achieve that near-white look? Grier and Cobbs note that "black women have paid fortunes trying to be white."[34] Having internalized the aesthetic preferences of U.S. culture, some black women go very far in trying to modify their natural looks by artificial means to conform to the light-skin, straight-hair ideal of the dominant white model. In the quest for beauty some try drastic steps—reconstructing face, hair, eye color, even bone structure—to look as "white" as they can and thus have a "ticket, and anything [they] want," as one female student put it. If securing white-sanctioned status is paramount, and if looking white is rewarded with status, a black woman's self-misrecognition and transformation into something closer to the white ideal by way of skin and hair lighteners, perms, relaxers, and hot-combs may seem a reasonable pursuit. Some white observers might observe this attention to physical attractiveness on the part of black women and suggest that many white women also spend much time and energy on appearance. Yet for most white women the "Barbie doll" standard is more achievable, if only by great effort including surgery, while it is always further off for most black women.

The white beauty standard creates great costs for most black girls and women—on a daily basis. For the majority, those who do not succumb to taking drastic steps to whiten themselves in one fashion or another, there is the constant struggle against white misrecognition and the necessary vigilance to protect one's own self-development and self-worth. Significantly, the Erkut and Marx study mentioned above suggests that black adolescent girls as a group have higher self-esteem than white girls, and that black girls' self-worth was more likely to be associated with positive feelings about their abilities and assets other than physical attractiveness. Given the constant assault on their self-images by the larger society and its mass media, how is this possible? In our view, the key is that the black girls were also the most likely of the groups studied to have an adult female—likely a mother, grandmother, or aunt—with whom they spoke about their problems and daily lives. Yet again we see the importance of the collective memory, shared knowledge, and extended family networks in the trials and successes of African American girls and women.

There is a need for rethinking prevailing beauty concepts in the United States, for decentering the dominant white standards and for rejecting constrictive uniformity. There is a great need for white Americans, particularly those in the mass media, to adopt an inclusive approach to beauty that includes a multiplicity of types of body character and attractiveness. African American women should be recognized by all Americans for the talented, beautiful, and creative human beings that they really are. Such an approach might mean not only fewer exchanges with the mirror and less money at beauty parlors but also increased productivity at work and, most important, a more equitable distribution of societal rewards by white decision makers and, thus, a more just society.

Chapter 4

Common Myths and Media Images of Black Women

Filled with engaging metaphors that unbridle the imagination, traditional legends and fairy tales continue to delight children and many adults. These stories are not only a part of happy childhood memories but often contain lasting, priceless philosophical and moral lessons that transcend the formative years. These stories transport children and adults into a world of fantasies, where the impossible is possible and fiction is reality. Such legendary accounts can be a getaway world and, for many, an escape from everyday life. Many adults remember and still enjoy telling fairy tales to children. Such fairy tales, Henry Louis Gates writes,

> function to order our world, serving to create both a foundation upon which each of us constructs our sense of reality and filter through which we process each event that confronts us every day. The values that we cherish and wish to preserve, the behavior that we wish to censure, the fears and dread that we can barely confess in ordinary language, the aspirations and goals that we most dearly prize—all of these things are encoded in the stories that each culture invents and preserves for the next generation, stories that, in effect, we live by and through.[1]

Even the terrifying stories of childhood can delight the moral imagination of Americans of all racial and ethnic backgrounds. Consider, for example, *Little Red Riding Hood* or *Snow White.* Such legends transmit to younger generations the dos and don'ts of a society, and as a means of social control lighten up the parental burden. The obvious moral lesson of these tales is that children are to be cautious. Yet, despite a delightful inspiration and priceless lessons, these children's stories are only tales and are usually known to be by their captivated audiences.[2]

The line separating myth from fact becomes seriously blurred, however, when *racist* legends wearing deceiving masks are accepted by white Americans as reality. For example, some white myths about African Americans are deadly when they are transferred into the collective white memory as reality and are transmitted to younger generations of whites as fact. In white fables about black women, these women are frequently associated in stories, in songs, and eventually in the minds of white readers or listeners with villains, while whites are often the heroes.[3]

Myths about African American Women: Sexuality and Attractiveness

Women in all racial and ethnic groups in the United States can be the targets of sexual myths and harassment. Usually the male behavior targeting women as sexual objects is intentional and reinforces other types of discrimination directed at women. Being a woman in U.S. society means facing stereotypes of women as sex objects, including the notion that most women intentionally invite male attention. Writing about the workplace, Lin Farley has defined sexual harassment as "unsolicited nonreciprocal male behavior that asserts a woman's sex role over her function as a worker."[4] Over the course of their lives most women face this unsolicited male behavior that makes them into objects of sexual interest or fantasy.

In a recent focus group in a southern state one African American woman comments on her experience with male reactions to her: "Some people don't know that they're being sexist, you know what I'm saying. They have not a clue. Men sometimes don't have a clue when you're walking down the street, and they're looking at your legs. Or they make a comment that that's being sexist." In her view much of this unwanted attention is unconscious. Many men do not reflect on the significant impact of their actions on women of all backgrounds.

However, black women endure a special kind of racialized sexism. Myths about wanton black women abound in this society. As one male sales executive from a northern city sees it, "For some reason white Americans . . . feel they can reduce a black woman to a sexual object, which is what they do to most women. . . . The white male privilege is known and accepted." Some white men, since the beginning of the enslavement of Africans in North America, have had a desire for the black Jezebel, for the mythological "jungle bunny," a crude racist term still in use among some white men. African American women have long been sexual targets for these men, particularly those with power. Privilege allows these men to try to actualize the sexual myth. The actualization in turn renews, protects, and rationalizes white male privilege, as well as the Jezebel myth. Even today, in the bars and fraternities of white male socializing there is sometimes joking about the sexual exoticness of black women. Jezebel imaging by white men can lead to sexual harassment or worse for black women in the workplace or other institutional settings.

Myths about the sexually aggressive black woman can even influence the thinking of some black men, although the stereotypes may take a somewhat different form. One of our male respondents, for example, laughs and explains how the increasing trend in interracial relationships may reflect some black women's aggressiveness.

> If you're a black woman you're in trouble finding a suitable black man and then if you are a middle-class, educated black woman, you really got a problem finding a black man. The pool of eligibles has to be absolutely limited, so it's a really serious, almost crisis proportion. And one of the inevitable outcomes of that kind of situation is the presence of more and more black women marrying white men. . . . I think that black women very frankly in that circumstance find themselves going after white men. . . . So, sure, I think that, at minimum black women like that make themselves available, if they don't aggressively go after, at least they have signs on them, you know, saying I'm available—should you be interested, should you be interested I won't say no. [laughs]

Even though the image here is not the crude version of white imaginations, and is presented with some humor, such attitudes help to actualize myths about black women and feed the imagination of both black men and whites who see black women less for their professional achievements than for how they fit certain myths of aggressiveness.

Advantaged white men may even reward such antiblack thinking and, as one female airline employee noted, encourage in black women behavior that perpetuates the harmful myths of gendered racism: "Black women, according to the white men who are in power, are something sexual, a sexual fantasy, so they will allow you to do so much just to play out that." Playing into myths of gendered racism may sometimes have short-term job advantages, but it is detrimental in the long run for both the individual and her community. The hiring decisions of white male employers or managers can be influenced by the received sexual lore circulating about black women, a point stressed by a male business manager: "If it's a white male dealing with a black female, and if that black female happened to be a very attractive female, she doesn't have to do anything. In other words, 'This is great, wonderful, maybe I should try to bring this person aboard.' . . . The thought process being that there's maybe something in that for me. I can benefit from this personally . . . in a non-business-related way."

To the extent that the professional success of black women depends on their evaluations by decision-making whites, black women judged to fit the preferred images of the dominant group may sometimes be assigned better ratings or given such rewards as lighter workloads or leisure time. For example, explained one male manager, "Within this company, the females that are attractive that are black . . . generally get jobs. The ones that are not, that may have qualifications, that maybe even can do the job better, don't even get considered." Conversely, however, most black women, especially daring iconoclasts, must struggle against their racial-gender conditions to achieve some measure of employment success.

One male television news anchor in a southwestern city asserts that the sexual mythologies and advances of white employers have very serious consequences for African American women:

> With women it's also a sex thing. If it's a [white] guy that likes to have affairs or whatever, the old slavemaster thing. Whereas with the black man, either he's going to be hired, if you're going to hire him, what are you going to get from him? It's like I'm not gay, so it's not sex. But with the black woman, ulterior motives, because if

she's on three months probation, that gives him a chance to check her out if she's going to be a part of what's going on. And if he makes advances at her, and discovers that she doesn't play that, then he can say "your check will be in the mail."

There is clearly concern and frustration in this man's comments. The gendered mythologies alluded to here may trigger in some white men an aggression toward black women that can lead to their termination from employment.

In summary, then, black female employees are sometimes expected by white employers and observers to live up to an image or a reputation that maintains their cultural devaluing and denigration. If white male employers choose, they may advance the employment mobility of some black women whom they find to be attractive, to the disadvantage of comparable black male employees. However, this supposed "success" at work may pressure the chosen black women into flirting or other sexualized behavior, which results in a moral defeat that can reinforce white fictions about black women. Most African American women do not give in to this discriminatory behavior, although they must struggle hard against white actions that are deeply rooted in the racist relationships of the past.

Racial-Sexual Myths and Their Origins

We have noted previously that during slavery African American women were routinely exploited sexually by some white men in positions of authority. Indeed, the diversity of skin color and other physical characteristics among African Americans is, to a substantial but unknown degree, the result of the large-scale rape of African American women by these white men. This exploitation of black women persisted in many areas of the South in the segregation period. The history of slavery and segregation and their contemporary relevance, aspects of collective memory, are constantly asserted in our interviews. One manager underscored the historical background: "That goes back, if you will, to slavery times, because black females were just a tool for white men to begin with. They would take their pick." A physician in a northern city reiterates this point: "The white men always had . . . the freedom to go to bed with black women, either as slaves or anywhere else." These comments can be set in the context of several centuries of U.S. history. The literature on slavery portrays a period during which African American women were common sexual targets of white men, such as white overseers and slaveowners. Oddly enough, these same white men insisted on racial segregation, asserting that "the Negroes should have their own life separate from that of whites."[5] During slavery, white men often professed being revolted by the physical characteristics, including body odors (usually from hard, sweaty work), of those whom they enslaved.[6] Somehow, nonetheless, white men suppressed this "distaste" and sexually exploited many enslaved black women.

After slavery, white male support for extreme legal segregation in the South and legal or informal segregation in the North did not keep white men from seeking exploitative sexual relationships with black women. During slavery and afterward white men have oppressed black women and men in different ways. The importance of slavery was underscored by a hospital technician in a major city: "This is the white slavemaster that basically castrated, lynched, tortured the black man while he had his pleasure with the black woman in the mansion. So, that right there tells you who the greater threat was to him in his existence." Slavery was riddled with torture and brutality toward enslaved women and men, and this brutality often had a sexual dimension. One director of a drug treatment program in the Midwest made this point: "The black woman, during slavery times, if she would go over into the slave house and lay down with the slavemaster, she got special privileges, okay? Whereas the black man, who got *forced* to lay down with somebody, still did not get those special privileges, because he was forced to do this. I'm not saying the black woman wasn't forced, either, but she got different privileges for doing the same thing." While they were sometimes forced to have children by enslaved women, black men were not, so far as we can tell from extant data, often directly exploited sexually for the pleasure of white men. (There may have been some sexual exploitation of enslaved black males, especially the young, that has gone unrecorded.) As a result, bell hooks suggests, most enslaved black men did not become the complete possessions of the white masters.[7] Seen in this perspective, African American men have long presented a greater threat to white male power and authority than black women.

Several respondents seem to be saying that black women and black men have long suffered terribly at the hands of whites, but sometimes in different ways. In the sexually exploitative process enslaved black women were forced to contribute to the myths held by whites about their unfavorable reputations as sexual players.[8] The crude, racist Jezebel legend is the product of a white racist misrecognition that constantly reinforces both white society's idealization of white women and its devaluation of black women.[9] This misrecognition and devaluing still lingers, revived daily in the white-controlled mass media.[10]

Other Media Stigmatization of Black Women

In Chapter 3 we examined images of beauty in U.S. society, including the images widely circulated in the mainstream media. In this chapter we examine some of the other aspects of the media imaging and treatment of African American women.

"They're unfair, grossly unfair," reply—if not shout—many black respondents in protest, when asked, "What do you think about the portrayal of black Americans on television or in white-edited magazines?" One male banking executive in a northern city was harsh: "We're always on the defensive. We're the whore, the prostitute, the pimps, the derelicts, the drug users. We're always in those 'favored' roles that the producer wants to put us in." Commonplace mass media presentations of black women in poor economic circumstances are deeply offensive to our respondents, who insist that the mainstream sketches do not accurately represent black men and black women, their struggles, or their lifestyles. Flowing through the narratives is frustration over disparaging portrayals in a variety of media contexts, as in the following statement by one female university professor.

> I'm very disappointed in imaging by the media of African Americans, and most certainly African American females. Not only from the media perspective of videotapes, but also commercials, and certainly the movies and made-for-television kinds of things and soap operas. Now, personally I think soap operas are some of the most ridiculous entities ever invented. They entertain a mindless public. [laughs] However, as far as the media is concerned, one of the things that the advertising companies tend to do is portray us at the low economic end of the spectrum.

While low-income or working-class black women frequently appear as moral or economic failures in the mass media, black women may also be unfairly portrayed at the middle level of the class continuum. The professor continues: "If we're portrayed as middle class, then they have us in a ridiculous situation of coming in first off, we're perfectly groomed, we come in from the office, we put the briefcase down in the kitchen and have dinner ready in twenty minutes, which is craziness. And that's not to say we don't do that, but believe me, we get out of the heels first." The white-controlled mass media may transform the occasional African American woman, like the lawyer wife on the old Bill Cosby show, into a superwoman who can handle with unusual ease countless situations that would be so demanding as to overburden any person in real life.* On rare occasions when her professional capabilities are recognized by white observers, the African American woman may again become a semifictional character, unreal indeed for having done too much. The implicit suggestion may be that, despite being fictive in essence, her attainments can be achieved by other black women if they will just work hard enough. This is yet another form of white misrecognition and stereotyping.

Why are there problems in the media's apparently positive depictions of a few black women as superwomen? While they are often successful in overcoming the pressures of multiple roles, middle class women sometimes fail, like every human being. The respondent above implies that a more honest media would abandon the false imagery and do black women credit by recognizing the full diversity of black female life-worlds, a recognition of the gamut of experiences inclusive not only of success but also of the trials and struggles through which this success was attained.

There are indeed many trials for successful women to overcome, as our respondents constantly recall in their detailed accounts. One administrator in a southwestern city delineated the pressures endured by a single black woman, including those who are professionals, in meeting daily parental and other family obligations.

> You look at a lot of the single-parent households. I mean, that woman has a lot of pressures. Not only does she have to go out and earn a living and support her kids, she has to push them, I mean,

---

*Most of the references of our respondents to Bill Cosby are to *The Cosby Show*, the television series in which Cosby played a physician whose wife was a lawyer.

she has to be the motivator, the breadwinner, everything. And have some sanity. And do some things for herself too. And, you know, along with being out there just dealing with, just the pressures of jobs, and everything else.

Although middle-class black women must manage role conflicts and other tough situations on a daily basis, that reality is either missing or dealt with inappropriately in the mainstream media. Whether or not she is elevated to the fictional status of a superwoman or pauperized as the welfare recipient so hated by many whites, conventional media portrayals abound in characterizations suggesting the allegedly loose morals or blemished characters of African American women. We are reminded yet again of the dominant cultural artist's commonplace racist depictions of African American women as intimidating and aggressive Sapphires or promiscuous and sexualized Jezebels.

Denigration Through Dishonor

Most television and film roles for African Americans fall into just a few groups. There are the athletes and entertainers, and there are the often stereotypical comedian and criminal roles. One female attorney spoke of being baffled by the media's insulting portraits of African Americans as morally debauched: "Oh, well, I'm very disappointed [with] a lot of the portrayals of blacks on television because it's always in some kind of a substandard role, or some type of a role that's not admired by the younger generation coming up, like a drug addict or a hooker or something like that." Others, like this executive secretary in a southwestern city, agree that the mainstream media portraits tend to denigrate African Americans by spreading derogatory stories about licentious black women: "There was a time when they were showing all of that, like Sambo and Buckwheat and Amos and Andy, and now, frankly, I don't think it's much better now. I was looking at a movie the other day. The black woman was a prostitute on the street, and the language that they used, even that was exaggerated. This woman was overreacting to the max. It's exaggerated." Television's maligning of black women is not new, as the old *Amos 'n' Andy* show, with its domineering black Sapphire, clearly demonstrates. Shows with antiblack stereotyping, both the old shows and more recent ones, are now generally available on videotape and are still being shown across the United States and around the globe.

Though some respondents see modest improvements in mainstream media presentations compared with the past, others, like the following respondent, a corporate sales manager, note the continuing impact of messages, conveyed to young and old viewers alike, about a morally unfit black woman: "Well, I think they're changing. You look at the quality of the shows you see. I still have a problem with showing . . . the women in short, tight skirts and they're either hookers or something like that. You see too much of that on shows." This version of black female devaluing and misrecognition is not limited to television, for it can be seen elsewhere in the mass media as well.

Sometimes, the tainted representations may be so humiliating to black viewers that they simply avoid or forget them. When asked about television shows that disturb him most, one professor in a northern city replied, "I don't know, I really try to forget these shows." People who block out what is painful benefit at least temporarily from the behavior, but there can be a negative long-term effect of forgetting what is painful.

While every population has reputable and less reputable segments, the mass media all too often feature the latter as typical of the African American population, shunning positive aspects of black culture and community, including very important success stories and role models. This critical point was underscored by a law professor: "To be sure, there are black criminals, there are black prostitutes, and you don't have to go real far to find a large number of them. I don't even dispute that. And I think that they should be portrayed along with everybody else. But it's the everybody else that's missing, because you don't see enough black families, you don't see enough black professionals, you don't see enough positive, enough black men who are honorable on television programs." The steady drumbeat of negative stories on the news and in other programming is frustrating to our respondents, the middle-class men and women who have achieved a great deal but seldom see themselves accurately portrayed in the mass media. Using the example of a television role, a female corporate manager in a northern city provides more evidence that media images of African American women are defamatory:

> Well, I don't watch a lot of television. I do watch things like *The Cosby Show* when I'm home and have the free time. I just don't

watch a lot of TV. Some of it I hate. Some of the black images I see, like Jackie, I mean, it's funny, it's entertaining. But at the same time, black women are being portrayed as very voluptuous and sexy. She's portrayed as, all she's interested in is men and sex and that. And I don't think that's fair. *The Cosby Show* is about one of the cleanest that comes along, and people have tried to pull that apart. So, it's just a problem. Why can't they just accept a show where the characters are black? Why can't we do the *Dynasty* sometimes?

As yet, the dominant media have not presented black women and men in serious dramatic roles centered in African American communities, on an ongoing basis, such as a major television series. The movie industry and other media have a similar bias in usually ignoring "everybody else" in black communities.

It is not just the content of the programs but what goes along with them that creates problems for African Americans. This respondent adds that advertising, such as on billboards, is a major problem and one with serious health implications.

I have particularly a problem with the media, the advertising part of it. Why is it, billboards especially, you . . . see billboards advertising the sexy type of woman smoking cigarettes? I get into a racial thing and a health thing with that. Always in the black communities, there are always blacks. I mean, like the woman, she's dressed elegantly, she looks nice, all of that. And she's seducing a black male, and she's smoking or she's drinking, one of the two. You go into the white community, you don't see billboards with the white woman seducing the white male on cigarettes and liquor ads. Think about it! You ride through [names neighborhoods], think about it. So, I hate that, and I know it's geared to that [black] community.

The seductive Jezebel reappears as a distinct silhouette not only on the movie screen but also in this advertising, often with a would-be elegance—tragically spoiled in this respondent's view by the propagation of legal drugs like nicotine and alcohol. Added to promiscuity, vices such as these are used by white advertisers as ammunition for twisted racial-gender presentations. Displaying these symbols of impurity in plain view of the black community leaves men and women, young and old, with a distorted image of black women that shapes remembrance. The images can trigger in many black viewers the memories of a racist past, while generating in some of the young and others less familiar with that past a certain devaluing and even disregard for black women.

Common misrepresentations such as these may be partially why this female manager reasons that "*The Cosby Show* is about one of the cleanest." Others, like a news anchor in a southern city, agree with this judgment:

> In terms of *The Cosby Show,* I think it has a lot going for it, in terms of the fact that there is a family intact, that you do have a loving relationship between the spouses, and between the parents and their children. I know of one complaint that's been made against it from the beginning, has been that it hasn't dealt seriously enough with topics that blacks in general have to face. To some extent, I'd have to agree. But at another level they deal with a lot of issues in a rather subtle way.

While clearly positive in its image of African Americans, *The Cosby Show* is problematical because of certain illusions about conditions for black families that it seems to suggest. One father discussed some of the problems such shows can create for parents and their children: "I do know that this is just entertainment. But my kids think it's the way we should live. That is unfair. It is unfair for me to explain to my son that, no, mom is not a lawyer, dad is not a doctor, and these things don't work that way. I think it's really sad."[11]

A few of our respondents also faulted some of the African American media for holding up the wrong role models for black communities. For example, according to a male corporate manager, popular black magazines sometimes play into the denigration of black women: "There are black periodicals that I don't look at for the same reason. I was looking at this magazine, I stopped subscribing [to] it one year when they had a gentleman on the cover as the 'Man of the Year' who had just walked away from his wife and his four kids for another woman. How do you make him *Ebony*'s 'Man of the Year'? So, you know, there are a lot of problems there." The subtle messages conveyed by this widely circulated magazine's endorsement of a family defector as a model of manhood are that wife and children need not be a black man's first priority, that a black man can abandon his family, yet still be celebrated or honorable. The magazine's portrayal of this prominent black man trivializes the significance of conjugal and familial ties, undermines black women, and makes their inferiorization by the dominant media seem more acceptable.

Fatness as Racial Stigma

The mythomaniac presentation of many black women as fat abets their cultural devaluing. The misrecognition that takes the form of the corpulent "mammy," such as the racist Aunt Jemima image long used on commercial products and in the movies, is a hoary stereotype among white Americans. Recently, it has been associated in many a white mind with black welfare recipients and other poor black women. As Patricia Hill Collins notes, "Portraying African-American women as stereotypical mammies, matriarchs, welfare recipients, and hot mommas has been essential to the political economy of domination fostering Black women's oppression."[12]

If one is a black woman, being seen as too fat can suggest a bad reputation because in the white public's view it is associated with laziness and a lack of self-control. The racialized too-fat images move the degradation of black women by whites beyond the strictly somatic into the realm of goodness and badness. One administrator at a northern law school tells of a conversation he had with his son about media misrepresentations of women:

> I asked [my son], I said, "Have you ever noticed that until, let's say, Phylicia Rashad, and I think there may be one other, but all the [black] females that are on television are fat?" And he thought about it for a minute, and then he couldn't think of any others that weren't fat, because all the females that they allow to have any [role] were fat. And that's the stereotype of the way people believe black women should look: fat, happy, and in the kitchen. But since they can't get them in the kitchen, they then just stick with the fat and black.

In the continental United States too much fat on any woman is commonly taken as a sin against the gods of the dominant culture. Fat is sin regardless of the possibility that for some women being large may be a matter of genetic inheritance, a personal choice, or agreement with a culture that views chubbiness as attractive. Like the values of beauty, values in regard to body size are greatly shaped by culture. For example, today native Hawaiian women tend to be larger than their *haole* (white) counterparts.[13] From the indigenous people's point of view, apparently, the larger women are the more beautiful their features, the more gracious their dancing, and the more powerful their songs. Larger native Hawaiian women are admired, and the presence of body fat does not seem a moral issue among the indigenous people of Hawaii.[14]

The too-fat question is different for African American women who look overweight on television because their somatic presentation is often made, by white cultural artists, into a matter of morality. This media imaging contributes implicitly and significantly to the myths undergirding black female devaluing and denigration in the larger society.

Additionally, consistent with their alleged moral weakness, African American women are often limned in the media as complacent or are forced into an odd or unflattering mode of bearing that, like fatness, categorizes and demeans. One male administrator comments this way:

> I saw a commercial last night that *really* offended me, from Roy Rogers, that had a young black woman on there who wasn't fat but her gestures were all purely stereotypical. She didn't remind me of the type of person who, when she talked, blurred her eyes, you know, unnaturally, but in the commercial she was *doing that*! And doing all these old-time gestures as though she was prompted to do them, and it didn't come off as being her natural self. It was a throwback to some of the earlier commercials, and it was *really* offensive, and I just flicked it off. But you find that all the time, and you find in television and in movies where white people are telling black people how black people act. Now who best can tell a black person how a black person acts? But there's that thing in television and in the movie industry where a white knows how a black acts, and will tell a black, "This is how black people act." And that's ridiculous.

There is an important insight underlying these comments. "Blackness," particularly as portrayed in the dominant media, is very much a collective construction of often too-fertile white minds. Indeed, blackness would *not* exist apart from the historical imaginings and constructions of white individuals and institutions. Today, whites still signal to these women and men how they *should* look and act in order to be appropriately "black" in the eyes of a predominantly nonblack audience.

A student at a southern university noted how even the films of one African American movie director sometimes have mimicked the dominant media's negative portraits of black Americans.

> Well, I know that Spike Lee has created quite a stir. He's putting in a lot of things that people think. And as far as I'm concerned, he's not saying anything that anyone has not said before. He's just putting it together in a very unique way. Sure, we are either pimps, or prostitutes. One thing I don't think it's fair, like I said, what's white is not always what's right. You do not have to have long flowing hair, a mane of hair down to your feet, or blue eyes to be beautiful. And I think whites have just instilled that. I don't think they portray us very, like people say, Spike Lee only presents one side, one point of view, showing us all down and dirty, and all our problems. He's not here to present every side, he can't do that. . . . So, no, I don't think those [images] are very fair.

From this student's perspective, like their white counterparts some black filmmakers act as executors of white society's will, honoring cherished if grossly deformed somatic and moral visions of African Americans—the "down and dirty," mythified visions, inclusive of criminal activity, curly hair, and fat bodies.[15] Indeed, "to earn a living, [even] African American performers and film makers . . . have had to conform to the stereotypes that audiences have become accustomed to seeing on the screen."[16] While Spike Lee also mimics and satirizes numerous white figures in his movies, more so than almost all other moviemakers, he does perpetuate some of the negative images of African Americans contrived so long ago by the omnipresent and powerful white cultural artists and mythmakers.

Why the Media Stigmatization?

There is a certain racial logic to the mainstream media's unfavorable representations of African American women. As one teacher explains, the portrayals fit the dominant society's outlook: "Sometimes white America likes to think that of you, because they feel comfortable with that image of you." These negative images of African American women are influential and accepted among most whites.

The false depictions of black women in the mass media, or the black actors who portray them, can become role models for black children who have few heroes to cheer. Yet for black working-class and middle-class children, rarely do the mainstream media characters look, think, speak, or live like their own parents and other relatives. One female school administrator from a northern city comments on the white-controlled media's comfort with misrecognition of the full humanity of black women and men:

> You watch TV now, and you see that our black men are pimps, beating up women, they're thieves, junkies, they're nothing. They're nobody. And it's really bad news. Again, the portrayal of our black men on TV, if you're a pimp or junkie, you're the role model, and our kids in the community want to be that pimp, that junkie, that's their role model. It's real bad. It's the worst kind of portrayal that we need for our kids. And the black women are always prostitutes. But from the research I've read, the average prostitute is basically a housewife or a schoolteacher. And you have the ones that own the stables are middle-aged white women, not black men.

Such negative and one-sided images can be dangerous for present and future generations. Moreover, this respondent notes that in their haste to devalue black women white cultural artists seem to play down or overlook the role of white women in prostitution in white communities.

In the light of the dominant media's negative and often insulting personifications of African Americans, one female professor advises: "Blacks are going to have to make a good statement. Anyone that's popular will always have to be a role model, because there aren't many, and I don't think whites understand us enough to tell us how to act." Because the middle class is seldom portrayed (or accurately portrayed) in the media, this professor is concerned that viewers, left with the wrong impression, may conclude what is projected typifies African American women and men. For that reason she asserts that a successful black individual is forced into public life and should assume the burden of leadership for the good of the larger community.

Media Stigmatizing of the African American Family

As we have noted in previous chapters, common portraits by white cultural artists of black life and communities have targeted black families as particularly problematical and disorganized. Periodically, influential white commentators, such as Daniel P. Moynihan and Charles Murray, portray African American families in a rather negative light. Like mainstream media depictions of black women, the common portrayal of the black family tends to be an illusion, one that is misleading, deformed, or unrealistic. One woman, a professor at a northern university, illustrates this point well.

> I think that you have many of the same stereotypes that you ever have had. I was looking at a story in our local newspaper just this morning . . . where they're talking about poverty, I think it's the front page, where there's, they talk about the number of children, [a] growing number of children in poverty. And there's a quote from David Ellwood who's at Harvard. He's written a book on poverty. And I've read the book, it's a fairly good book. And the quote basically says that there's a growing number of children in poverty in America, and they aren't all in ghettos, either, you know. They're not all black.

In spite of this fact, she adds, this newspaper got the image wrong.

> But the picture on the front page is a picture of a black family living in this inner city and showing *their* poverty, you know. So that you get those stereotypes continually. Just as most people think that a larger number of people on welfare are black. Certainly it's true that in proportion to our proportion of the population, there are a larger number on welfare, but the myths never get dispelled by the media. Ever. And I think that picture on the front page, you look at it. It's a prime example. It's typical. So I think that we still have all of those myths still very much alive in the media, and in every place you see it.

The use of photographs of black individuals and families to illustrate media stories about poverty and welfare is commonplace, even though the majority of the nation's poor families are *not* black. The image of who is poor or on welfare in the average white mind, including the well-educated white mind, is not to be set aside simply because the data contradict that imagery. Sincere fictions abound when it comes to poor Americans.

Reflecting on more positive portrayals of African American families in the media, this university professor continues with a pointed comment on the scarcity of certain images of black communities. She begins with the first Cosby show:

> And when you get black families portrayed in a, say, "better life," it's more like the Cosby sort of thing. Which doesn't meet, which isn't like most black families, either. [laughs] But then I'm not sure that you ought to expect television to portray anything realistically. I don't think they portray any family realistically, so why would they ever portray the black family realistically, either, you know. [laughs] So that it's there. I think the realistic images and the nonracist images, you have to look along the way to find them. So I think how most, many white Americans, view what blacks are really like is that they're either all high-powered, high-earning sports stars, or movie stars, or some sort of celebrity singer, or they're crack dealers or welfare mothers or something. And there aren't any ordinary black folks. So I think my answer is that I think that just in all the media magazines or whatever you find a lot of stereotypes.

While *The Cosby Show* was the highest rated sitcom on national television in the decade of the 1980s, it provides a misleading portrait. Like real black women, the real black family, whether it is middle class or working class, is largely unknown to white America. Where are representatives from the majority of "ordinary folks" who make up most of black America? This social and demographic reality is hidden behind a veil composed of white stereotypes about black families and their supposed values and behavior.

As with other African Americans, the professor roots certain sincere fictions of whites in centuries of past oppression in North America, including slavery.

> You have a society that's racist at its core, from the time of slavery on, and it's never delivered itself of that. And then whenever you

116

have any set of behaviors or set of problems that are associated
predominantly with blacks, like some of the drug stuff that goes
on in the inner city, it, for most people, because they don't put
social power in any given context anyway, it only exacerbates the
news about race, you know, and allows them to continue with
the stereotypes. So I don't know how we can combat that, I
think it's very complicated.

Once created, stereotypes have a staying power through the generations. Negative white images of African Americans, as individuals,
families, and communities, persist because they have never been chal-
lenged in a way that delivers the majority of whites from the recurring and reinforced distortions of their own minds.

Basically agreeing with the previous respondent, a hospital technician in the South observes how false depictions of the black family
seesaw from one extreme to another.

I think the way blacks are portrayed, it's a total farce. You have
from one extreme, you have the Cosby family, the happy-go-lucky
Negro family that's made it. To me, all you're looking at are white
people in black faces performing on television. So, that's one extreme. That may be true to a certain extent, that may be going on,
but it's not a true representation of the black experience in America. Then on the other extreme, you have the crook, criminal, prostitute, dope dealer types. That's another false image. That too is
going on. But again, that too is not a true representation. And
these white-edited magazines and these black magazines, again you
have a false image. . . . Again, it's a total farce, and they don't represent what the black masses in this country [are] really like.

Neither vision of African American families does justice to the circumstances of most black families. There was general agreement
among our diverse respondents on this issue. The lives and experiences of most African Americans are not currently portrayed in the
mainstream media, nor have they ever been accurately portrayed by
the whites who generate the prevailing societal images at any given
point in time.

Commenting on the range of shows portraying Americans over several decades, a male salesperson in the North says:

117

Well, at least we're not seeing *Amos 'n' Andy*. But I think that also there's a problem. I like Bill Cosby, I love Cosby. And the show has some redeeming social values. But also the show does a disservice, because the vast majority of blacks, even middle-class blacks, do not have that opportunity, and are not in the same realm as a Bill Cosby. It gives whites a distorted picture of black family life. And probably 5 percent of us, maybe 10, have that opportunity, but the vast majority do not. So, the picture is distorted in that end. This is not to take anything away from Bill Cosby, [but] I think he puts some family situations that are not [all that realistic]. I don't watch *227* that much, but they've done some redeeming things. They show reruns of *Good Times*. That bothers me now, it really does. All the laughing, the joking, it bothers me. I used to watch it when it first came on, but as I see it again, I just, it stinks, to tell you the truth. So, I don't think we've gotten a fair hearing. I don't think we've gotten a fair trial on television. There have been some notable exceptions, but on the whole, it's been, well, I won't say it, but extremes.

The distorted picture that whites get of black families from presentations like *The Cosby Show* has been documented in some recent research. Many white Americans, about half according to recent polls, still see African Americans through stereotypes of laziness and lack of effort.[17] The inequalities faced by African Americans are not seen as substantially the result of discrimination by white Americans. Television presentations like *The Cosby Show* feed these white misinterpretations of society. Whites often pick up from this type of media presentation that any black person can "make it" if they will just get out and work hard enough, just like the adults on the show. Researchers Sut Jhally and Justin Lewis conducted focus groups with white Americans who had watched *The Cosby Show*. Many saw it as presenting a "world where race no longer matters." Generally favorable in their attitudes toward the show, whites were able to watch it and "combine an impeccably liberal attitude toward race with a deep-rooted suspicion of black people."[18] Among our black respondents, a female attorney in a northern city sees some amelioration in images of African Americans on television, but she is still disappointed in what is portrayed:

On TV I think the images of blacks are improving, but that

doesn't mean that I want to give them any credit at all. That means that I want to give us credit, and say that, you know, we've put our foot down and we're tired of seeing maids and butlers. We get to see policemen, but we don't see doctors. We see very few lawyers. We see very few fit mothers, other than the Huxtable family. We see very few families, very few grandparents. I'd like to see, just blacks as they are, not so exaggerated, or one black in a total white cast. And of course, they have to be that great, oh so faithful friend, which to me is the same thing as an unpaid slave with the loyalty to the white person.

Our respondents recount how television and films often feature black characters in morally or socially degrading roles, as apparently unfit for positive family interaction and normal family life. Occasionally, some respectable black families surface, but, as the respondents convey, besides the Cosby-type families there are few black roles that are sufficiently honorable to disrupt negative white notions of the black family.

As we have underscored throughout this book, in our racist system African American women and men are frequently not recognized for who they really are. Their talents, accomplishments, and burdens are often invisible to many whites. It would be disconcerting enough if the white failure to recognize the full humanity and life experiences of black women—and of the black family—were confined within the borders of the United States. However, the U.S. mass media's globalization of the deformed portrayals of African Americans is a major source of concern for a high school principal in a southern city: "It's absolutely amazing about how Hollywood and New York have actually killed the black family and the black image to the whole world, since Britain gets our TV and things like that—and Australia." Many videotapes of movies and television programs portraying black Americans in a negative light are shown around the world every day of the week. In this way people across the globe who have never met an African American pick up the hoary racist stereotypes crafted in America.

As frames of reference for universal impressions, the media's contorted depictions harm the black family's feeling and aura of itself. One female college student remarked how the media echo the prevailing white attitudes and legends about black character.

> People make these films because they figure that's all that white people can relate to, and that may be true. But then again, you know, why not challenge white people? But I guess the industry all, the people with their own money go with a sure thing, you can't challenge white folks on their attitudes and stuff. It's horrible, because nothing's innocent, everything is done there for a purpose, in the media especially, I think. And it's not innocent. You can't blow off what you're seeing, because so many people, all they do is watch TV, and they learn from TV, so it's very dangerous. See, that's why I want to go into films. I thought about TV first, but I thought, realistically, there is no way, no way, that I could write for TV that I would want to, because you have to appeal to the masses.

A likely reason for racist portrayals of African American individuals and families is the mass media's yielding to the cravings of a demanding white public. "A racist society requires a racist media to disseminate these values and beliefs to a mass audience."[19] But also at work is the mainstream media's own insouciance about the circumstances of black families, be they working class or middle class. This lack of concern is serious because, as the school principal explained above, demeaning portrayals are commonly spread across the globe, miseducating people not acquainted with African American families, people who have no other standards for judgment.

A central problem is white control of what is created in mass media presentations. This control can have general and personal effects. In a probing commentary, one schoolteacher sheds more light on the media's control of certain societal views and values.

> My mother's name is Beulah, and I remember the show *Beulah,* with the black maid. And my mother was like, what's wrong with the name Beulah? But it has a negative connotation because she was a burly maid. And my mother couldn't get a person named after her because of the way that was portrayed on television. There's nothing wrong with that name. If that maid was named Sarah, nobody would want to name their child Sarah. But I think that whites have so much control of us, sometimes we just give up. I think we do have a lot more control than we think we do.

Honoring a respected predecessor by repeat naming is a vital element in many family traditions and memories. The transfer of names from one generation to another is one way many families preserve their heritages. However, parents who wish to protect their offspring from ridicule might refrain from naming them after a predecessor, no matter how venerated, if the predecessor's name was dishonored by association with a degraded position or, worse yet, has become a symbol for that degradation. Passing the name down the generational ladder might hinder its inheritor's social and economic progress, so that a small but important part of a generational bridge is not built. This happens because disturbing connotations are placed in the minds of viewers, nonblack and black, by an often thoughtless, mythifying media.

The routine moral and spiritual belittling and defaming of black women and their families by white Americans and white-dominated institutions shape the remembrance of audiences, young and old, nonblack and black, and produce moral lessons with consequences as real, lasting, and painful as the outcome in the case of the dishonored name Beulah. In the case of common white constructions of African American women, men, and their families, the lines separating fact from fantasy are often not detectable. Old legends, wearing the deceiving dress of reality, are effectively transmitted to national audiences and believed by white Americans, and even by some black Americans. As they are communicated worldwide, these legends nourish global illusions about African Americans—which can come back like boomerangs in the shape of new nonblack immigrants to the United States with preexisting antiblack attitudes.

Conclusion

A few sharp strokes here, a few dark tinges there, refining the tableau of stigmatization and devaluing, a white cultural artist, dirty paintbrush resting between teeth, rubs his hands together with pride. His strong but duplicitous trompe l'oeil looks incredibly real. Crafty mass media productions often depict African American women as pauperized reprobates and underachievers, as the producers of weak families, or, on occasion, as exaggerated superachievers. Even in the latter case, the superachievement may be portrayed as questionable, even suspicious, because more than likely it is a succès de scandale.[20] Differences otherwise significant in African American communities, differences

121

between triumph and failure, between virtue and vice, now matter little because the negative misrecognition of the black woman is fixed and, as in our white artist's tableau, apparently genuine.

In media-oriented cities like New York, Los Angeles, and Las Vegas, if not in all U.S. cities, there seems to be a white determination to create numerous media projects that implement the moral devaluing and stigmatization of African Americans. In such places Mammy, Jezebel, and Sapphire are celebrated in spite of the presence of information to the contrary, not to mention great white corruption in these very cities. Not only do white disciples of this propaganda exude a faith that true images of black woman are revealed in their distorted phantoms, they also ignore the unpleasant impact of their racist images and misrecognition. White illusions and remembrances are preciously guarded because they are valuable to the preservation of the dominant society's persisting racial hierarchies.

Chapter 5

Distancing White Women

As we have seen in previous chapters, in many organizational settings, such as places of employment, African American women and men experience the pain of being social outsiders. They face a broad range of everyday discrimination, with recurring reminders of traditional segregation and exclusion. Often they are kept from social recognition, important positions, and significant rewards in predominantly white settings. For black women in traditionally white workplaces being marginalized and dehumanized is a common experience. When our respondents speak about work-climate problems with white women and men, they do not speak in generalities learned from the mass media or from books but offer direct accounts of the discrimination and mistreatment they face in their daily rounds.

Racial Conflict in Organizations

While the tensions and frictions between white women and black women and other women of color occur in many institutional settings, the workplace is perhaps the most common site for struggles. Instead of coalescing against white male oppressors, black and white women are often mutual adversaries, as one black female executive observes: "Ah, job competition. I think it all centers around jobs. And they [white women] see us as being counted, we can be counted twice, we can be counted twice as both a minority and a black, and so they're entering the labor force, and they're interested in jobs that we're also interested in." Some white women may hold a grudge against black women. The suggestion here is that some whites resent black women's "twofer" status in the job market, the double advantage allegedly provided to employers. Nonetheless, when compared to the gender inequality confronting white women, black women's social inequality is more complex, particularly given the manifold sources of racial inequality, which include the actions of white women.

Callousness and Discriminatory Treatment

In discussions of racial discrimination, including those in the social science literature, one often gets the impression that the main perpetrators of racial antagonism and discriminatory actions in the United States are working-class whites. Indeed, the hard-hat, working-class white male is perhaps the leading national image of the white racist bigot. However, we have found in our individual and focus-group interviews, like a few other researchers, that this conventional portrait of white bigotry is seriously inadequate if not misleading.[1] While there are working-class bigots and discriminators, whom our black respondents sometimes mention, these are not the principal concern in most institutional settings. In these everyday places it is *middle-class* whites, men and women, who turn out to be the major perpetrators of discrimination.[2]

"I'm going to tell you" about white women, asserts one successful business entrepreneur in a southwestern city. She describes white women as particularly treacherous: "She's more vicious than her male counterpart. She is much more vicious than her male counterpart could ever be. Most of the discrimination, things that I have heard of in the past two years, have been committed by white women." In our interviews the specific actions of white women encompass a range of negative and, less often, positive, responses to black women. The everyday callousness typical of many white women is painful for black women. The specific expressions of this callousness vary, ranging from marginalization at social gatherings where white wives accompanied by white husbands dismiss black women, to white women addressing black women so oddly or curtly that it humiliates, to white women withholding professional guidance or promotional and other employment opportunities from black women.

The disparaging of the racial "other" takes subtle and blatant forms. Simple recognition may not be forthcoming from whites. For example, a female scholar at a major educational institution recently reported this incident to us: "My white female secretary introduced me to her grown daughter and her granddaughter as 'a nice lady I work with.' I was stunned! Am I not a college professor, a Ph.D., one of her employers? I would have *never* been dismissed that way in the African American community." An African American woman's position and accomplishments were disregarded, were misrecognized and not "seen." The contemporary misrecognition and callousness of white women fit into a historical pattern of relations and one-way communication between white and black women captured in the writings of black scholars like bell hooks, Toni Morrison, and Audre Lorde. Lorde writes, "The history of white women who are unable to hear black women's words, or to maintain dialogue with us, is long and discouraging."[3]

One black woman, a supervisor, was critical of white female administrators who do not supervise people of color properly. In her experience there is no difference between white female and white male supervisors: "The end result is going to be the same, I'm going to struggle, either way." She recalls one of several difficult experiences she had with a white female executive who seemingly was determined to intervene actively in her community involvement: "I was selected to serve on the grand jury. She had problems with that. She even wrote a letter to the administrator about me serving on the grand jury, and [asking] was there any way that could be prevented. . . . Well, she was just a racist and just the idea that I was involved in all of these different things openly and publicly just really bothered her." Capturing more details of the incident, the respondent provides support for her view that unfair treatment is at play in this case.

> I managed to get a copy of the letter. After the assistant administrator wrote her back that, no, there was nothing to prevent me from doing that, she called the judge. The judge wasn't in when she called, and she left a message for the judge to call her back. And when the judge called her back, she wasn't here. But he left a message that he was returning her call. So I reported everything, and that's what she doesn't like.

In this report from a black woman's experience we see an example of a white woman wanting to shape the life of a black woman, in this case outside work. This was one of several such incidents she reportedly had with her supervisor. In these examples a white administrator seems to have been protecting not only white space at work but apparently some type of privileged space in the judicial sphere. Using her chance to share her viewpoint with a higher authority, the black woman took assertive action in her situation, defending herself well against the attempts of the white woman to impede what the respondent saw as important community involvement. Her grasp of the situation led her to significant countering responses. Significantly, she spent effort in documenting the series of events. This type of documenting action is part of the repertoire of responses that many black women and men develop to cope with everyday antagonism and discrimination from whites. While some whites might see this documenting as a paranoid response, experience with whites makes it clear to most African Americans, in workplaces and elsewhere, that such caution is necessary.

Dealing with discrimination on a daily basis requires the development of a broad range of coping and countering strategies by all those who are targets for white actions. Numerous respondents describe the strategies they have had to develop to deal with whites in the workplace. In a recent focus group a government administrator relates:

> I think that racism runs between subtle and blatant racism, and I've . . . had both. . . . I don't know which is worse, the white females or the white males. I mean, I guess that it all boils down to the same thing. And I have, especially, and I guess maybe I see it more with the white females, [who] don't like to deal with me. They like to try to circumvent me, and go through other people to talk to me. And the most recent case, is not this week, but about a week ago. And the white female, she had a problem with the way we were structured, at one of the commission meetings. And, as opposed to talking to me about making a change, she went to my supervisor. And of course, you know, he doesn't deal with stuff like that. . . . And, actually, she didn't call me back, and I know why. Because I think part of her problem is, historically she's always just dealt with people the way she wanted to deal with people. And she has a reputation of getting her own way.

Then she describes how she dealt with this white woman who did not want to deal directly with a black administrator:

126

And I caught her one day in the hallway, and I was really very nice to her. And I think she was really surprised, but I was nice. Because, see, I think . . . even though you know a person is racist, there still is a way to handle people like that . . . because you still got to get the job done. And, by the time she and I finished, she was a happy camper. But the bottom line is, she also realizes that she can't circumvent me, you know, she has to deal with me, whether she likes it or not.

While much energy had to be expended to secure fair treatment, this black woman had a partial triumph in the end. Contending with everyday racism is hard, particularly when the antagonist is of one's own gender. However, sharing a gender position does not necessarily breed understanding because of historical conditioning. We see here, as in previous chapters, that discrimination frequently calls forth a black response, one that is rooted in many decades of accumulated learning and experience among African Americans. These everyday experiences with white Americans and the countering strategies are commonly stored in the collective memories of families and communities and are passed down from one generation to the next.

Hostile and Stereotyped Remarks

In various organizational settings across the United States the array of negative comments and actions endured by black women at the hands of white women is apparently as great as those endured at the hands of white men. In the workplace the negative remarks directed at black women by white women reflect the commonplace racial credo, and they are one more way whites manipulate or demean the status and lives of black workers. A human services manager spoke about a young white woman at work who sometimes used the phrase "you people." The manager then explained that she educated this white woman about the offensiveness, however unintentional, of such remarks:

And it's not because I dislike white people, I don't have a personal grudge against white people. . . . I've seen white people who are intolerable, and disrespectful toward people of color, and so when they deal with me, I'm as sharp and as harsh as I need to be, and make it very clear that I choose not to make them comfortable.

Popular myths of white superiority, the dominant racial credo, partially account for the common usage of multiple-meaning remarks objectionable to black Americans like "you people." The usage here signals lack of civility on the part of a young white speaker, whom the respondent feels would benefit from some education on this matter. One way that African Americans respond to apparent white antagonism is to try to understand what lies behind comments in specific situations. Their further response is often contingent on whether they think the whites involved can benefit from active intervention, such as being educated. Some whites, such as the young, may earn a gentle response, while others require a harsher lesson.

In many cases phrases like "you people" distinguish "othered" groups from persons of honor, the aliens from the citizens. The usage here—an implied disdain for this black professional—signals to the respondent a dearth of civility on the part of the white speaker. Despite white speakers' discourtesy, and negative effects on black listeners, expressions like "you people" hold their place in the dominant lexicon because they undergird the racial stratification and inequality so favorable to whites. Though scattered fragments of the broader racial discourse, such language contains and sustains dominant values influencing white thinking. The usage separates good from bad—an "us," the elite, from a "they," the subordinated group. Such special phrases perform a subtle, symbolic, successful violence against people of color. This symbolic violence shapes thought and, ultimately, social structure, just as social structure in its turn inspires racist thinking and language.

Idioms like "you people" may not seem harsh to white speakers addressing African Americans, including educated speakers too familiar with their own surroundings, language, and thought to be fully aware of the surroundings' maleficence for its black participants. Since the 1980s many white commentators have attacked the new hate-crime regulations at some universities and similar ordinances in some cities for restricting and regulating hateful speech that, however vicious, they argue is protected by the First Amendment to the U.S. Constitution. However, what these white critics may miss is that vicious epithets and similar verbal comments hurled at people of color by white Americans are usually intended to be very harmful and that they can have as severe an impact on their targets as physical attacks. Liberal whites, who recognize the harsh epithets are designed to be hurtful, often miss the point when they suggest that the answer to hate speech is simply "more speech" to counter the epithets. What they miss is that such verbal attacks are often part of a larger, hostile racial climate that does serious psychological and physical damage to its targets. Significantly, there has been some recognition of this broader impact of hostile verbal attacks in a few recent court decisions. For example, the U.S. Court of Appeals for the Third Circuit handed down a decree that pervasive use of such phrases as "you people" and related epithets are enough to prove that a workplace has a racially hostile climate. This decision reportedly has spurred a number of corporate officials to change regulations on discrimination in their workplaces.[4]

What to a black listener may be clearly invidious, or reflective of a white speaker's individual racial bias, is a reflection of a broader racial indoctrination and animosity that contributes to the difficulty some white women and men have communicating with or accepting the professional guidance of black women. This point is manifested in the comments of an administrator in the North:

> I've had problems because being a black female, I've had to be responsible for having a white male working under my direction, and that did not work. White men do not want to take direction from black women. . . . Now, I'm having the same problem because I have another, a white woman who's scheduled to come into our program and she has a doctorate also, and she has told [people] that her concern is that she would have a problem taking direction from me, having me tell her what to do. So, it's a problem. It's a problem that white folks have not come to grips with. They still have the plantation mentality, the plantation mentality is alive and well.

White male or white female, the problem is often similar. An effectual plantation mentality preserves an old, historically dominant misrecognition of an inferior black woman in the contemporary white mind, thereby thwarting their occupational authority.

In some ways white women seem to be a greater problem than white men. One young black professor recently underscored some distinctive problems created by white women: "One difference is the added jealousy white women feel toward black women—the way we dress, carry ourselves, et cetera, even the fact that our spirituality keeps us grounded, all of that causes jealousy."

Faced with workplace marginalization and dehumanization, black women could often use assistance from privileged white women. Solidarity with white women could help alleviate black women's experiences with gendered racism. But such solidarity is rarely offered. Most black and white women are separated by divergent racial biographies and histories, and they come into conflict in the workplace and many other institutional arenas. Drawing on their own cultural legacy, and privileging its interactive styles and stereotyped images of others, white women may view African American women as "too aggressive" or "too loud" in everyday interaction. For their part, African American women draw on everyday experience with white women and often come to see them as "exploiting" or "insincere" in interracial interaction.[5]

In addition, African American women may suspect that they are sometimes being used by white women primarily or exclusively for the latter's interests and status goals. Cross-racial conflict is not a new problem in the history of relations between white and black women. Writing on the relationships of slaveholding women with their enslaved black servants, one historian has noted how white "mistresses could be the very devil. A mean mistress stood second to no master in her cruelty, although her strength was less. . . . From my reading of the diaries and private papers of the slaveholders, I have sadly concluded that the racism of the women was generally uglier and more meanly expressed than that of the men."[6] Moreover, some slaveholding women who were activists supported the cause of black women slaves to further their own religious and political goals.[7]

The superior racial attitudes reminiscent of plantation life linger today in the attitudes and practices of many white women. In a 1980s study of private household workers, who have long been an important group among African American women, Judith Rollins found that these workers mostly toiled for white middle-class women, who used the labor of black women to free up time for their own activities.[8] These white female employers emphasized various types of racial deference. For example, they usually used only the black woman's first name, from the first conversation, but expected the black woman not to respond in kind. These white women treated black household workers generally as "inferiors."

From the early days of slavery, through legal segregation, to the present-day home or business workplace, black women have frequently felt the controlling power of white women who do not bond with them. Indeed, in recent African American fiction the portrait of a white woman "who exerts power over the lives of black men and women to secure a measure for her own self-worth appears frequently."[9] Abiding slave and mistress continuities and memories destroy the potential for nonracial visions of gender, and arbitrary racial factors interfere with white women's legitimate goals of gender equality by destroying the possibility of cross-racial cooperation among women of all backgrounds.

Given the dominant wisdom and indoctrination, white women, while attentive to issues of gender, often miss or dismiss the collective experience of black women with gendered racism. The gap separating black women from white women is wide, indeed, as can be seen in the cogent language of one entrepreneur from a southwestern city, in language reflecting her rage and resistance.

> It pisses me off about white women talking about comparable worth. Where in the hell is our comparable worth? We've been out here in the damn job market all this time, they haven't talked about our dollar matching against [the] white male . . . about our equal rights, and I will not join their movement to help them get where they're going until they help us, black women and men. And I'm not going to separate black men from us, because I think a lot of the friction we have comes from them. You know, not just white women, white people, they pit us against each other. They tell [black] males that the reason you don't have good paying jobs is because of the black female. They lie.

This entrepreneur blames prejudiced and insensitive whites not only for racial discrimination but also for fueling controversies between black men and black women. White women's obduracy in seeing the question of comparable worth only in gender terms seems guided by their racial identification with white men. Their conformity to traditional racial notions and ideologies isolates them from black women. The evasion of the reality and meaning of racial inequality, on the one hand, and the ostracizing of black women, on the other, reduces the hope of these groups of women collectively resisting common white male oppressors.

Not all barriers to mobility encountered by black women in employment and other settings come from these white women. In addition to barriers created by white men and women, there are some created by black women in positions of authority. A few of these women periodically display callous and selfish attitudes toward other black women trying to move up the employment ladder, according to a female entrepreneur:

> Well, I have not worked that much with white women, as I have with white males. But I have worked with black females who act like white women—who, I say, were hired to keep us in our place. And they dangle in their face and gave them a little forty- or fifty-thousand-dollar-a-year job, and they would do anything to make sure they maintained that forty- or fifty-thousand-dollar-a-year job. And that means if they have to cut your neck off, they will do it. And I have seen that in the workplace, as a matter of fact I have experienced it.

As a long history of sociological analysis indicates, pressures for conformity in many employment settings are pervasive and intense. Black female employees are not exempt from all the usual pressures, as well as the pressure to abandon black interests in favor of white definitions of conditions. When co-opted, some black women may participate actively in restricting the opportunities of other black women, and they may thus participate in the perpetuation of the hierarchies and barriers of racism. They also lend support to false but lasting white "wisdom" about racial matters. Middle-class black women (and men) who succeed in moving into positions of authority face the constant dilemma of conforming too much, or too little, to the dictates of white-framed organizational norms and understandings. It is not surprising that, in keeping with that organizational reality, the actions of some black women toward their fellow women parallel those of prejudiced white women.

Friction with White Women in Other Settings

Sometimes, the encounters of black and white women outside the workplace result in friction, molding further the cultural estrangement long inspired by the ancient slave plantation mentality. In the illustration that follows, a professor in the health sciences tells of the poor service she received while shopping.

> I was in an exceptionally good mood one day. I went into my grocery store and I wanted to return some VCR tapes. I had opened one of the three that I'd purchased and it wasn't functioning properly, so I was going to take them back and I had my receipt in hand. So I waited for the person in the booth. There were two white women in the booth, both under the age of thirty. And one of the things that I noticed, as a woman over forty, is the lack of respect among white females thirty years and under, and certainly white males that are in the adolescent group. So I politely waited for them to finish waiting on this white grandmotherish type, and I took my turn at the booth. One person turned her back on me and sat on the telephone; the other person started to work on some bookwork right below me. And I politely looked at my watch; I let five minutes pass and I'm still standing there, and I said, "Who do I get to help me here?" And the woman looked up at me, that was directly in front of me, looked me straight in my eye and said, "I didn't see you." I was furious.

In her discussion this woman makes it clear that she has recurring problems with white women, such as those in sales positions. She makes evaluations out of experience. Her gentle way of acting did not impress the sales attendants in this case. It is likely that making a fuss would have caught their attention, producing a favorable outcome for this shopper. Yet fussing might also have triggered in these clerks the misrecognition of the black woman as threatening, as a "violent black." Indeed, such a black reaction might have been what the white clerks anticipated or wanted. The dilemma facing this black woman, a clear example of "damned if you do, damned if you don't," reflects the perverse and confusing character of the racial messages sent to people of color in this white-dominated society. Being recognized as a human being worthy of respect and fair treatment is at the heart of positive social interaction. This incident again brings to mind Ralph Ellison's portrayal of white reactions in his book *Invisible Man:* "I am an invisible man. . . . I am a man of substance, of flesh and bone, fiber and liquids— and I might even be said to possess a mind. I am invisible, understand, simply because people refuse to see me."[10] The theme of not being seen in stores is common in our interviews and in other recent research studies. The everyday experience of black men and women, including those with high achievements, is that many whites refuse to recognize them as human beings deserving of full respect.[11]

Some white readers might suggest that this particular incident is relatively minor and might argue, correctly, that on occasion white women also experience such poor service. Critics might contend that the professor is overreacting or is paranoid. Yet, when putdown episodes such as this become *daily, lifelong routines* in the lives of black women, as is often indicated in our respondents' narratives, these bitter fruits change moods from good into bad. This woman describes her reaction as "furious" despite being "in an exceptionally good mood" that day. Such a psychological reaction is stressful and over the long term probably has serious personal, including health, implications.

Such episodes are more typical of the black experience than of the white experience because of the dominant group's power in many places and because of the obsession with racial and cultural whiteness, which excludes from the boundaries of humanity those who are regarded as "others." This white action or inaction, in this case for a professional woman, is commonplace in the reports of African American women. The daily encounters of black women with belittling by white women and men are not random, not trivial, and not simple oversights. Having absorbed the dominant logic, these white salesclerks apparently believe themselves to hold a special power not shared by African Americans and not counterbalanced by a black person's educational credentials or patience and tact in a situation.

Throughout our chapters we have seen that white actions, those of both women and men, reflect certain feelings and fictions that are revealing about whiteness itself. These understandings can be overt or concealed. Sometimes, they are so deeply hidden that, as Frankenberg found in her interviews with white women, it is "difficult for white people to name. . . . Those who are securely housed within its borders usually do not examine it."[12] The white women Frankenberg interviewed made it clear that whiteness entails more than negative stereotypes about African American women and men. It involves feelings and emotions that lie at the heart of the white self. As a result, antiblack imaging and animosity can have a venomous aspect, as in this case.

134

As we have seen in the case of the workplace, verbal responses to African Americans by whites can be negative and aggressive. Whites, women and men, periodically demonstrate differing shades of arrogance and varying symbols of estrangement to the black women they encounter, as in this account of an offensive remark made by a white woman to one of our respondents, a designer in a major city.

> I travel a lot, and it's just little looks and maybe offhand remarks. I was in a group of people in therapy once in an overeater's program. . . . I was the only black person there. We were sitting at the table one evening, having dinner, and this white woman said—she was making a remark about something else—and she said, "token black." Then she looked at me and clammed up, because I was the only black person there. And I became angry with her, and told her I'd deal with this in court. I don't become violent or physical or anything . . . and it would be better if she didn't make any more remarks unless she had something she was willing to give up, because I would sue her for it. So it's things like that I do to people; it kind of scares them off. I kept all the [white] guys on my job from bothering me the same way. I'd ask them, "Now, what do you own besides that pickup truck and that big hat and those boots you got on? Because it's going to be mine if you keep fooling with me." So I usually try to scare people off.

Ideally, members of a support group should set aside personal differences in their quest of a common goal. However, as one sees here, deeply anchored racial traditions can convert initial solidarity into an unsupportive reality. Probably a faux pas, given the white woman's own astonishment, the "token black" remark suggests this type of racial categorizing is embedded in white thinking. This gaffe indicates that, while white and black women share gender, they are disunited in their struggles for justice, in part by racial sentiments that surge, as in this case, when least expected.

Contending with racialized comments and other harassment requires that one's repertoire be in place. Countering actions can range from verbal replies to court suits. Whether real or not, threats of litigation can intimidate some whites, forcing them to think twice about abusive conduct. However, no matter how successful the countering strategy is, the energy cost of having to respond and keep one's response repertoire in good order is very great for black women and men.

At social gatherings, opportunities arise for making new contacts and strengthening old ties. These social activities can assist one's individual or family mobility, for often on these occasions important information circulates and networks develop. However, at many white-organized activities black women, if they are invited, tend to be integrated superficially. As a nurse in a southern city noted, even when white male guests converse with black women, white women remain aloof.

> I find the white women are more defensive than the white men, in a social gathering. The white men are more aggressive and friendly toward the black women, and the white women sit back and [get] angry about the situation. Because, like in the Cub Scouts, I'm able to talk to the husbands, while the wives really won't talk back or just refer you to their husbands.

Instances of white male friendliness toward black women may of course only be transitory and not an indication of personal or social acceptance. Moreover, this congeniality of white men may sometimes reduce the possibility that black women will be able to communicate with or establish potential networks with white women.

Major Differences Across the Color Line

Since the reinvigorated feminist movement of the 1960s many women, black and white, have debated whether the women's movement has encompassed, or can encompass, the fundamental interests of African American women. One problem in many such discussions is the failure to understand the different structural and historical conditions that black and white women face. There are several important ways in which their situations differ. An executive in a southern city underscores one major difference:

> I think that there is a newly sort of developing schism between Anglo women and black women, I don't think there is ever a very strong relationship there. I mean, there is just a schism there because of race. But the part of the women's movement, I think there were hopes that because there were some common problems there

that the two groups would unite. But because our problems are somewhat different, I don't see white women really, really thinking of black women as allies, they see us as competition. And, there is a difference in the issues. Our issue is not men, our issue is the system, our issues revolve [around] the system, and so sometimes, feminism for white women is very different. Ours is centered around jobs, they're centered around men, and so I see a shift in developing there, if there ever was a closeness.

This executive postulates the possibility of closeness but envisions a growing alienation between black and white women. Different collective memories shaped by past and contemporary experiences blind white women to the plight of black women, who are victims of both racism and sexism. As this respondent sees it, the major goal of many black women is getting into jobs that have in the past been off-limits to them because of racial discrimination. As we noted previously, many white feminists see male spouses' actions as central to women's problems, such as by not allowing them to develop careers outside the home, while black women are more likely to view the men at home as allies against a hostile white society.

This point was underscored some time ago at the 1977 Conference on the International Woman's Year in Houston, where a Black Women's Action Plan was presented by dissenting African American women. This statement asserted: "Moreover, as black women informed by our past we must eschew a view of the women's struggle which takes as its basic assumption opposition to men, as distinguished from organizing around the principle of opposition to the white, male power-structure's perpetuation of exploitation, subjugation, inequality and limited opportunities based upon sex or race."[13] In other words, the goal of the feminist movement should be to challenge an oppressive society that is generally founded in, and operated according to, both racist and sexist principles.

As this participation of black women in a feminist conference indicates, the concern of black women with issues such as racism and workplace discrimination should not be taken to mean that black women are not for full equality of women in the larger society. Most are strong advocates of women's equal rights, including in employment. African American women have long been advocates of women's rights issues, as were abolitionists Sojourner Truth and Harriet Tubman in the 1800s, and educators Anna Julia Cooper and Ida B. Wells in the late nineteenth and early twentieth centuries. Most of the black female (and black male) abolitionists in the 1840–1865 period supported women's rights, although most considered white racism to be the societal problem needing immediate attention.[14] In recent decades, research studies utilizing opinion surveys have found only small differences between black and white women on women's rights issues, with substantial majorities of both groups adopting strong women's rights positions on specific issues of concern.[15]

Nonetheless, there are important disparities in the respective situations of black and white women, which help explain the racial tensions in the contemporary women's movement. A female supervisor describes some distinctive problems that black women face just by virtue of their racial-gender attributes:

> Dealing with the children, relationships, the workplace, all of those are problems. When the school system, the school system was not set up to educate our kids. When a system negates your whole history as part of the curriculum, then it wasn't set up for you! [laughs] So, you know your children are not being properly educated, that's something you have to deal with. The school systems here have nothing to offer these children, so that's another problem, trying to motivate them and keep them in school. You try to motivate them to try to get them to stay in school, that is a hell of a job. Then the first time they stub their toe, they [whites] want to kick them out. They want to put them in some kind of suspension, all these kinds of things take place. And who has to go to school and try to deal with this problem? Dad is not going. Black women are the head of more households. Now, if your child is sick, even if that child is in day care, if the child is sick, day care doesn't want him, and they don't want you missing from your job either. But if a white woman's child is ill, you can hear them making all kinds of excuses around the office. She had to go, they can understand that, but they can't understand why you have to be with your children.

The major institutions of this society tend to negate the history and experiences of African Americans. This includes most school environments. Though employed white women, like employed black women, handle multiple roles, black women are more likely to be single mothers, and the latter often deal more or less alone with myriad problems of their own and their children.[16] For two-parent African American families, the role of wives in dealing with racial-gender and other matters is complicated by the domino effects of their husbands' negative racial experiences on black families. White women do not face these racial woes but instead benefit, whatever their class level, from many and diverse white privileges.

Asking a question to one of our respondents in the North, a black interviewer noted how the script is different for white women: "I've often heard white women with the feminist movement screaming to get out and work, and people will tell me, 'Well, black women have been working all along.' " The respondent, a high school teacher, adds her view.

> I've heard that. My mother always worked, and she still always did household stuff. I find that most incredible now. As I can recall as a kid, she was up at five o'clock making breakfast for us, and then we all went to work. And then she left the fields half an hour before us and made dinner or lunch, and then she was back when we were back. And then at the end of the day when I was so tired I could hardly move, she came home and made supper, and cleaned up the kitchen, and some time in there she did laundry. Now, I don't know when she had time to do that. We didn't have a washing machine for a long time. And she still worked. And that was true for most of the women in our area. I don't know so much about what they did in other areas, but I know in the South, black women have always worked, they worked out of necessity. And if they stayed home, it was simply because they had too many small kids and there were enough older ones to go out and work in her place so that she didn't have to, but she wasn't staying home as a luxury. She was staying home because somebody needed to stay home with all those small kids and so she got elected.

Black women and white women, taken as groups, have different work histories.

In recent decades the organized feminist movement has generally reflected the interests of white women, including wives and mothers who have found the male-dominated home anything but a haven. The pathbreaking 1963 book sometimes given credit for stimulating the contemporary feminist movement, Betty Friedan's *The Feminine Mystique*, addresses "the problem that has no name," the central problem for U.S. women: bored suburban wives who are not able to get out of the home to develop jobs and careers because of male-determined definitions of their femininity.[17] Friedan's definition of the situation is not the way most African American women, given their historical experience outside the home, would define liberation in this society. Indeed, contemporary black women do not appear in Friedan's analysis.

Since the beginning of African enslavement in the Jamestown colony in the early 1600s, most women of African ancestry have had to work outside their homes for much of their active lives. They were forced by slavery or, later, by economic exigencies to participate actively in the workforce. Historically imposed, multiple roles are thus integral to black female lives, creating distinctive experiences and necessities. Today, many African American women cannot identify with a white-centered feminist struggle to enter the workplace if that means women seeing "success" as being able to decenter their families in their lives. Indeed, many black women have longed for the luxury of having more time to spend with their families.

The understanding among black women that many white women are less encumbered and more advantaged can create resentment. Nonetheless, there is some common ground between black and white women who find themselves to be working mothers, as this respondent added later:

> I don't think it's any more difficult for black [women] than it is for [white women]. It's difficult being a working mother. I don't know how we manage to do that, but we do. I drop my daughter off in the morning for school, I have to pick her up in the afternoon, she doesn't have bus service. I have to help her with her homework. I have to do my schoolwork. And then I had a part-time job, so I was doing that too. So, it's a lot. But if you want to do it, you can do it. It's difficult. If it were easy, anybody could do it. That's my favorite line!

All working mothers handle a double shift.

Because of the omnipresence of racial burdens and barriers, the black male respondents in our sample, as a rule, view the situations of black women as different from those of white women, as did this elected official in a southern city: "I'm not one of those that happens to believe the struggle of black women is the same as the struggle of white women, because you're still black. And I think there are more similarities in the plight of black women and black men than there are differences. . . . The obstacles of racism are the same. They're not different." Because of centuries of racism African American women have long had strong links to black men. As we noted previously, this makes them less likely to accept certain traditional overtures of white feminists. As racial solidarity transcends gender solidarity, the continuing significance of race to U.S. society is yet again highlighted. A male engineer puts it in a similar way: "If you're going to be discriminated against, nine times out of ten it's because you're black first."

While sympathetic to the gender discrimination faced by all women, a male graduate student in the South reiterated how the advantaged position of white women is deeply anchored in U.S. history.

> If I'm understanding the feminist movement correctly as wanting to include white women as minorities, meaning that they can also vie for positions in affirmative action programs, certain job opportunities, educational opportunities, that's a definite dilemma. Because you realize that America has always been and still is a sexist society. But it also, more consistently and more principally, has been a racist society. You weren't enslaved because you were a women, you were enslaved because you were black. You weren't not admitted to major universities because you were a woman, you were not admitted because you were black. Women received voting rights in 1920. That was a long time coming; the times were even longer for the blacks, before it became hassle free. To a certain extent, white women need to be appreciated and be included in some type of aggressive policy that involves sharing of the American pie. But to put them in the same boat as black women and black men is not fair, because the same historical limitations have not been imposed on them as on blacks.

There is much sensitivity here to the sexism faced by white women. However, racism takes first place in the liberation struggle, as it is seen by most of our female and male respondents.

Still, the acute awareness of the centrality of racism for African

Americans does not mean that black women do not see and oppose sexism in their own communities. Black men can also be a problem for black women, as a supervisor at a hospital explains: "The problems the black woman faces are totally different from the problems that the white woman faces, because not only is the black woman oppressed by the system, she is also oppressed by her own counterpart. The black male oppresses." Black women face a racially oppressive system promoted by white women and white men, and they also struggle against the gender discrimination of black men. In addition, some black male stereotyping of black women—as when some black men adopt a white female beauty standard—stems from effective socialization in dominant racial ideologies. Moreover, black women sometimes feel left out when it comes to the development of public policy. Sharon Griffin has put it this way: "When the issue is sexism, traditionally, white feminists often do the talking. When the issue is racism, traditionally, black men do the talking."[18]

We should recall from our discussion in Chapter 3 that an additional source of tension between black and white women is the perception of some black women that black men are being "stolen" by white women. Clearly, many African American women are very concerned about interracial relationships involving white women and African American men. Frequently it seems that a well-publicized case of a black male sports figure or other celebrity is a trigger for extended discussions in black communities about the dating and mating of black men and white women. Central to the concern of many black women is the reported shortage of eligible black men for relationships, as well as the fact that white women already have many advantages from their privileged racial status in the larger society.

Supportive White Women

Our respondents do, of course, speak of white women who have been helpful or friendly, despite the bleak prospects for such support and cooperation. As a volunteer worker in a southwestern city notes, "There are several, quite honestly, white women in this community who have been mentors as well as opportunity makers for me."

Mentoring for Skills and Education

Other respondents cited the help or guidance they had received from supportive white women over their lives. Note the testimony of a black female professor at a major university:

> [One white woman] was a tremendous influence on my life in encouraging me to finish up my master's, to seek additional education, and to get involved in community activities. . . . The other influence in my life is still there as far as a white female is concerned, and that's my present boss, the dean. . . . She has always been encouraging, as far as me and my particular professional goals, and I think for an administrator, displays an inordinate amount of understanding. And that's not to say that, we don't always agree, that we always agree, but the issue is, she listens and she responds. And she may be accused by a lot of people of being a lot of things, but a racist is not one of them.

This professor is appreciative of the respect and recognition accorded her by two white women. She reasons that interpersonal respect and regard bridged the racial distance and neutralized disagreements or made them more bearable. This report suggests that old-fashioned politesse is neither dated nor superficial, but rather a neglected, though desperately needed, human requirement, one that needs serious consideration when we search for a viable solution to persisting problems of disregard associated with the persisting color bar.

Other testimonies can be found in some of our interviews, with some black women acknowledging the contributions of a few white women to their personal careers or success. They offer scattered examples of how that support has been instrumental in their pursuit of certain professional skills. One woman, who works for a department store chain, reported much blatant racist and sexist harassment by several white men in her employment situation. However, she found some assistance from a feminist group:

> I didn't know who to turn to when I was having so much trouble

on my job, and I think if I had been able to reach the NAACP—
and I did try calling and nobody answered the phone—that they
wouldn't have been able to give me the support that I needed. And
the NOW organization did that for me with support group meetings, and I've tried to meet people and talk to them about it who
are going through the same thing I was going through—I am
going through, rather. Feminists, they're doing a great deal for not
only female causes but for minorities in general. They're doing
something for minorities.

In particular organizational settings some white women have
worked hard to help black women and other women of color. There is
some history of mutually supportive relationships between black and
white women, such as in the early days of the abolitionist movement
in the nineteenth century. It was during the movement for the aboli-
tion of slavery that a group of women, white and black, became convinced of the need to eliminate gender as well as racial oppression in
the United States. Moreover, while it is clear from our interviews that
white women are a major source of discrimination and pain for African American women, some white women are clearly working for
racial change. In speaking with whites at lectures and seminars given
around the country, we have found that those who show the most
interest in problems of racial discrimination and in eradicating racism
are disproportionately female. Why this is the case is a matter deserving future research.

Making Friends

How might the tensions between black and white women be reduced?
Our female respondents offered a few ideas about this difficult but
critical matter. As these women examine and evaluate the situation,
black women and white women are estranged not because racial differences are inherent, but because of white (male) society's misrecognition of the positive attributes and rights of both groups of women.
A number of our respondents see building relationships across the
color line as important, although they also recognize how difficult
this is in practice. Indeed, judging from our interviews, positive en-

counters and friendships with white women occur all too seldom for black women.[19]

Still, a better understanding of cultural attributes routinely distorted or shunned could cause the racial strain between black and white women to subside. This point is developed by a black woman who calls for whites to draw closer to, and listen to, black acquaintances.

> In terms of what white America could do—I think, just try to understand us better. I think we have to live in their world, we have to understand their etiquette, the way things are done. We have to understand that when white women get their hair permed it turns curly, and when black women get their hair permed it's straight. That's something that I know because I had to assimilate myself into the white world. White women don't understand about hair and makeup, and just little things like that, because they haven't had to learn our world. And I would just ask them to, you know, if you do have your "black friend," do sit down and talk about some of the issues of black America to try and get an understanding of where we come from or why we do the things that we do, or why we say the things that we say. And just try to understand us better.

Understandings can be increased across the color line, but not without much effort. Cross-cultural exposure, a recognition of the real humanity and life-worlds of black women, might reduce in many white women the effects of prevailing gender-racial misconceptions and, ultimately, the resentment expressed in discriminatory actions. Still, there is a difference between having black acquaintances, what the respondent likely means by "black friends," and having real black friends with whom one can exchange candid dialogue.

Several respondents spoke about the barriers that a few black and white women manage to overcome in order to engage in positive communications and friendships. In a recent focus group in the Midwest one nurse speaks of a white woman with whom she eventually became friends.

So, I didn't like her okay? Then one day I got to talking to her, and me and her are like sisters now. We're the best of friends. . . . It's not like they [whites] don't like you because of who you are or what you are. But they have been taught not to like you because you're black, you know. And it's from their parents. I had a white girlfriend. I have a white girlfriend at work. You know what she told me and my father one day? My father would have her come over on our lunch breaks, fix her greens and corn bread. She had never had it before. Fixed her greens and corn bread. She said, "If my father knew I was in a black person's house, he would probably croak right away and then totally disown me." Because he told her, "Wherever you have a black person, you got a problem." And this is how she was raised, to believe that blacks were nothing but trouble.

Friendships can and do take place across the racial boundary in workplaces and other social settings, but these relationships are very difficult to create and, once created, to maintain over time because of the social and family pressures, most commonly from the white side of the friendly association. The animosity toward African Americans expressed by one generation of whites often comes from what they have learned from the previous generation. There is a collective memory of white Americans that carries many negative images of black Americans, and these images have rarely been directly confronted in major ways by any of the educational or mass media institutions of this society. Token multicultural courses in schools, moreover, cannot offset the years of parental socialization in matters of racism. As a result, negative images linger on and pollute not only the minds of whites who might try to make friendships but also the cultural air throughout the general society.

In a recent field-research project one of our graduate students, Tiffany Hogan, interviewed several pairs of black and white women who were involved in close friendships across the color line.[20] Not surprisingly, she had some difficulty in locating close biracial friendships. However, from those she did locate the interviews were very revealing about the character and importance of bridges across the deep racial chasm. For example, in one interview a black banking executive speaks of her relationship with a close friend who is white.

What is different about the relationship that I have with Mary, as

146

it pertains to race, is that I found in Mary [a person] who . . .
could be a white friend. But that we could talk about the fact that
we were different, that our relationship did not have to solely be
built on how we were similar. Our relationship could also include
how we were different. That, because of who Mary is, we could actually be intentional and could actually talk about this phenomenon;
that there are issues that I have along racial lines, that I didn't
have to pretend that, "Oh, can't we all just get along?" It wasn't
just going to be a "get along" kind of relationship, as much an opportunity for me to really grow and learn about other aspects of my
relationships with whites that weren't positive. I felt that here was
someone who could now be, in a different way, quote-unquote, a
real white friend.

Clearly, "real white friends" are not the same as white acquaintances
at work or school. Real friends are those with whom one can share
deep concerns and serious problems, including in this case matters of
racism involving whites. Cross-racial friendships like this one mean
that much or all of the social distancing of black women by white
women that we noted above has collapsed, and the white member of
the pair is willing to discuss seriously the racial issues that not only
divide the nation but also cause great pain in their recounting, for
both the black and the white parties involved.

Another of Hogan's pairs of friends included two teachers, one
white and one black. In a joint interview the white teacher describes
their cross-racial friendship.

We just always felt comfortable with each other. There has always
been a bond there, that keeps growing through the years. We can
say anything to each other [black teacher: "Yeah"] and feel comfortable that we are not going to get laughed at or [she makes a face]
"What did you say that for?" [black teacher: "Exactly"]. You know,
if I said something that she wasn't comfortable with, she is going
to tell me. And I feel comfortable saying something that I want to
say or need to say, knowing full well that I am going to get acceptance, or the knowledge that I need to know to understand what
had happened, or to handle something.

The interviewer summarizes and interjects, "There is trust around that issue?" Then the black teacher replies: "Exactly. And so when I always talk about her to family or to friends, they can just tell, by the way I talk about her, that how much I love her and how much she has been a positive in my life, especially here in this town. If it hadn't been for her being here, I don't know how I could have survived some things that I have survived." Again, we see that acquaintanceship is not the same as a close friendship in which one can "say anything" to a friend without fear of hostility or rejection. Being close friends across the color line is a matter of building comfort and trust, and doubtless this requires many hours of discussions of difficult issues, including racial issues, in many different settings. Not only recognizing racial and cultural differences, but accepting and even welcoming them, is perhaps the true meaning of racial integration. The comments of Hogan's pairs of friends provide important clues for how this racially troubled society, and particularly whites in positions of authority, might begin to resolve the racial problems that are likely, increasingly, to tear the society apart. Among whites candidly recognizing and acknowledging the reality of racism is the first step to building trust across the color line.

Conclusion

Over the last few decades white women have entered the private worlds of white men, including employment settings in virtually every town and city across the United States. As a result, some white women have gained a modicum of power vis-à-vis white men, and small numbers have risen to positions of authority in corporate and other workplaces, as well as in other social settings such as education and politics. Given this rising influence, these women now have a critical role to play in the continuing degradation and dehumanization of African American women.

Ideally, viable solutions to gendered racism include the significant contributions of committed, genuinely nonracist white women. Yet most white women still misrecognize African American women and nurture gendered racism passively—by distancing themselves from issues affecting black women—or actively, through their own injurious words or blatant and subtle discrimination. The passive neglect of African American women can be seen in many places other than our interviews, as recounted recently by professor Barbara Phillips Sullivan.

> I joined other members of the Black Women Lawyers Association of Northern California in attending the annual dinner of the predominantly white California Women Lawyers sometime during the 1980's. The guest speaker from *Ms Magazine* purported to talk about the experiences of "women" and peppered her remarks with humorous vignettes to which most of the audience responded warmly. But, we (and our table contained all but one or two of the African-American women in attendance) became decidedly silent as the vignettes continued. It became clear that the speaker was describing solely the experiences of upper-middle-class white women. I do not begrudge her telling stories about the life with which she was familiar. The sticking point was that she failed to acknowledge the race and class specificity of her stories. She never once acknowledged the racial or class character of her stories. She claimed implicitly that the experience of upper-middle-class white women was the defining experience of "women."[21]

When many white feminists speak about women, they, implicitly or explicitly, seem to mean white women. Indeed, in the first decade or two of the recent feminist movement women of color were all but absent from leadership positions in major organizations. For example, in 1977, and again after the election of 1983, there were no women of color on the board of the National Organization of Women (NOW).[22] At the important 1977 Conference on the International Woman's Year, the previously mentioned Black Women's Action Plan argued that because black women have different experiences with institutional racism, and a "different future from that of white women, it is doubtful that anyone else in the United States can or should speak for them."[23] While there is a growing concern about this matter in the mainstream women's movement, there has as yet been no resolution, primarily because of the difficulties many progressive white women have in dealing with the nation's great racial divide and, doubtless in many cases, with their own racial socialization.

Persisting white racism has terrible costs for all women, men, and children who live in the United States. Racial discrimination is still widespread. Racial suspicion is everywhere and penetrates virtually every aspect of the society. It looms large in the minds of whites, blacks, men and women. Active and hostile words and actions can surface at any time in the most unexpected of places, in places where black women might otherwise expect support and shared ideals. Despite the fact that some white women contribute to the dismantling of gendered racism, for most white women their distancing from black women and their acrimonious words and actions indicate that suppressing gendered racism is not their collective will—and that perpetuating gendered racism is. The long racist histories of white men and women, and the conflicting histories of white and black women, have left a harsh racial-gender legacy. History provides clues for white women's contemporary distance from black women. Most white women's strong racial bond with white men is a negative statement about their often troubling views on black women and about the importance of equality and justice for all women.

Chapter 6

Black Families: Goals and Responses

Closeness to extended families can help black women and men absorb and counter the many damaging impacts of racial oppression. For several decades field research has shown that extended family organizations play a central role among African Americans in coping with life's difficulties, including racism.[1] For many African Americans the extended family is the center of a very positive and important support network. In a recent focus group a hotel executive recounts: "I have been fortunate. I have not had to go out and look for friends because I was born into a family of friends. I have six sisters and a mother. So, when I get ready to go shopping, I don't have to call up anybody. We are tight in the family." While our respondents are generally enmeshed in extended families, and draw on them for positive support, they also note threats to this traditional family structure. In part, this may be the result of economic and social mobility factors. However, those we interviewed suggest that, to some extent, a gradual weakening of many black extended families comes as a consequence of a shift from traditional communalism to increasing identification with dominant values of individualism. As one female professor at a southwestern university explains,

> I don't think any of us can be successful until all of us have the same opportunities to do that. Therefore, the whole structure which black America was built on has been an extended family helping process. As one gets to the top of the bucket, they reach back and

help someone else up. And I think that we have moved somewhat
from that position to just "me and mine," instead of looking at the
community at large, and what do we do in order to help all of us.

Then, as if giving a warning, the professor added emphatically:
"None of us have made [it] until everybody has. Everybody won't
make it to the same degree because we're individuals and [have] individual differences, but everybody must have the same access to that
opportunity." Advocated here is not an ivylike dependency of each
family member on another, but, for the benefit of each, a careful
preservation of access to the means of achievement by all members for
the group. Access needs preserving, for each member to advance, and
for each to retain her or his own success within the family context.
The cooperation of members within an extended family or larger community makes this crucial preservation of access more likely.

From this perspective togetherness and helping are critical to individual advancement. Each community or family member benefits
from the support and success of others. Individual decisions and actions promoting the well-being of others are worthy personal invest-
ments. Such a life model, which suggests that successful individualism
means successful cooperation, is distinctive, and unlike certain models
proclaimed by the dominant white society. In our view, this strong
collectivism of black families and communities deserves much more
attention than it has earned in most mainstream analysis of African
Americans.

The Extended Family in Black America

Although the professor speaking above appears to be focused primarily on the role of cooperation for socioeconomic mobility, in our interviews one sees other women and men discussing various types of
support and gaining from close association with their own families,
including extended families. Family systems vary, as do their definitions. Elmer Martin and Joanne Mitchell Martin have described a
black extended family as "a multigenerational, interdependent kinship system which is welded together by a sense of obligation to
relatives; is organized around a 'family base' household; is generally
guided by a dominant family figure; extends across geographical
boundaries to connect family units to an extended family network;

and has a built-in mutual aid system for the welfare of its members and the maintenance of the family as a whole."[2] Yet, indicating they are aware of differences between systems, the authors add, "Our definition grew out of our personal membership in families of this nature and our observations of similar families."[3] A somewhat broader definition of extended family is provided by prominent family scholar Harriette Pipes McAdoo: "The term *extended family* does not imply that all live under one roof but that non-nuclear family members are in close interaction with one another, exchange goods and services and keep in close or periodic contact with one another."[4] This definition accents interaction and not necessarily propinquity. Regardless of nearness the healing effects of participating in extended kinship units for those who are members cannot be overestimated.

Black families have long received negative images and bad public relations in the United States, mostly because of the aggressive efforts of white scholars and commentators in publicizing problems, both real and alleged, in these families. In a now famous 1960s report, social scientist and U.S. senator Daniel P. Moynihan wrote of black female-headed families being pathological and a serious retardant to the progress of African American communities.[5] This commentary was, and is, not unusual, for most aspects of black life and culture have been viewed more or less negatively by many white Americans, including teachers and scholars in academia. The exceptions to this rule are mainly positive comments about black abilities in certain limited areas, such as music, entertainment, and sports, which whites generally consider to be proper black provinces.

Attacks on black women and their families have been periodically resurrected over the last two decades, by Moynihan and now and then by conservative pundits like Charles Murray. Such analysts frequently claim that there is a distinctive subculture of poverty and welfare dependence among black low-income families that is the main barrier to their developing more successful lives and relationships. The call of these pundits is for black families to imitate white families, which are alleged to be much healthier and more viable. Black women and men need simply, according to much white advice, to become "harder working" and more "moral," like most white Americans are alleged to be. While the focus of these analyses is ostensibly on the poorest African American families, somehow many white commentators, politicians, and media analysts have communicated to the general public notions that "problems" of single motherhood, "wild youngsters," laziness, squalor, and welfare dependency are characteristic of a majority of African American families. This anti-black-family imagery has so spread that a majority of whites polled now see the poor and welfare recipients in the United States as mostly or typically African American.[6]

Some social science research strongly suggests otherwise. A majority of black families do not have the catalogue of negative characteristics the white commentators are accenting. The majority of black families are working-class or middle-class families, and the majority of these are viable and struggling to make a living against great social and economic barriers, including pervasive racial hurdles and obstacles. Nonetheless, according to many white commentators and politicians these racial barriers do not play any significant role in the problems faced by African American families. Most also ignore the fact that African American families taken as a group exhibit strong and positive values in support of family creation and maintenance.

Significantly, some social scientists have recently demonstrated the presence and significance of viable and strong extended families among African Americans in the past.[7] These family structures were generally maintained against the enormous challenges presented under slavery and segregation. In the 1990s still other social scientists have shown that extended families and traditional family values are prevalent among African Americans in the present. "Today, relative to whites and even to some ethnic groups of color, the Black community shows a higher level of multigenerational households, fosterage of kin and nonkin children, care for dependent family members, respect for elders, religiosity, and sacrificial efforts for the upward mobility of its members," according to Robert Staples and Leanor Boulin Johnson.[8]

Research shows that most black families are not isolated from important networking with relatives. The extended family unit is still significant for the majority of African Americans today. When needed, extended families, which often include close friends, protect black women and men and restore them to wholeness.[9] Extended family units in many societies, including the United States, include adopted relatives or "fictive kin." These are recognized, for example, in the common usage of "aunt" and "uncle" in African American communities to refer to emotionally close but unrelated persons.[10] As Peggye Dilworth-Anderson explains, "Fictive kin can be as important in the black family as those related by blood. Boundaries are also permeable and flexible in black families. People can move in and out of several families and have numerous siblings or 'play' siblings and parents."[11]

Evidence of even broader fictive kinship may also be seen in the tendency of African American women and men to use appellations such as "sister" or "brother" for unrelated women and men. In addition, some research suggests that middle-class African Americans have larger networks of kin and fictive kin than low-income African Americans.[12] In general, moreover, fictive kin are reported not to be as common among white families.[13] For various racial and ethnic groups, the research literature suggests that socioeconomic mobility usually does not destroy the importance of extended families for these groups.[14]

Extended families and fictive kindred mean that most African American women, including those in the middle class, have support available when experiencing life's difficulties. African American women (and men) seek out kindred and fictive kindred in times of need. In previous chapters our respondents voice their concerns about and experiences with many difficulties in employment and other organizational settings, in the mass media, and in dealing with white women and men in places throughout the society. After looking at the scale of the difficulties that they face, one may wonder how most of them have survived and, as a rule, somehow thrived. They manage not only to contend against gendered racism and the stresses associated with it but also to make significant contributions to this society, both inside and outside the home. One major reason for this surviving and thriving is the extended family.

The Many Strengths of Black Families

As many African Americans see it, the model of the ideal family can and should diverge from a common family model accented by many whites: the social needs being different, the family composition and operation may also be different. Culture is adaptive and a mechanism for human survival and actualization, and thus it dictates that a group not adopt values and conceptions that do not harmonize with its requirements. For African Americans, this reality is accentuated by the fact that their cultural adaptations are also a culture of resistance against racism. One successful female entrepreneur in a southern city addresses this matter: "I don't use white standards to determine what family is—that is, a husband, a wife, and boy and a girl, and two cars in the garage and a VCR, and a Cuisinart. . . . If you use their standards, see, we're caught up in the mores and the standards and the values of their system." The respondent implies that materialistic values lead to the development of a certain type of nuclear family, which in turn appears to reinforce materialism. The smaller a family unit, the larger is each share of the rewards and the greater the potential for wealth accumulation. Conversely, the larger that family unit and the more restricted its pool of rewards, the smaller is each share and the more limited is the potential for wealth accumulation. It seems that the smaller nuclear family system can offer more possibilities for individual financial success. Yet, suggests the respondent, this type of nuclear family, with its distinctive accoutrements, may not work well for African Americans, because it neither corresponds nor responds well to their specific structural and historical realities.

Instead, the entrepreneur strongly suggests that an extended family model responds better to black Americans' social and economic situations. She cautions that African Americans should be mindful not to adopt the dominant conception of family:

> We need to stick to our own value systems like we did back in the other era, because as long as we did that we had strong family ties. Because, see, a family to me does not have to be the husband and the wife [only], it could be grandma there, the aunts . . . we all know about the extended family. . . . So, we always have had that extended family thing, but because of the way the economy is and how mobile [it] is, a lot of us are not even near our families.[15]

By each member becoming involved in the well-being of the others, in spite of difficulties, the extended unit can help its constituents cope with and share the distinctive burdens and barriers bequeathed by U.S. society to black Americans. A support system is needed that goes beyond husband, wife, and children to include distant relatives, fictive kin, and close friends, particularly those whose successes and failures can teach lasting lessons. This larger circle can add to the system of shared knowledge, with a generally positive impact on each member's coping abilities.

There is indeed a long history of a helping tradition and of beneficial collectiveness in African American communities. This tradition is strongly rooted in the extended family, as a number of historians have demonstrated since the 1970s.[16] Writing about the period of slavery, John Blassingame makes clear how old this tradition is.

> The family, while it had no legal existence in slavery, was in actuality one of the most important survival mechanisms for the slave. In his family he found companionship, love, sexual gratification, sympathetic understanding of his sufferings; he learned how to avoid punishment, to cooperate with other blacks, and to maintain his self-esteem. However frequently the family was broken, it was primarily responsible for the slave's ability to survive on the plantation without becoming totally dependent on and submissive to his master.[17]

From the beginning the African American family was *the* haven in a heartless and racialized world. Notice too that, even with its members splintered off, the family of the enslaved African Americans provided them with much needed emotional security and social or economic support.

Family maintenance despite disruption or separation points to a bonding and spirituality that early on transcended socially constructed boundaries. Historically, this spirituality of African Americans has facilitated the development and maintenance of extended kinship. A female psychologist in the Southwest describes it this way: "The more things change, the more they stay the same. See, as you get to a certain age, you realize that history repeats itself." She reiterates the comment later in her discussion. She suggests in her interview that despite some historical transformations the basic pattern and requirements for African American families are still the same. The reference to age suggests the wisdom of hindsight not possible for younger generations. Lapsed time means that the older cohorts have the reservoirs of deep insights and reflections that are passed on as critical collective memories and knowledge. This reflection indicates, as the entrepreneur says, "we always have had that extended family thing."

Spirituality and Black Families

A male psychologist in a southern city emphasizes the primacy of kinship for African Americans, and the contrast between their spiritual approach to life and what he views as a white preoccupation with materialism.

> Now, black people are more spiritual, our thinking has not been dichotomous, there's been middle ground, a kind of spiral. We believe in relationships. I don't know whether it was African tradition, all I know is what happened in America you had a lot of extended families, where there was a lot of love and concern and helping and working with, and trying to do for each other, and not for ourselves. And see the white man's situation is very selfish, everything for him, whatever it takes for that one person to have power. They're power hungry, power crazed, they want power and they want money. Money gives them power.

For African Americans as a group money and power matter less, says the psychologist, because their tradition of spirituality and sharing are counter to a single-minded or individualistic accumulation of capital found among many whites. The psychologist adds:

> We have not been power oriented, where one person can take over a corporation . . . they don't need it but they just do it, getting those billions of dollars they can never spend. We haven't been like that, we get a little bit and we share with our neighbors, our bread and our meat and like that. Some of us like me, wouldn't know what to do with ten million dollars, because we'd be giving it away so fast, we'd probably never accumulate that much. We don't need but $100,000 to live on and we're satisfied. We don't have to have a big house, and mansions and rooms we never use. We don't have all that. We've never been a people like that.

The role of spirituality and moral values in the lives of African Americans is clearly stated in this powerful commentary. These collectivist values have been found in other research on black communities.[18] And while black males and females have had a somewhat more difficult time "in establishing and maintaining stable relationships" during the 1990s, most field research still finds familial bonds to be very important.[19]

Most whites, including public commentators and politicians, do not understand the deep need that most blacks share for family relationships, their altruism toward kith and kin, or their nonchalance toward the acquisition of power. Part of black spirituality is the tendency to forgive whites who do harm, as the psychologist notes: "They don't understand why when we have a chance to kill them we don't. When we get into office, have you noticed that when blacks get into public office, they never retaliate, they never take advantage of whites. Many whites are afraid to let blacks get into office, few of the blacks will pay back. You've never seen any situation at any time . . . where a black paid back. But the white man will, he will get you." Not only are many whites hostile to blacks, this psychologist maintains, but many also tend to be insensitive to their needs, or poor judges of their finer human qualities. Cooperation and associated behaviors like forgiveness, which facilitate cooperation, are missed or misperceived by most whites, including media commentators. For many of the latter, and for some scholars, perceived family vices take precedence over real family virtues and values. While there are certainly exceptions to the rule propounded by the respondent, there is a remarkable ability among African Americans to forgive and·move on. Our respondents associate this with a distinctive spirituality born out of long experience with trying circumstances and rooted in age-old traditions.

For black Americans cooperation could not in the past and still cannot be abandoned, for it is one of the critical social mechanisms that has promoted individual and collective well-being. Cooperation has been one key aspect of African American life and culture. Many whites, it appears, give a different meaning to these behaviors. A psychologist notes: "They mistake kindness and gentleness for weakness and they want to be strong. We had to stay together during slavery, and work together in order to make it. They've never had to do it. And so, it's still a part of us to be that way. And we're very uncomfortable when we don't function that way."

Such lack of concern for the greater collectivity may show up in the practices of many whites that seem so impolite or uncaring—characteristics noted not only by our respondents but also by many international observers who have visited the United States. If power and wealth are deemed central, and if competition and aggressiveness are critical to their achievement, large-scale kindness and gentleness may be seen as obstacles and rejected. Placing one's own needs above those of others, and related behaviors indicative of a lack of respect for the larger human circle, are values that are certainly questioned and critiqued in the European philosophical tradition, yet they seem to remain central for many white Americans, including many who appear in the lives of our respondents.

By contrast, most African Americans value relationships developed and maintained with collective concern, kindness, and gentleness. It is in these relationships, including those in immediate and extended families, that African Americans find the backing and comfort they need in order to function in a troubling world. Hence, the same behaviors that for whites may seem a disturbing interference with upward mobility are for blacks necessary and worth cultivating.

Growing Up in Black Families

One does not have to talk very long with our African American respondents to understand how important extended families have been in their upbringing and in their success in dealing with a difficult world. A manager in a northern town describes some personal benefits that she derived from being in a strong extended family: "First of all, I think my upbringing, my parents, and my extended family were very influential, especially in my educational goal, and anchoring me in a solid foundation, and helping me know how to compromise, and just giving me a good sense of work ethic, educational ethic, a sense of right and wrong, and a sense of purpose and duty." This woman is appreciative for her extended kin's teaching of first lessons about societal dos and don'ts. She speaks of acquired cooperative skills, the give-and-take that facilitates the development and maintenance of relationships. Also appreciative is a female social worker now in a northern city who acknowledges personal benefits she accrued from supportive extended family and community networks.

> I was raised in the South; there was much more community, and extended family, not necessarily blood relatives, but sort of a community taking care of you. I think that foundation was very important to my educational and personal attainment. And then the fact that my mother and my uncle and my grandmother recognized that I had potential at a very early age, and my mother stressed the importance of an education. And she used to say, if you get a good education, no one can ever take that from you. She said, they can

strip you, they can disrespect you, but they can't take that from you. My uncle, who was educated, has his Ph.D. in education, influenced me greatly. I used to spend my summers with him and my grandmother.

Then she adds a thought about others in her community who helped her:

I think the fact that I had teachers who were concerned about me, saw that I had a lot of potential, and nourished me, and made sure I found out about programs like Upward Bound, and was exposed to college for two summers when I was growing up. So, that influenced me.

In this summary of early learning real and fictive kinship play an active role in a young person's socialization and educational opportunities. Not only extended family members but also teachers, playing a parentlike role, were part of that informal social structure. "Sort of a community taking care" describes that experience well. In her interview she also points to some movement away from this traditional community involvement to a greater focus on "me and mine," like some of the other respondents, and suggests that today's teachers often do not play a close-up role in the growth of children. Indeed, one problem for many African American families and communities has been that there are fewer African American teachers, those teachers with experience and collective knowledge about being black in America, in the public schools today than in previous decades.

Our interviewees include women and men who have faced family situations that many social scientists would, albeit too casually, label as "broken" or "disorganized." Even in these cases, however, kinship and fictive kinship ties often made positive contributions to the respondents' personal growth, as they did for this college-educated telephone operator in a western city:

When I was growing up—my brother and I—our parents were divorced at a very early age. So, our extended family had to take on more of a responsibility as far as rearing us, as far as being supportive to us. This kindness and support from a very early age built some very strong foundations of confidence, self-esteem, the ability

> to take risks, the ability to differentiate myself from the world. . . .
> Like I said before, as far as the role of family and friends, I grew
> up with a large, extended family network, and my friends also
> played a very important role in that they gave me the very founda-
> tions of which I can overcome these barriers. This foundation was
> built on self-respect, love for myself and my brothers—the ability,
> the self-esteem, the ability to know that I am a good and worth-
> while person.

These extended kinship networks have particular significance in the
socialization of young people whose immediate family has one parent.
The physical presence of grandparents, aunts, uncles, nephews, nieces,
and close friends is conducive to the development of a collective memory of the family and therefore can nurture a strong family identity.
Where memory and identity might otherwise be lacking, black youth
benefit from being in and identifying with the extended family network. There they acquire a sense of belonging from which to draw
strength and valuable knowledge for dealing with everyday life. Additionally, they may benefit from the support of this larger unit in other,
unexpected ways. Our findings about the importance of extended families for socialization have been confirmed by other researchers.[20]

In addition to providing a sense of worth, there is also historical
and generational continuity to be gained by young people associating
with members of their extended families. The presence of these members, or memories of them, can provide young African Americans with
reflections on their life-world and a pool of models from which to
draw values and responses to difficult and challenging life situations.
A business salesperson in the North explains, "My children especially
have been in a world where they haven't experienced the things that
I've experienced. I try to relate to them the struggles that have gone
on, so that they will remember also that, hey, where we've come from,
and they can appreciate where we are." Although most parents may
try, some may not teach clearly this important connection to the past,
a point a college student underscores, saying, "A lot of parents make
mistakes because they don't inform their children of the past."

The presence of an extended kinship network seems to be, for the
most part, very salutary. Where one fits in the world can more clearly
be recognized. There is a sense of security in being part of a larger
kinship whole. In such a context, personal and social identity is more

easily developed and maintained. Family history, especially oral history, is more easily transmitted. When younger generations distance themselves from their extended families, they are also separating themselves from family histories and important reference figures. This distancing can block or retard the full development of a collective memory of the family that is likely to be crucial to shaping identity.[21] The absence, or near absence, of that collective memory and identity can make young people more vulnerable to ahistorical and negative portrayals of African Americans in the media. Lacking the familial and historical contexts, some younger black Americans have fewer resources to use in refuting negative propaganda. A professor at a northern university made clear the importance of this connection with the past in relating the story of a group of close family members at a recent family reunion, who were talking about values transmitted over time. His ancestors had been slaves, and he recounted that the family members talked of how these slaves had "a great sense of family. . . . They lived through Jim Crow, through the Depression, and found their way through the sustaining concepts, the sustaining philosophies, the sustaining wisdom, love, family, and support." Family reunions and similar gatherings are good settings in which to develop or renew beneficial connections and memories essential to all people, including the young and particularly those who are growing up with one parent. These reunions may well include close friends as fictive kin. The presence of an adopted, fictive kin segment in a large extended family unit might perhaps elicit in many whites a sense of public exposure and discomfort that they would not feel within an isolated nuclear family. However, for black Americans the strong and shared loyalty evident within the larger kinship structure seems to protect members' privacy as well as help them heal racial wounds.

Further illustrating the significance of a large kinship network for younger generations, the previously quoted telephone operator explains how successful role models have given his life more direction.

> My grandfather, he got his doctorate in chemistry, and is a retired professor now. He tutors college students. My uncle is an engineer. He is now at a western university, and he is the head of the . . . engineering department. My mother is my strongest, my best influence, my rock of success. She has not [only] single-handedly raised my brother and I, but she has provided us the opportunity, the

chance for an education, the chance of a better life, through proper encouragement when needed, nutrition, a nice place to live. You know, those things that a lot of us don't have a fair chance at.

Being from a divorced family, this man was not only helped by his caring mother but also by the guidance of other relatives, guidance he found very beneficial. He is one of many respondents who, recognizing that the extended kinship unit may not be quite as strong as it once was, praises its benefits and shows evidence of its impact on his own life. The conception of an ideal black family as extended kinship network, and the benefits acquired from it, may be what triggers our respondents' often strong commentaries on these issues. Developed in the midst of recurring racist experiences, concern about the presence and persistence of strong kinship networks seems warranted.

Particularly in their "sense of obligation to relatives" the respondents' own feeling of kinship with these family members is evident. One example is in this comment from a male newscaster in the South; when asked about family goals, he immediately expressed concern for the well-being of young relatives:

> Well, again, not being married, not having children, I don't have goals for a family per se, like people who are married with children have. I think because I don't have my own immediate family, I am always striving to help the rest of my extended-family members. I have two nephews who are teenagers now, and my brother is a single parent who has his two sons. And I'd like to help him get his sons well on their way to a good education, so they can get a good job, and things like that. I'm very family oriented in that respect.

Judging from the comments of our respondents, black adults who are single are often very family oriented. For this man family and extended family seem synonymous. Though he speaks of nephews, he sees himself simply as "family oriented." His discourse and that of many other respondents suggest the looming presence of an extended family structure in thought and action. Although it may not be as large as it was in earlier decades, the extended kinship network still represents a welcome refuge from personal troubles, including experiences with racism, and a place where much support is given and much education takes place.

Relying on Families to Deal with Discrimination

As our respondents have so often said in this and previous chapters, the extended kinship system that is a part of African American tradition is still relevant to interracial difficulties and situations. Today black families, including extended families and fictive kin, remain critical havens from a racist world, places one can go to receive solid support and coping advice when necessary. Strategies for individual contending and coping with racism often stem from commentaries and advice given in family gatherings. The telephone operator remarks on what takes place even at an otherwise festive occasion: family members "meet together to talk about how we're going to deal with discrimination . . . mostly at Christmastime. The Christmas season, we talk about discrimination." Holiday settings like Christmas are convenient times for important discussions of everyday experiences and unusual events. As entire families gather, they share stories of positive and, sometimes, not-so-positive experiences. One can imagine the not-so-positive accounts causing members to relive vividly those experiences—whether their own or those of others. The festivity of the holiday season may buffer the discomforts in these candid discussions.

According to those we interviewed extended families are commonly required to provide lifelong support. In a recent focus group in a western city a female professional emphasizes how important the extended family network is for solving racial or other problems.

> Somehow when I share with my family, which is what I have done all of my life, it seems to dissipate. And I get feedback, and I get the kind of support I need to handle the problem effectively. So, that's the first place I go. As a matter of fact, when it just happens, I always call my mother, call my sister, call a friend. I start processing it right away, and getting feedback. . . .

Later in the interview, this woman probes further on the virtues of large families in times of trouble:

> My family is critical. Because I have such a very, very large family . . . I have a very, very, *very* large support group too. I mean, I consistently seek and maintain relationships that allow me to handle whatever I have to handle. . . . When I came to this city I was basi-

cally twenty-one years old. I didn't have a family here. And I have a very, very large extended family. So they are critical to me for *everything* that I have to get done. No matter . . . even for making a decision about buying a car, buying a home. I mean, my family, I mean I will write just to ask their opinion, whether I do it or not. They are very, very critical.

Some of the extended network of family and friends may be nearby, while others may be farther away. Still phone calls and letters create the highway of communication for dealing with a range of issues, many of which have to do with ordinary life decisions.

Home is also where you can go when you need to let go of your anger, including rage over racism. A female training specialist in a focus group put it simply: "Sometimes, I just go home and vent. And they let me vent." Numerous respondents mentioned how family members were important in dealing with racism they faced as they went to work or otherwise traversed historically white arenas of action and interaction. One secretary reports her family's advice on matters of recurring prejudice and discrimination:

> I think my family is very supportive. . . . My father is more like, "Maybe you should ignore it and turn the other cheek," where my mom is like, "Report it." You know, so I . . . get it from both sides. . . . I think these are things that I should tell them, and these are also things that they should relate to me about their experience so that I can distinguish what is racism, what is prejudice, and how to deal with it. . . . I think we have a lot of individuals today who don't even know [how to recognize racism]. . . . Somebody in that family should have brought that out to these individuals. . . . This is important for families to sit around, and let them know.

The collective memory of families and communities not only helps a person to evaluate what racism is but also what are the useful strategies for fighting back. Accounts of negative encounters with whites should, in this woman's view, be shared and assessed in the sympathetic and reassuring context of kinship.

Dealing with unsupportive or hostile whites every day in workplaces and other social settings has both cognitive and emotional aspects for both perpetrators and targets. When asked how friends or family had helped him in dealing with discrimination and its frustrations, a male manager at a major corporation replies:

> I think just primarily by being a sounding board and allowing me, or reminding me, that I know how to handle that. . . . Just being a source of listening and another shoulder and somebody who understands what we're all faced with. . . . So we have to continue to work together. I appreciate my family and my friends being there to console me when I'm really hostile and emotional enough to go out and do something really asinine, and you've got to have somebody to bounce that stuff off on.

Here again we glimpse the high costs of racial discrimination for African Americans. It is clear in our interviews that these costs include not only psychological consequences such as the toxic emotions of hostility and rage but also physical damage such as stomach diseases and heart attacks. These costs must be faced and handled on a daily basis.

There are of course numerous ways in which black individuals and families handle the stresses of everyday life, including the steady acid rain of racism. Some of our respondents noted the role of laughing at adversity within family and friendship settings. By making light of serious discrimination, they are able to protect themselves a bit against the costs of racism. The old cliché about laughter being "good medicine" seems to apply for African Americans facing antagonistic whites in their daily rounds. However, a heavy reliance on families to deal with stress and anger over racial discrimination can have a serious price for family members, as a social services coordinator makes clear:

> So many times, after you've experienced an eight whole hours of discrimination, either directly or indirectly, it really doesn't put you in the mood to go home and read that wonderful bedtime story. You're just tired . . . and really, you're crying on the inside, and you may not really want to admit to yourself, you know, because all of us like to think we're in control of what's happening to us. And I think we all deal with it differently. And that anger sometimes buildup, and you're not even aware that it's there. So the moment your spouse, or your child—if there is anything that may seem like it was a belittling or demeaning, you responding to them with a level of anger even that really is inappropriate for the situa-

tion, but what you're really responding to is that eight hours prior to getting home. And so many times you are dealing with—they are the recipients of that energy that you had to store up, that anger from that whole day. . . . We bring all of that baggage home, and then we wonder why our relationships are in trouble.

Racial discrimination not only is a matter of "eight whole hours" of individual suffering but also is often very wasteful for families and communities. Serious discrimination commonly creates great anger and frustration in the immediate target and can have a domino effect as the anger is vented or explained in family contexts, where the other members of the family may also have their own struggles with white Americans to recount.

The social scientists and commentators mentioned above who have discussed problems in African American families in recent years usually focus on "broken" families or related family issues. As a rule, most of the responsibility for such family difficulties is placed on the family members for their failures in maintaining the right family values. However, in this mainstream literature on African American families we have seen little significant analysis of the severe negative effects of everyday racism on African American families and communities. As the women and men we interviewed make very clear, everyday experience with hostile and antagonistic whites saps some of the energy needed for maintaining ordinary family life and for building strong communities. Of course, a majority of African Americans have somehow been able to create and maintain effective families and communities in the face of this racism. They have often done this by exerting almost superhuman efforts, which have an impact on their lives in other areas, such as their personal health or their ability to maximize their contributions to the larger society.[22]

Home As One's Space

We have pulled apart our interviews so far to show the several important dimensions of black family issues as seen by our respondents. But we do not wish to leave the wrong impression. Individual human beings do *not* live lives in one dimension at a time; they live them in a holistic field, over periods of time. Many family dimensions come together in that place called "home," that place and space where mentions of whites and white machinations may be backgrounded or be entirely absent, and where familyhood, sisterhood, and brotherhood are strongly foregrounded.

We see the conceptually separated family dimensions coming back into a very positive whole in this probing account of a government administrator speaking to a focus group in a western city:

> In our particular family, we are very fortunate to have acquired property ... for all of us in the family.... And I hope that we use that property as a foundation to propel the next generation into a much, much higher quality of life than we've had. But I also want to see the necessary discipline, and see that as a family tradition, rather than something you think [is] some entitlement program just because your last name happens to be [name], and to keep that drive in our family, to keep the respect in our family, and to keep the love in our family. Because we are, as sisters and brothers, we are one of the most [tight] units I know. And this became so very obvious to me when our father died, how our parents had managed to raise us, all of us, in one home and, yet, we all ... have individualities, and we all play certain roles in our families at different times, we are all supportive, we are all very honest with each other. I just want to see that *always,* because it's such a solid foundation, and it's so grounding. I mean, like [Jane] said earlier, we've always had sisters to talk to. You have those folks who knew you before you knew you, so there are no secrets. You can be very honest, and very open, and in an atmosphere that, you know, is going to go to everybody.... But, to keep that closeness going, to keep the goals going, and to keep the achieving going. That is just one of the most important things that I see our family is doing.

Here is a holistic portrait of key dimensions of black family life—the extended family; closeness and interpersonal honesty; the collective memory; persisting values of love, respect, and discipline; the solid foundation of family support; concern for and property accumulation for future generations; and individual development within the collective whole.

The focus in this account on black values suggests that one must be careful not to exaggerate the importance of experiences with and concerns about white Americans and white racism in assessing the family life of African Americans. While we have necessarily focused on the many and serious impacts of racism on black women and their families—and this topic has certainly been neglected in the mainstream social science literature—we want to make clear that not everything done by these family members or in these black families is developed in relation to white Americans.[23]

Family settings provide much more. If a black person wishes it to be so, a family gathering can be a space where she or he does not have to think about or talk about whites. Indeed, it is likely that white-related issues are marginalized or absent in most family discussions most of the time. As is true for other Americans, long hours are spent just reveling in the joys of kin, children, friends, and spouse's companionship. Ordinary family problems are also confronted. Families are places where family and friends are honored for and of themselves. To think otherwise can reflect the same arrogance that nurtures everyday racism. Moreover, outsiders, black or white, are usually absent in such places. And, when invited, friends who are white may not be seen as white, thereby losing some or much of their racial character. They are simply close friends, well-wishers, and celebrants of family vitality and relationships.

Troubles in Families and Communities

We noted in the opening of this chapter that the strong extended families of African Americans are under some pressure in the United States today. Our respondents frequently alluded to this pressure and were concerned about the future. For instance, one entrepreneur praises the numerous benefits of the extended family system in black communities, but she also worries that large segments of black America have moved away from this traditional family framework: "But we don't have that [strong sense of extended family] too much more anymore, because it's 'I, me and mine. I want to stand alone. I made it, you ain't made it by yourself.' It's so individualistic [a] thing, like I-got-mine-and-you-get-yours kind of syndrome." This remark is similar to that of several respondents who used language about an increasing focus on "me and mine" among African Americans, which represents some shifts in the traditional sense of collectiveness. A school principal in a southern city shares his successful family experience and memories of the recent past:

> When I was coming along, there was no way you would put a family out when there was help needed, nor would you put a family member in a nursing home. When the grandpapa died, and the grandma got a little sick, then grandma came into somebody's house. You brought her a bed and everything else, and you get a room for grandma. You didn't put her in a unit. As far as I'm concerned—and safely I think my wife can say too—if your mom is too good to come in this house, you've got to go. My mom comes in here ... she needs me. If you can't help me, you've got the door.

This educator's use of the past tense reflects his concern that the family function about which he speaks so highly has been weakened somewhat in black communities as well as in the larger society. In his interview he further links this weakening somewhat to racial "integration." He is apparently concerned in this comment about the institutionalization of aged African Americans with white Americans in nursing homes, a public solution that in his view is better kept private. In black communities, as in some other American communities, grown children are their parents' old-age insurance and contribute to their well-being in later life. Previous social science research has demonstrated that caring for aging parents is an expectation in black families and that parent and child roles are often reversed once one attains middle age. Without their children many elderly black Americans would be without a home.[24]

Again one is reminded that for African Americans as individuals, and as a group, to function at their maximum a family structure of greater size than the nuclear family is generally required. Like this educator, a health professional in the North notes his sadness that some family traditions are weaker today than in the past: "One of the big differences between years ago and today, as far as black people are concerned, is that we had a tremendous extended family. You couldn't do wrong because Mrs. So-and-So went to your church. And word would get back, before you got back home, that you were around the corner breaking glass or doing something you weren't supposed to, or you were disrespectful, you spoke disrespectfully to somebody. We don't have that anymore, much to our detriment." The respondent longs for a more traditional "good Samaritan" structure. There is a longing for a community "family" cooperating to take care of its members and transmitting that message to all concerned, like a sign outside some homes indicating to children that inside their safety is guaranteed because they are supported by the community. Each individual and family taking responsibility for every other individual and family is being threatened by contemporary social changes.

A manager in a northern city echoes some previous respondents, noting the importance of the community as extended family and expressing sadness at what she sees as a loss of some sense of community.

> It's stressful because my young children don't have the support in the community that was once there. I have to ask the neighbor downstairs would she help watch my little girls when they're outside playing, and I'll watch her little girls, but I have to ask. When I was younger, it was an accepted fact when all of the children were outside playing, everyone was taking the responsibility to be aware of the children. Therefore, again as I said, if someone fell they could ring anybody's doorbell. You know, "Miss Jones, So-and-So fell, could you come out, because I live way up the street." It's not like that now. In fact, we have to say, "Grandma lives on the other end of the street, I will let Grandma know that you're outside, and you can run up here, or run down to Grandma's house." But not necessarily tell them that they can run across the street and ring anybody's doorbell.

Again, we see the suggestion that the community is not as often a larger extended family as it once was, at least not as a matter of course. Nonetheless, there is still social support for children playing outside, in the form of grandmother down the street, as well as in neighbors who watch, if only when asked and reminded. Note too that in the last two comments the concern is not so much for the extended family itself but for the larger community family that once was stronger than it is today.

Many white scholars and pundits have blamed the changes in black families, including the extended family networks, on internal matters within black America. However, we have already noted some of the outside pressures that have forced some families to change. Another reason that some black families cannot provide as much broad support as they once did is that, to quote a female newspaper publisher in the Southwest,

> The white boy will take your job just as quick as you can blink your eye, and all of that [middle-class affluence] means nothing. If anything you're so out there in hock, that you will shortly be back where your momma and daddy came from, if not sooner. So, as a result, the reality of that I think is causing some minority community people, middle-class blacks, to realize that they've got to put something in, in order to get something out. . . . I think so many people are struggling just to survive, because they do have that standard of living, because they do want a nice place to live and that costs money, they do want nice groceries, they do want nice clothes. Not really anything extra, but just to keep that standard of living means working two jobs in some cases, or wife and husband working. And what happens to the education of the child? And what happens to extracurricular activities?

Some of our interviewees protested the mimicking of the hyperconsumerism proclaimed so often by the representatives of white society. Yet that is not the major economic problem for African Americans today. Concern over the family's standard of living is a part of the black American situation, and a middle-class family's well-being may require taking multiple jobs by several members of the family. However, as this woman sees it, the central problem is that in trying to keep one's middle-class standard of living even black Americans with resources face a serious threat of racial discrimination from whites and from white economic control.

Black Women's Hopes and Goals for Their Families

One might expect, given their negative experiences with white Americans in the workplace and other sectors, and the partial weakening of the extended family, that black women might be pessimistic about the future of their families and their children. Yet, despite daily lives steeped in harsh racial realities, the women we interviewed still work for, plan for, and dream of a thriving future for their families.

Educational Goals

As we have seen in previous quotes, mothers and fathers work for

173

and envision a good education as the key to success for themselves and their children. These hopes and aspirations are expressed by one mother, a college student at the time of her interview: "My family goals—I want my children to be able to finish high school with good grades and participate in everything they can participate in the meantime, and also go to college. Not just to *any* college, but to any college that they really want to be able to attend, and hopefully will be accepted in those colleges, and in turn we'll be able to afford to pay for whatever college they want to go to." Not only is a choice of colleges important to this mother, but she also intends to make sure there is financial coverage for this educational objective.

This ambition for children's education is shared by another mother, a teacher in the North:

> I have an eight-year-old. And one of the things I stress to her is the importance of getting a good education. Once you have that, all of the other things will follow. And that's something that nobody can take away from you. And I always tell her, the other kids can do good, but you have to do better, and the reason for that is because you're black. And I just want, one of the things that I would like very much for her in terms of reaching my goal, is to have success, for her to be an independent individual, who is self-supporting and can take care of herself.

A good education ranks high on most black women's lists of wishes for their children. This accent on education is generally strong in black communities. Accumulated knowledge buffers the effects of being black in the United States, so mothers often drill that idea into their children at a tender age. A few other field studies have found this to be the case. For instance, in interviews with black women in the United States and Holland, social psychologist Philomena Essed found that black children are taught at an early age about racial discrimination by their families.[25]

Mothers teach girls and boys early about the stigmatization of blackness in a white-dominated society, and how education—a possible means to greater power, though certainly not a complete buffer—can reduce its effects. One of these mothers, a banker in a northern city, finds classroom experience incomplete without one's reflecting on that experience.

I'm divorced; I have just one child. I see in her things that I saw in myself growing up, and I'm trying to help her achieve those goals. I want her to experience more things than I have. So, therefore, I am not pushing her, but I am encouraging her to venture off. I'm a believer in not so much being [in] or experiencing school but knowing what you experience, learning something from what you experience, whether it be in the classrooms or going out into the country.

It is likely that this concern for reflection on experience comes out of this executive's personal circumstances and, doubtless, the collective experience of her extended family. Much has been made of the importance of encouraging and studying human reflectivity in recent social science theorizing, yet in our interviews we find it coming from those with grassroots experience.[26] Note too in the last few commentaries how successful individual achievements are again put into a family context and how views are shaped within the context of black identity and collective memory. As one mother concluded, "You have to do better, and the reason for that is because you're black." This advice suggests that a strong black identity assists in understanding white-racist myths, helps one to demystify these misrecognitions, and therefore enables one to do better and achieve success in spite of daily obstacles.

Asked about family goals over the next five years, those of a female optician in a southern city are also educational. She wants her children exposed to diverse cultural experiences, among other things.

I'm married, I have two children, ages six and four and a half. My daughter is in a Spanish . . . program, and I hope to see that she, by that time, will be speaking Spanish fluently. And the only thing that would make those changes is actually the environment, of where she might be taught, this pilot program in the city. Because the morals of the children that she's around are just as important to me as speaking Spanish, because I could also go to another, have her to take a class as far as speaking Spanish. Those are available for children that age now. But I just have her in public school, which is a magnet program doing that.

As far as my son, who is four and a half years old, I would think that he would have caught up to my daughter's intelligence, he would be into the more science level because he's very much interested in science. And she's more interested in zoology, and right now they're both in those kinds of programs in addition to the school that they're in now. So, five years from now, hopefully they would be involved in programs in the city that will start working toward their educational goals.

Whether expressed for her daughter or son, this mother's objectives and wishes for her children are well developed and focus on multicultural experiences, a concern that is common among middle-class African Americans. Her expressed goals for the children are similar and not at all gendered. We also see here an explicit reference to a good moral environment, which is a clear or implied concern in many of the respondents' comments about their current and long-term family goals.

When mothers (and fathers) speak about goals for their children, they often mix pessimism with hope and accent the importance of personal persistence in the midst of many discouraging realities. Hope is evident, yet again, in the wishes of a nurse in a southern city for her children:

> I plan to help my oldest fulfill his educational needs, which is tele-communications in college next year. And my younger one, I plan to boost his education in any way possible, like sending him to enriched programs, which is like at the colleges in the summertime, and enrolling him in different computer things that'll help him excel in any way we can. And try to get him into music classes. I hope to start him in some kind of foreign language class on the side that we can get him to take before he gets into the molded stage.

Again we see a concern for breadth and multiculturalism as part of children's essential upbringing.

Ambition for education, like other ambitions, cannot alone end the tribulations and barriers of everyday racism. As these mostly well-educated respondents regularly testify, white society's negative or hostile reactions to one's color persist despite one's education. Because education can often increase awareness and thinking about racist conditions in the larger society, it can create and nurture deep dissatisfaction, offsetting some of education's beneficial effects. Long ago, the great abolitionist Frederick Douglass remarked: "Learning to read had been a curse rather than a blessing. It had given me a view of my wretched condition, without the remedy. It opened my eyes to the horrible pit, but to no ladder upon which to get out. . . . Any thing, no matter what to get rid of thinking!"[27] Yet although education can have this unpleasant effect, it is a major tool for dealing with the barriers of racism, precisely because it helps develop that awareness. Asked whether she thinks education will be valuable for her children, an airline representative responds in this way:

> That's another thing that I'm questioning now. That's what I've always heard. But I also know just because they're black, they can have the same amount of education and work twice as hard, but the racism is still going to be there. And so, not that education is a panacea, but at least they will be as prepared as white America has said that they should be. So that won't be something that they'll [whites] have, some excuse that they'll have to deny them something. So if they've got everything that they said they had to get I know they're going to change the game plan, but at least they'll have what they're telling you have to have now. And so, I guess, that's my goal, just to get them through school, and I guess that just means that my secondary goal is just to be financially able to do it.

This poignant comment is similar to that expressed earlier by a teacher who warned her daughter that she must do better because she is black. Here too the respondent implies that she advises her children to be well prepared—even as she acknowledges that white society's game plan may change. Throughout our interviews there are references to the ways in which whites, particularly those in decision-making positions, change the "rules of the game" just as large numbers of African Americans work out how they can meet those social requirements. Indeed, this issue of unfairly changing the rules of the workplace as black Americans enter has been at the heart of some of the nation's most important civil rights debates and court cases.[28]

Although more schooling is not seen as a cure-all, education is still expected to positively counteract some of the harsher effects of being black in America and to produce rewards for the respondents' families. As a result, most parents seek more and more education for those in their families. African Americans are among those Americans who give the most attention to the importance of education, at the personal and family level and at the national level, such as in support for expanding government funding for school programs. One distorted aspect of public discussions of educational matters in the United States lies in the fact that African Americans, both women and men, do not get as much public credit as they deserve for being such strong supporters of education.

As African American mothers and fathers plan to meet important educational goals, they show the significance of family memories, values, and bonds for themselves and their children. Their good spirit of kinship leads them to care greatly and to hope mightily for the short-range and long-term good of their families. Setting these high goals for their families, in turn, helps family members to have higher self-esteem and to heal personally from racial wounds. Strong educational aspirations and their implementation become part of the solution to encounters with everyday racism.

Business Goals

Not surprisingly, our respondents have other major goals and plans for their families, such as this administrator in a nonprofit organization who wants her children and extended family involved in a solid business enterprise. She dreams of collective effort and notes that her husband "has a small business right now. He'd like to be able to build that business and be able to get other family members from other parts of the country and work in that business. We would like to be well-off enough to help some other people in the family. That's our goal." Surfacing again is the spirit of sharing and a drive for family cooperation, cooperation which in itself can be healing.

A family enterprise is also the goal of one female entrepreneur:

> My husband and I work in our business together, so we have a very close-knit family, very, very close-knit, and I have one three-year-old daughter, Mary. And I'd like for her to get involved in the business and really understand how business works, and maybe even have a business major when she goes to college, I think that would be a good idea. And eventually, if she wants, to eventually work in the business and be an entrepreneur."

178

Note how the focus continues to be a better family future in terms of a collective well-being rather than on accumulation of capital or individual success in isolation from the family. An orientation toward the collective good of families and communities is apparent in the discourses of these middle-class respondents. As this businessperson relates her design for her daughter to larger family contexts, she adds a criticism of some African Americans for looking too much outside the community for assistance. She mentions that Asian Americans have started many businesses "in black neighborhoods. And I don't want to discriminate against anybody, of course, but the whole point is, it would be nice to see blacks owning businesses. Not only in their own neighborhoods, but I mean other neighborhoods as well, but that would be a nice start."

Continuing, this respondent offers reasons for the apparent absence of African Americans in business in spite of the many benefits to be accrued from participation in such business ventures.

> Blacks have been excluded from the mainstream of business for so, for centuries I guess you could say, four hundred, three hundred years, and so they haven't really been taught that working for yourself and being an entrepreneur is really one of the ways to go. It's one of the avenues that they can take. They've basically just been taught you just go to work for somebody else, and hope that you get a nice job, and that's it. It's fine to work for somebody else. I'm not knocking that, I'm just saying that in terms of being an entrepreneur and working for themselves, it's something that their parents never had an opportunity to do in a lot of cases, so they weren't taught that.

As she sees it, a historical lack of access to, or familiarity with, business enterprises keeps black Americans, including black women, from engaging in these important activities. The respondent hopes her daughter will embrace such a career and become successful, while also fulfilling an important need for the black community. Again the good of the community and the good of the family are webbed together with the personal good. The interdependency of individualism and collectivism is again asserted.

Current data show that only a modest percentage of women who are self-employed are black (just under 4 percent).[29] For some black women business ventures may seem a fertile, and relatively unexplored, territory for new efforts to support themselves and their families. Indeed, there seems to have been a shift over the last decade among middle-class African Americans toward more emphasis on building businesses in black communities, seemingly parallel to a de-emphasis among some African Americans on traditional integrationist strategies for social and racial change.[30]

The respondents' dreams, goals, and plans for their immediate and extended families can yield positive and healing effects not only for individuals and families but also for the black communities surrounding them. One's own efforts, as in a business enterprise, can be more than a vehicle for individual financial success. They can have meaning as part of a family heritage to hand down to the next generation. This point is summarized in the succinct comment of one woman in a southwestern city: "I want my business to grow so I can give it to my kids."

Other Family Goals

Asked about goals for their families over the next few years, a number of other important objectives and hopes besides education and business were specifically mentioned by our respondents. Some family goals are more general, as can be seen in the following comment of a woman counselor: "I just want health and happiness and . . . I want my son to have a little easier time than his father did. . . . But, I just want health and happiness for all of them, and I want my son never to feel like, you know, he is not as good as, or he can't make it." The spirituality of African Americans is suggested in this sense of respect for the most important of human goals: personal and family happiness and well-being. Significantly, a consuming desire for material goods and affluence in themselves is very rare in responses to questions about the goals and future of families.

The dialogue between several women in a recent focus group in a western city makes clear the way in which family goals often permeate the thinking of African American women. By observing their interaction on these matters, we see how each one builds on and amplifies the comments of the others. This is a major advantage in using focus groups in assessing how people think about matters

180

such as family development. In the discussion in this group a reporter first expresses wishes for her future family's well-being. Her ambitions cover a range of issues: "I don't have a family per se. If I have future children, I just want them to be decent human beings. . . . But, I'd like them to be happy. I'd like them to be 'unscarred.' Go out there and prove that you can do so. . . . That's what I would like if I ever marry and have a family." Even those who are single seek broad happiness and spiritual goals for themselves and their families, actual and potential. In some cases, like this one, the hopes for well-being are tempered with a recognition that racial scars await most African Americans.

Another reporter adds to the conversation and focuses on goals regarding her parents:

> I can't even think past next week so far as marriage and children, but I definitely want to be in a position to take care of my parents if they ever needed it, you know, even if they didn't, you know. My parents have done so much, so much for me and I'd like to give them back at least like a small amount, a very small amount to them. And that's like a big priority for me. That's something that I sometimes worry about.

In spite of the concerns that some African Americans express for the weakening of extended families, including the problem of putting parents in nursing homes, several women in this focus group make it clear that they feel grateful to their parents and plan to return to them some of the good support they bestowed upon their children. The last respondent's sentiments received an immediate response from a business owner who, turning to the reporter, explains what parents generally hope for and expect from their children.

> But if you are a nice person, you become successful as far as you want to be, that will give them back what they want. That's all most parents want for their kids. It's to give them the tools to do well with, and succeed, and not have to worry about them, and I think that if you would do that, you would give back to your parents more than they've ever given to you, in their eyesight. We want the best for our kids. We want them happy and to be able to survive in today's society. If you prove to your parents you can do that, you will give them back.

The reporter nods, showing her appreciation for the advice, while another professional woman expresses similar concerns for her parents. Despite having sacrificed so she could obtain her education, her parents would not accept her offer: "I wanted to pay my mom. They paid for my college. . . . My mom [said] no, no, no, we just want you to be OK. . . . Take the education that you got . . . and be able to be successful." The business owner then reiterates her point about a good parent: "She's given you the tools. Now, it's up to you to do something with it, and that will pay us back. Do something with what we've provided you." We see interesting interaction among the participants in this focus group. They build on each other's comments, creating a palimpsest texture on the issues of families. Older, and with grown children and grandchildren of her own, this business owner is giving advice to two younger women whom she has just met. She responds to their comments as if they were her own younger relatives. This interaction is a good illustration of how fictive kinship works among African Americans. Doing something with one's education, the business owner emphasizes, would pay parents back. As a fictive parent speaking to younger women, she speaks for the black collectivity and is representing the larger community of parents. Her advice to younger women is abstracted from her own extensive experience with and understanding of families and that larger black community. Collective memory is again drawn upon and transmitted.

Our respondents accent a range of family and individual goals, including good health and happiness, ownership of a successful business, and education. The latter goal is particularly emphasized, for they frequently see knowledge as a form of personal and family liberation. Whatever their objectives, most clearly want a better future for themselves and their immediate and extended families. They recognize that these goals must be achieved in the face of daily encounters with unpleasant or hostile racial experiences. They are also concerned about actual and possible transformations of the strong extended kinship system among African Americans into a kinship system that is more nucleated or individualistic. Such a transformation is one that most want to counteract in their own actions and efforts.

Conclusion

For African American women the habit of surviving for mothers and families is linked to the struggle to thrive and succeed under adversity not of one's own making. When asked about her dreams for her family, a female entrepreneur in a recent focus group in the West replied in a vein that sounds very patriotic:

> I think my children know who they are . . . and I think they know that you can succeed in spite of everything that we have said here today. In spite of all the negativity, I still think America is the best place to live. Because, if I have the strength of character to overcome somebody else's view of me, I can do anything I want here. And I can be anything I want here. And I think my kids now understand that, they know it. I am trying to provide a legacy for them to step into and give it to the next generation.

The patriotism expressed here is rather different from what one often hears from white Americans. This African American patriotism is closely linked to family concerns and futures, and money and materialism are not a central issue. For her and our other respondents maintaining and reinforcing an African American legacy and collective memory that can guide, bond, and lead to success are far more important. Goals and aspirations for a successful family future, despite myriad racial obstacles, are evidence that African American women as a group strive to transcend their collective memories of racial oppression and cultural degradation. In spite of threats to their vitality and structure, family and extended family are still survival armature for African Americans in the present, as they were in the past. The ambitions, objectives, and dreams black women and men have for their families help to keep that extended family structure very much alive and keep most respondents, as individuals, strong.

Chapter 7

Motherhood and Families

Today fathers proudly announce to families, friends, and colleagues that "*We* are pregnant," "*We* are expecting." Yet, no man has ever given birth to a child. While after a child is born some men successfully play a nurturing role, even then these men are not capable of carrying out true motherhood. "Motherhood" comes from the Latin *mater,* which means origin, nurture, fount, or woman. It is women, thus, who can undergo the full range of experiences typifying motherhood. Though partly biological, these experiences are more importantly social.

Before a birth these experiences of motherhood include feeling the first heartbeat, the movement that indicates the presence of a separate life, and a deepening bond between the new life and its female carrier. After birth, these experiences include mothers teaching first lessons in survival and giving first feedings, even as fathers may passively look on. It is usually mothers who record the dates and times of first life events—a first burp or smile, a first step, the first tooth gained or lost. The connection between mother and child is deep, unique, and the foundation of social life. These events, which for unrelated persons outside the family may seem insignificant, are especially for mothers worthy of notice, kept in scrapbooks and family albums, later to become family relics and sites of memory. While it is certainly the case that many fathers attend closely to these events, in most families it is mothers and grandmothers who are the primary keepers of accumulating memories. (Though we focus in this book on the role and responsibilities of women and mothers, we recognize that fatherhood as protector of collective memory is also important and deserves much future research attention.) Portraits in the mind are gradually added, here and there, and preserved. From time to time they are visited and revisited with affection, by parents, siblings, extended family members, and close friends.

The Significance of Motherhood

Motherhood is very significant for African American women wherever they reside. Character and courage are connected to a woman's successful performance of that role. No matter how lowly what a woman does, if done for the benefit of her children it becomes worthwhile. Although social scientists and public commentators have often presented harsh and false portraits of African American mothers, the collective memory of African Americans views motherhood positively and prizes it highly. Consider, for example, the old spirituals of enslaved African Americans. Some of these famous songs closely associate mother with home and native land. Being without a mother is like being an expatriate. It is an experience of isolation, loneliness, and a form of alienation. "Sometimes I feel like a motherless child, a long way from home" makes motherhood synonymous with origin, refuge, and home. This is consistent with its Latin etymology.

The Early Years

In our interviews black women and men mention their mothers often, spontaneously praising them, glorifying them, and openly expressing gratitude for sacrifices and teachings. "My mother. My mother. When I was coming up, she was very strong with me and she always would tell me that I could do whatever I want to do if I wanted to pay the price," replied a financial planner in a southern city when asked who was most helpful to him in achieving his life goals. In reply to the same question a banker in a northern city also gave thanks to his mother for her constant support and encouragement: "My mother pushes me constantly to make it, because she knows what she had to go through in life, and what my father had to go through." Such positive statements about mothers and learning from them were echoed strongly by several participants in one of several focus groups with black women in a western city. When asked, "What should black women do to end racism?" without hesitation one mother, an administrator, replied, "Motherhood! Motherhood!" Others in the group agreed. What they seem to mean is that through teaching and nurturing mothers hold the power to change how their children are affected by racism in society.

Later Years

The care and close attention of mother for child at the dawn of life is only the beginning, though it is indicative of the role a mother will likely continue to play throughout a child's life. Ordinarily, the critical guidance that typifies motherhood lasts, and so lasts mother's transmission of important values and memories to the offspring. Events that mark a life take various forms and have varying significance at different stages. For example, young adults face problems that are dealt with by drawing on motherly guidance. In a recent focus group in the Midwest a nurse recalls how her mother taught her to handle racist and other troubling incidents: "I just smile about it. You know, it used to bug me when people didn't like me—black or white or otherwise. But [in a] conversation with my mother, it's like, 'Well, are they paying your bills? Are they, what are they doing for you?' 'Well, nothing.' 'Well, what difference does it make? Everybody is not going to like you.' "

Recent markers in one's life may be seen as more worthy of attention, capturing the importance of a new moment. These new markers include graduations, weddings, and family reunions that often accompany them. At least in the here and now, these may supplant the joys of earlier years, of that memorable series that started with the child's first smile. But this shift in focus is only temporary. Eventually, new markers too become past and are placed in perspective. They too come to represent moments in a chronology of life events, a chronology that tells the story not only of one individual but also, in part, of an extended family. An individual's stories are shaped by the experiences of others within that family, just as the others' experiences are shaped by the individual's stories.

It is women, in our case black women, who are usually central to the collection, recording, and remembering of old and new markers within extended families. While others in the family—fathers, sisters, brothers, grandfathers, aunts, uncles—certainly contribute in major ways to these recollection activities, it is mothers and grandmothers who fill in the majority of the blanks, because they usually have primary responsibility for the care and guidance of children and families. The unique position of mothers within the family, and the usual closeness to their children, facilitate remembrance.

Motherhood is not, of course, always harmonious. Mother-daughter and mother-son relationships are rarely perfect. This may be especially true where the social context is one of oppression or austerity. Whatever its source, family conflict may strain the mother-child relationship to where good motherhood cannot be fully active. Conflict can have a negative impact on the transmission of collective memories to kith and kin.[1]

Later in life adult children, especially daughters with families of their own, now the keepers and transmitters of a newly combined memory, typically consult again with mothers, mothers-in-law, and grandmothers about family past and present, seeking from them precious items for safekeeping—the secrets, good and not-so-good, that are relevant to well-being because they give meaning to individual and family lives.[2] For example, an executive discloses in a recent focus group a family secret she has learned recently: "I still maintain that because of where we came from, and because of where I fit into the family, I *should have known* that my great-grandparents were slaves. I thought it happened y-e-a-r-s ago . . . like Egyptian time, years! . . . The way I was taught you'd think it happened in 1865 B.C." The teaching of actual family history adds context for, and often reinforces identity in, individual lives.

In another focus group a female business owner stresses teaching children about their history and other important matters:

> I think that [teaching black children] is critical, and the mother seems to be the person, the black woman seems to be the person that all that stems from. I don't care what the black man is doing, I don't care how hard he is working in the family, for the family, that comes from the mother. It does, and I think that's where black women have dropped the ball lately. [Interviewer: "So the mother is the center of the family?"] *Yes,* she *is.*

Knowledge gained from mothers strengthens the bridge between family of origin and one's own family, between past and present. It is common for events, traditions, and secrets to be transmitted matrilineally, from mothers to daughters and daughters-in-laws for the benefit of posterity. These traditions are seldom shared with persons outside the extended family network. If there is sharing, it may be done reluctantly or partially, as is the case with favorite recipes, because recipes and their special contents are a family thing. They are of the home space, the private domain. Likewise, family events, old secrets, and traditions with their special content build loyalty among family members, because they are derived from a certain commonality—at its best a commonality broad enough to encompass distinctive individuality.

This common denominator is like a family grammar or family language. Consider the following statement from a male researcher at a southern university: "My mother was an excellent role model for me. She achieved, and I mean people in our family achieved. If you were a [gives family name], you were supposed to make good grades. And you were supposed to achieve. So whenever we went to school, teachers would say 'Oh, he'll do all right, he's a [gives family name].' " Here a common denominator of shared principles links together a family, whose name is recognized by teachers because of successful performance. The similarity in values shows they belong to the same family group. Like others in our sample, this respondent credits motherhood for the family's common language of achievement.

Keeping alive the memory of kinship experiences links mother to child, sibling to sibling, and all to the extended kith and kin network. The common language contributes to the making and marking of family, of family longevity and cohesion, and, over time, of community cohesion. It attests to an underlying similarity in at least some of the experiences of a family. Thus, it can be central to developing and strengthening individual and family identity. It tells those who are noted in family landmarks—those whose names appear in scrapbooks, whose pictures are in albums—that they are important. For grown children the recorded memories of early life events show they *were* important years before they could notice or remember. It reminds family members that they are worthy human beings with a circle of people interested in their well-being and likely to share kinship memories and accumulated knowledge essential to coping with life's troubles, including those associated with racism.

This may be one reason why family scrapbooks and albums are so important in the homes of black Americans. These records provide evidence to an individual and to others that she or he is a chosen member of the extended kin (sometimes friendship) group. But albums do more than this. Jacques Le Goff reminds us they are significant because they express "the truth of social remembrance." They help pattern group experience, show continuity, and unify. Le Goff concludes, "there is nothing more decent, more reassuring and more edifying than a family album" that preserves the collective memory of a family group.[3] Maurice Halbwachs long ago suggested that, like people, groups like families have the capacity to remember.[4] Typically, it is women who keep and order these scrapbooks and albums, and they perpetuate family meanings in the process.

Even in the absence of family albums, scrapbooks, and similar tangible souvenirs, important life markers will likely be remembered and recounted later in the form of stories by mothers and grandmothers. Even well-intentioned men have a tendency to forget many of the family landmarks, in the same way that many tend to forget anniversaries and birthdays to the disappointment of wives and children. Mothers and grandmothers collect and recollect family events and pass along accumulated wisdom. Sad events and good events—mostly the good ones—are noted no matter how small. They are added to the precious family collection. Events and bits of accumulated wisdom are treasures to be stored and recounted. And whether formally recorded or not, albums and scrapbooks or not, it seems that especially women, and most often mothers, record and disseminate the collective memory of African American families. They are thus decisive in determining the identity of posterity and community.

Variations of Motherhood

Not all motherhood is the same. Each type of motherhood has a different character depending on a racial or ethnic group's experiences and on the needs created for family and children by the conditions of the surrounding society. As social contexts vary, so will the content and form of maternal teachings, as will the contributions of fathers and others in extended families to family teachings. Even though loving guidance remains a basic principle and primary responsibility of all motherhood, there are variations that should be noted. For example, motherhood is very important in both Caribbean and African

American cultures. However, in most Caribbean countries whites are a minority, and institutions have developed that primarily serve the black majorities. As a rule, racial prejudice by whites is not as obvious or prevalent as it is in the United States. Therefore, mothers can function differently, with the involvement of other family members in rearing offspring still active but generally less of a necessity for survival. Although here too the memory of slavery may be revived on occasions, that memory has a less direct, or less conscious, relevance to the everyday lives of black people in the Caribbean. In this setting one would expect less need for a motherhood that includes direct racial socialization of children, because everyday interactions are primarily with other black people. Indeed, it is whites who often must learn to adjust to the black majority.[5]

In a society like the United States where skin color is a critically important marker of social position and guides the distribution of major social and economic rewards, and where institutions are designed to support the color line, there is a great need for groups marked by this racism to build special knowledge and develop special competence to deal with situations related to persisting prejudice and discrimination. In such a society women must develop the kind of mothering that shapes their offspring for survival and gives them special tools to counter racial oppression. This training becomes a special obligation for mothers. Also in such a society the involvement of fathers and other family members as supporters and protectors of motherly nurturing is even more central to successful motherhood and the transmission of collective memories.

Variations in mothering are also found within the U.S. context. We noted in Chapter 2 how, for black women in the nineteenth-century Northwest, being a homemaker or full-time mother was not even a choice. "In striking reversal of white middle class norms, 'good' women worked for a wage to bring their loved ones together."[6] In that place and time African American womanhood took a distinctive form. These working women had different responsibilities and practiced a different kind of motherhood mediated by their circumstances than many white women, especially those in the middle class. Though still a loving approach, they found themselves in a different economic and racial context. Working motherhood likely required, where available, active participation of the larger kinship unit in the socialization of children to complete the part of motherhood that was unfulfilled.

Mothering still varies for black and white mothers today. For black children and young adults experiencing problems unique to being black in white-dominated society, the content of a mother's guidance will likely include, as it did in the nineteenth-century Northwest, ways of dealing with everyday intolerance and discrimination. Most family groups provide constituents, children especially, with tools to deal with difficult racial situations.

Good socialization, good mothering, means giving these children special tools. In a recent focus group in a western city an entrepreneur underscores this point. When asked what black women should do to end racial oppression, she replies: "I think the first thing that black women need to understand is that you cannot control what somebody else is going to do, OK!? You can only control how you react to it. What black women need to do is to teach their children from the very beginning who they are, to have self-esteem, to get education and knowledge, because knowledge is power, to try to keep their families together. I think to teach respect." Such an ambitious list reveals the many complexities and tough situations faced by an African American mother. From this point of view the role of mothers is to educate and train children to know when and how to respond to attacks on their selfhood. This training can develop from a mother's knowledge of the racial experience and responses of other kin such as grandmother, grandfather, brother, or sister. Like photographs in the family album these responses are accumulated and passed along, generation after generation.

Teaching these responses is but one responsibility of mothers. In order for motherhood to function well and be successful, its messages must be understood and accepted by younger generations. The teachings must be effective. Mothers' messages about how to respond to racism may reach younger people who are already exposed to whites who contradict the teaching of a caring motherhood. One gleans from the respondent's comment a wish for control not only over individual black responses but also over the everyday racial problems themselves, with the help of a strong motherhood.

Connecting Past and Present

Motherhood not only passes on the memories of one lifetime but also frequently refers back and draws on the experiences of ancestors and tells that important history to the offspring. Grandmothers are particularly important in passing on collective memories and wisdom. They frequently maintain multigenerational albums and scrapbooks, and they are often there with wisdom and good advice.[7] In a recent focus group in the Midwest a nurse assistant mentions survival strategies for dealing with whites: "Kindness will kill a person. My grandmother told me that so many times. 'Don't get upset. Don't fuss. Don't argue with them. Just smile at them.' " And a senior planner in a focus group in the South also cites her grandmother, in another context.

> I think the family is, is vital, because, you know, that's where our behavior is learned. It all starts at home, and I think it's important for it to work the other way around—for us to, to help them. You know, for everyone to support each other. And one of the things that my grandmother always said is that you can tell what people think about you by the way their children treat you. They might smile in your face, but their children are real lukewarm. They don't care a thing about you. Because their children hear what mom and dad will say after you're gone.

In this view families are critical repositories of definitive learning about life and interaction. Here is a common reference to the passing along of family wisdom from grandmother to grandchildren. The foremothers pass along accumulated knowledge and recount family narratives and stories again and again.

The history of ancestors is of great importance. A retired professor in a southern city explains: "Most of our history was handed down, verbally. See, my mother talked to me about people being lynched and how it was, and I felt it, and I had this rage." Memories of the past, passed along by mothers, grandmothers, or other relatives, are not always pleasant. Many are very painful and disturbing. Examples of disturbing memories include those of slavery and of lynchings, which have taken place as recently as the early 1980s. There is much knowledge about concerning brutality suffered by previous generations of black Americans to transmit to later generations. Such events are painful to hear because the experiences are those of real people, of ancestors whose lives were cut short by circumstances beyond their control. Absent the brutal oppression of white Americans, these African American ancestors could have accomplished much more than they were able to do for their own families and could have done more economically and otherwise to enhance the positions of later generations. Such memories may be accompanied by a deep sense of great loss among the rememberers.

Unlike many white teachers and others who might place dark shadows on the character of those who endured racism and on their progeny—changing facts and manipulating historical knowledge—most black mothers, fathers, and other relatives can remember at least some of the important family and group history. Parents, especially mothers, can transfer to kin even a disturbing memory in ways that will offer a balanced view, buffering the worst effects and shifting responsibility for these experiences from those who have experienced them to the white inflicters. Mothers can bring an introduction to these events with as much guidance and understanding as is possible, with the principal goal being the exploration of a family's positive and persisting roots.

In a recent interview one mother, who works as an administrator, made the problem of entrusting whites with black history very clear.

> I say we [black women] have to maintain strong family units, that are educated in historically based, based in the history, know their family's history, know their group's history, and more importantly, raise strong black children that are not afraid to communicate and set barriers. And raise children who are not followers, children who are natural born leaders. And support our children. We have to make sure our children are educated and our children are aware, and our children have the tools to go out and survive in a hostile environment, that's not only racist but, these are issues they are going to face, and I think that we need to prepare ourselves for that role and prepare our children for it. . . . Black issues should be taught in the family as opposed to in the classrooms, because I am never comfortable with white teachers doing black history. Some do a great job. . . . My sister and I went to Egypt, and we came back . . . so I was invited to speak to a class about Egypt. I get to class and the teacher had prepared the students for my coming, and to ask me questions. So I did what I saw, what we experienced—the pyramids, the whole Egyptian thing.

This should have been a very positive experience for all concerned, both the children and the adults. However, the white teacher apparently had a negative image of north Africa in mind.

> When I got to the teacher, she looked so disappointed. I could not understand. So, she asked the kids to ask me questions. And the kids didn't. Finally, the teacher said: "So, what's the illiteracy rate, in Egypt? How many are starving to death in Egypt? How many are living in the streets in Egypt?" I mean, as opposed to the cultural things, the museums I saw, the universities I saw, the monuments I saw, she wanted me to tell the children about the poverty. And so, when we begin to entrust our history to other people for dispersion, I am not comfortable doing that.

She then adds that this experience confirms her view that important history lessons must be taught by black parents in the family. In black communities motherhood normally means the telling of ancestral stories, to incite the interest and pride of family members in these events and teach useful lessons to kin, so that they will understand why these events happened and place them in family and societal contexts. Thus, a time line is developed for the benefit of future generations. In a focus group in a western city, one woman describes her own mothering, saying, "I am trying to provide a legacy to them to take it to the next generation," illustrating again the impact of motherhood on the collective memory of later generations.

Inactive motherhood can mean that distorted memories are passed to black children and young adults through the agency of certain whites, such as social workers or teachers, and prevail over memories of important ancestral achievements and traditions. Damage can occur when an individual's knowledge of family or the community of families comes substantially from the agents in the social institutions that protect the antagonistic white memory of racial matters, and not from knowledgeable mothers and foremothers. Once absorbed, the outsider-oppressor's memory can have a harmful impact on individual and family identities. Inactive mothering leaves ample room for historical distortions, stifled self-esteem, and blocked achievement.

In cases where motherhood has failed to guide well, as in the case of a family separation, and where there are no good substitutes—female relatives or a nurturing father—there may be little understanding of this history and of family landmarks that sustain and protect individual and family identity. What were mother's words of wisdom? What did she and grandmother or father consider important? Why did they think these things important? What were their accomplishments? What worked for them, and what did not? And most importantly, what can be learned from their experience?

In spite of the clear benefits of active motherhood, moreover, one must recognize that success for offspring is not guaranteed simply because of motherly guidance. Even active motherhood competes with the numerous outside white agents, with their negative images and memories that may distort or reshape, in many ways, the teachings of good motherhood. Whatever the case, it is likely that motherly guidance and the presence of a family's collective memory will reduce the effects of outside distortions and societal propaganda about black lives and families.

Understanding One's Roots

Teaching children who they are means taking them back to their roots, tracing the common paths traveled by others before them. A female respondent speaks eloquently about the importance of knowing the history of African American women often gained from one's mother and other relatives.

> I took a cruise across the Atlantic Ocean, so I had the opportunity to cross the ocean in a ship. And I got a real bad cold, which means to tell me I wouldn't have made it, and when I read about Harriet Tubman having to walk from Georgia to New York City, when I hear about the [vengeance] that black women took, the whippings that they took, I didn't have a problem. They are holding me up on their shoulders. There is no way I can . . . because they have given me too much. We have been given far too much. We have been given so, so, so very much. I mean the sacrifices they made, mine is just a drop in the bucket. Mine is nowhere near . . . so, I would never cry about being a black woman in this country, because I owe too many folks way too much to cry.

The heritage of African Americans includes not only early Africans' experiences in North America but also experiences on the African

195

continent. Despite their sometimes mixed origins, the experiences that our respondents have described are often related in one way or another to the African part of their roots. Their experiences continue to be linked to that African origin. St. Clair Drake has explained that central to the everyday coping processes of African Americans is "their identification, over a time span of more than two centuries, with ancient Egypt and Ethiopia as symbols of black initiative and success long before their enslavement on the plantations of the New World."[8] Moreover, the recent overthrow of the racist apartheid system in South Africa has oriented black Americans even more strongly to the liberating actions and histories of their African brothers and sisters. Our respondents periodically speak of looking toward Africa as a place of heritage and of liberation. Today, a symbolic return to the continent and its achievements, preferably guided by loving mothers and other relatives, allows a broader view of one's ancestry and permits an understanding of today's experiences in light of yesterday and an envisioning of a future where one has more control because of that cumulative experience.[9] A symbolic return to the African continent does more than trace the collective memory of racial oppression that links African Americans. Visiting Africa reinforces an identity independent of the history of oppression.

Still, answers to "Who am I?" and "How did I get here?" will eventually intersect with issues of past and present racism. Knowing the history of racial oppression helps one to complete the historical road traveled and aids reflective retrospection, but by no means does that capture the total memory that is important to building self-esteem.[10] Writes one social scientist, "The absence voluntary or involuntary of collective memory of peoples and nations can result in serious troubles of collective identity."[11] Thus, a symbolic return to the African continent and its history and civilizations—through education, travels, visits to museums, or family stories, scrapbooks, and albums—helps protect family and collective identities. Today as in the past, this symbolic visit to African sites and memories can begin in the home and is often guided by mothers and grandmothers.

The government administrator quoted earlier described a visit to Egypt that gave her a strong connection to her African past, a sense of which she tried to pass along to a class where a white teacher apparently had a negative and stereotyped image of Egypt. In her recollection this woman made clear that she was unwilling to let whites control the teaching of that history: "I am not comfortable doing that. I believe it should be taught in schools, but I am not comfortable [with whites teaching it]. I think *home* is where it has to be." In the United States home is critical for passing African or African American history to the next generation. In a black-majority country, say in the Caribbean, teaching this important history need not occur mostly in the home. While mothers and fathers may occasionally mention the exploits of African or national heroes and heroines, these need not be discussed inside that setting. Institutions other than the family, especially the schools, are given that primary responsibility.

Let us illustrate by looking briefly at the Caribbean nation of Haiti. Virtually every Haitian recognizes January 1, 1804, as Independence Day, as well as many other important dates in the country's history. They remember Toussaint L'Ouverture, the black slave who led the successful revolt against French colonial rule, and other heroes of that history of liberation. Some recall this because they studied history in schools, while many others have gained this knowledge from popular culture or national celebrations. These markers unify a country and families within a country; they define all participants as part of one Haitian nation and community. Recalling these historical markers is also useful to the many thousands of immigrants in the Haitian diaspora. Immigrants to a foreign country like the United States are empowered by their remembrance of Haitian holidays and history. They too are defined by that historical experience and are linked symbolically, in this sense becoming one people.

Whether one is Haitian or African American, knowledge of one's general and family history empowers one, even if only bits and pieces are remembered or the details are forgotten or vaguely recalled.[12] We have previously noted that the life stories of former generations are not always pleasant. These stories can be seen as analogous to mothers using old chipped tableware on an important occasion, despite new plates being available, because this tableware served a previous generation, someone dear like a favorite aunt, a grandfather, or grandmother. For its owner, the old tableware tells a story that is worth preserving.

In general, one might expect collective memories of the past and of distant ancestors to be less appreciated in the United States—a society said to focus heavily on the present, the immediate, or the near future, and to discourage encounters with the past—than in other countries.[13] The United States is a society where honoring the dead does not seem to be as common as it is in many other countries. Where the new is king and the old quickly discarded, the past too has reduced value.

For a contrast, let's return to the example of a family table where, despite new dishes being available, old, chipped ones are used; they have become part of a family heritage because they symbolize hard times and difficult experiences, as well as victory over them. They are seen with pride and affection. They are important because they bring back memories of a grandmother to whom they used to belong. Through these items, grandmother is still present, her experiences still alive and real, and the times in which she lived are also alive, at least in that family's memory. Such are the sites of memory that for African Americans bridge past and present.

A Sense of Control

By linking present, past, and future through guidance of the young, collective memory can liberate a group by giving it a sense of control over its history and ultimately the present and future lives of its people. This may be why the previously quoted business owner expresses her disappointment that mothers have let

> a certain percentage of our children, go. . . . They [are not given] the background and the training they need to be able to deal with the world, because you look at India and everybody is the same color but they have the caste system. . . . No matter where you are in the world you are going to run into situations where you could conceivably be discriminated against, not just black and white, but religion, or "I am richer than you are," or "I came from this side of the track, you came from up on top of the mountain, or from down the bottom of the mountain." There is something. . . . But what we need to do to change that is to teach our children how to live, and be successful *regardless* of the situation they find themselves in. Strength of character, belief in God, get them back to church, because I think a lot of kids, I see that's where all my strength comes from.

From this vantage point it is important for black children and young adults to know that their mothers, fathers, and grandfathers have encountered problems similar to theirs and have handled the problems, as well as to know how they handled them. This accumulated knowledge must be included in the rearing of offspring. As others have noted, this respondent insists that the central figure for this rearing is the black woman: "I think that [this teaching] is critical, and the mother seems to be the person, the black woman seems to be the person that all that stems from." As many of the women we interviewed see it, motherhood is a principal link between the past, the present, and the future. Women are viewed as heavily responsible for the socialization of children. They must not only pass along the memories, habits, and rituals of previous generations but also instruct children in their daily practice as they train and nurture them. Children learn that they are a part of the same community, that there is an underlying logic to their family habits.

Family control of the family heritage is at stake here. African American children benefit from being told about habits and practices that served previous generations well, that are tested, and that may still be relevant—or about other practices, not so successful, that should be avoided.

In Chapter 3 we discussed the issue of beauty, its many consequences for the self-esteem of young black women, and pointed to a study that finds a positive correlation between children's knowledge of black contributions to history and children's choices of dolls. Black children are more likely to want and select dolls that look more like themselves when they are aware of African American history. This study supports the general point that knowledge of relevant history can strengthen identity and empower an individual. Where history is silenced or distorted by a dominating society, motherhood and fatherhood have an important part to play in teaching African American history to daughters and sons.

There are other ways for mothers and fathers to control and preserve a collective memory of the extended family and of family and personal identity. Repeat naming is one. First names are often given by mothers. Mothers may name children after a respected predecessor and will usually avoid passing on names of persons they do not like. Many mothers create their own innovative names, especially for their daughters.[14] Through control over naming, mothers bring past into the present and give a family the opportunity to reconnect with valued predecessors. The surname also helps to keep the family heritage alive, if in a small way.

Previously, we discussed the importance of family albums. In many different racial and ethnic groups, although fathers sometimes take many photos, often it is the women who insist that important life-marking photos be taken for family albums. By virtue of their closeness to children they usually desire the photographic record.[15] It is usually mothers who, especially during the holidays, have photos sent to family members and close friends. They are often behind the framing of letters that list family achievements. They are able to see continuity in a family. In addition, it is usually women who send or keep holiday cards year after year, and who send special notes to family members and others at holiday time. Women preserve the mementos, such as old ornaments and dolls, especially if they are made or given to them by a family member. They may add these to the previous collection, hoping to pass them down to the next generation of families. The latter, if these values are still important and the collective memory was successfully transmitted, will do the same. Mothers tend to keep old dolls, baby dresses, baby teeth, the not-useful-to-anyone things from life. Day after day, through these and even more important practices, like the teaching of history and building of self-esteem, mothers shape the collective memory of their children, the identity of their children, and eventually of citizens. While men and other relatives frequently support and protect motherhood, it is motherhood that typically prepares, maintains, and facilitates visits to the sites of collective memory.

Conclusion

In this chapter we have seen our respondents celebrating once again black women, but most especially mothers. While all members of a family, both the immediate and the extended family, are usually involved in the preservation and teaching of collective accomplishments and memory, in most of our respondents' accounts it is mothers who have an ongoing and central responsibility for family remembrance. They are central to the collective memory of the family and its passing to younger generations. The obligation to use the collective memory to empower black children so they can develop a strong identity and use that identity to fight societal racism rests heavily on black women. Because women, especially mothers and grandmothers, often hold much of the memory of the black family, they also hold much of the collective memory of the black community, for communities are at base composed of families. Moreover, in a larger sense, the general history of African Americans is in their hands.

Yet we would be misrepresenting the views of our respondents if we did not underscore the fact that they do not position women alone in the process of collective memory and historical remembrance, either in the past or in the present. Motherhood functions best when supported by fatherhood. For example, an insightful entrepreneur in a focus group in a western city highlights the importance of fatherhood, saying:

> We [black women] also feel that we are going to be ones who are going to have to raise the family and the children, et cetera, and so we go ahead and get about our business. . . . But I think younger black men are not nearly as supportive of black women, and I think it's because maybe they've been surrounded so much by black women and not enough by powerful black men who can say "This is how men [should be]." Like my husband used to tell my son, "This is how men are supposed to treat women; you never saw me treat your mother like that."

Fathers are very important in the everyday rearing of daughters and sons, but especially for sons. The quoted father is asking his son to follow his example and to respect wifehood and motherhood.

Our respondents are also clear that in the process of preserving collective memories and community histories mothers are ordinarily backed up and supported by fathers, grandmothers, and other close relatives such as aunts, uncles, cousins, nephews, and nieces.

As we have heard in our respondents' own voices, African American culture carries history as this history carries culture. For the most part people agree on basic points: that history should be remembered, that names of historical heroes are familiar and ought to be passed along to children or that a certain holiday is special and needs to be celebrated. Remembrance, even of half-forgotten facts, can give people the strength to go on. Recall Jean Brierre's play discussed in Chapter 1. In that play two Haitian girls gain strength from remembering their foremothers and feel positively, not only about their past but also about themselves. This applies in the United States as well. In such social contexts foremotherhood intervenes constantly in the teaching of important historical knowledge and of constructing a personal identity that can foster survival and success.

Chapter 8

Finale

As they have for centuries, African American women and men today face a complex array of racial barriers created by white Americans in all major institutional settings across the society. The barriers they face can be seen in a number of different areas, including several delineated in this book: the workplace, school settings, societal images of beauty, and various media stereotypes and portraits. To deal with racism in these areas African Americans have developed an important array of survival and countering strategies, which are webbed together in what we have termed an oppositional culture. This webbing together has meant the development of a culture of resistance positioned against the many threats of the dominant society. Oppositional culture is rooted fundamentally in families, including extended family networks. At its heart are collective memories that have been carried for centuries in critical social networks. Our data also make clear that the experiences of black Americans sum to more than a listing of encounters with whites. The accumulated experience and knowledge involves much more than dealing with white hostility and discrimination. As we have often noted, the sense of peoplehood among black women and men is undergirded by persisting collective memories that are constantly reinforced in extended family interactions.

Black Women at Work

Work is central to the lives and self-esteem of most adult Americans. Being employed or unemployed has a significant impact on both families and communities. Black women experience the usual barriers and trials that all workers face in earning a living. Yet for black women racism and gendered racism remain widespread barriers, which are added to the other workplace difficulties. Occupational ceilings, perceptions that they are incompetent, and excessive demands from whites are common. In work settings black women often lack mentorship, are intentionally isolated by whites, or are seen as unintelligent "twofers" who hold their positions only because of some type of affirmative action.

Yet, our respondents report that, despite the harsh workplace treatment, black women are sometimes more acceptable to whites, especially white men, as employees than are black men. As these whites apparently see it, black women seem to pose somewhat less of a threat, can be controlled by virtue of their gender, and are more acquiescent. Black women's more common presence in some traditionally white workplaces may be intentional, a white manipulation that can result in strained black family relations. In a society that promotes patriarchy, the white preference for black women has consequences for black women, men, families, and communities. Not all our respondents accent this view of a less threatening black woman, however. Some emphasize how strong black women, especially those outspoken about racial barriers in white-dominated work settings, can also pose a serious threat to white men.

The experiences of African American women in the workplace are in some ways rooted in the past. On slave plantations and under segregation black women suffered at grueling labor, usually without the opportunity to protest working conditions. As we have seen, this history of enslavement and legal segregation is still alive and maintained in collective memories. Today, however, many black women do protest their workplace conditions. Indeed, using various strategies, women work hard to maintain or recapture their dignity. A designer in a southern city explains what it means to respond to racism and how, as a consequence of it,

> Everybody worries. They treat me a lot better. Mainly they stay away from me because they're afraid that these things are going to slip off—that they don't seem to be in control, the racial remarks and things, so they just kind of stay away from me, or quite a few of them do, the really bad ones that I wouldn't want to associate

with anyway, and the others are just like they always have been friendly. I find it amusing. You have to know how I treat these people to understand why I laugh. Everybody that knows me laughs about it. "Stay away from her, she's crazy" [laughs].

A successful response to racism can give one a sense of personal control. Control means not letting oneself be too affected by white actions, but thinking, acting, and feeling independently of whites and their actions. Control means trying to transcend the racist experience, thereby having charge over what affects one's life. Each such response adds to the general knowledge that contributes positively to the collective memory and benefits present and future generations.

Concepts of Beauty

Concepts of beauty are another area of daily life where African American women face widespread gendered racism. Long ago, western thought and science chose what was to be defined as beautiful and what ugly. These definitions persist, as the white-maintained beauty rule still requires that one's skin be as fair as possible and that other physical characteristics be of a certain type in order for a black woman to be accepted. The arbitrary beauty definitions have consequences for all black women, and especially those who strive to fit that image despite messages they receive through dolls, magazines, films, and television, that this white beauty prototype is out of their reach. The toy and media cultures that reach many black children and young adults often celebrate negative images and somatic definitions of black women.

Our respondents acknowledge that there are contradictions in the attitudes and actions of whites, as when some white women imitate black women, and some white men find black women to be attractive mates. But, these are exceptions. The fairer-the-better rule generally prevails for whites, reproducing the past and protecting the established racial hierarchy so engraved in the white memory and so important to white advancement. Here too black women develop ways to successfully counter false images, using the special knowledge passed on to them by grandparents and parents. Success is suggested because even where physical attractiveness is threatened, self-esteem can remain intact if there is knowledge of one's roots and a focus on talents and achievements rather than attractiveness. This knowledge and focus act to establish balance by helping black women deal effectively with persisting attempts by a racist society to destroy their self-esteem and introduce self-doubt. Caring parents and teachers transfer this important knowledge about history to their students, as a male teacher and counselor in a southern city explains:

> I tell the students I work with that you have to strive for the best and accept nothing less in you, and to get to that point, you have to know your culture, you have to know your history. I try to get them to love reading, to thirst for getting knowledge outside of the classroom. I try to stress to them that their education is the only thing another person can't take away from them, that their education is on them. I try to stress that responsibility is theirs. Education is not something that somebody gives you, education you have to go out and get. And the education that I try to stress to them is not only knowing that math and knowing that science, but knowing your African roots. You know, knowing your roots here in America as well as knowing your African roots. I mean, that's the only way we're going to be able to get over this self-doubt.

That some black women have difficulty finding mates may well be related to the way they are portrayed by the society; some potential mates may be focusing more on beauty as defined by white society than on important achievements and history. Yet the prevailing standards of beauty are defined by those who have the greatest power, and this process reflects the existing racial hierarchy. As our respondents emphasize, there is a need to rethink dominant beauty standards to make them more inclusive. There is a continuing need to teach African American children, girls in particular, to focus on their talents and achievements, their history and culture instead of the mirror, and to encourage them to develop a sense of their deep family and community roots, which can increase self-esteem.

Media Portrayals of Black Women

Media myths that denigrate black women still abound in this society. These myths can be harmful when they are transferred to generations of black and white children as reality. One popular myth is that of the sexually aggressive black woman, the "Jezebel." This image grew up in early historical periods. During slavery, even as white men alleged being repulsed by their slaves, they still exploited black women sexually. After slavery, especially in the South, sexual exploitation continued. Yet it is black women who inherited the poor reputation, not their white male oppressors. Here again, one is reminded of the racial relevance of the past for the racial present. The Jezebel myth is no more than a lingering figment of a very old white imagination.

There are other common forms of media stigmatization of black women. Black women are often depicted as fat, probably because many whites equate fat with laziness and lack of self-control. This stigmatization can have serious consequences for both black and white children. On television black women are often presented in negative economic or moral terms, representations also noted by and offensive to our respondents. While sometimes they are portrayed as "superwoman"--a depiction that may initially appear positive to some viewers--superwoman is not an accurate representation because these women both succeed and fail. The respondents want honest media that present black women in a way that takes into account both successes and failures--the whole gamut of their life experiences.

The stigmatization of African American women is not limited to television. Most of the movie business behaves in much the same way, presenting black women in secondary or stereotyped roles. Advertising stigmatizes these women too, promoting the sexuality image as well as legal drugs such as alcohol, potentially shaping young people in black communities.

Black families also suffer from stigmatization by the media. Portrayals of black families on television are usually not realistic. Black families often illustrate television stories about welfare, even though this may contradict the facts in the news reports. Again such images can have a negative impact on children. In general, the mass media deny black women, men, and families their dignity. These women and their families are transformed into something they are not. The talents and achievements of black women are often ignored or negated. Moreover, such negative portrayals are broadcast around the world to people who, because they have little basis for comparison, probably take these images at face value. The views of audiences are shaped worldwide. Whites, who have an important stake in the outcome of these portrayals, generally control what is created and presented and thereby perpetuate racist images, memories, and histories.

Black and White Women

While solidarity with supportive white women can help alleviate some effects of gendered racism, black and white women are often adversaries. Black women frequently report callousness and discrim-inatory treatment by white women. The expressions of that discrimination vary, from marginalization at social gatherings to white women concealing critical information from black women or blocking promotions of black women. These behaviors, which are often evident in the workplace, extend outside work as well. In certain respects they are reminders of plantation life, where many white women not only shared the racist attitudes of white men but are reported by some historians to have often been more cruel toward their female slaves than white men were. Differing collective memories discourage cooperation between black and white women. Moreover, though at times black and white women seem to experience some of the same gender problems, the problems of white women do not include gendered racism. And white women generally benefit from being close to white men in ways that black women (and men) cannot be. Exceptions were noted by the respondents for white women who work to end racism, and they acknowledge support they have received from some friendly white women. Nonetheless, close relationships between black and white women are not common in the United States.

Black Families

In our chapters we have often separated out key aspects of the lives of African American women for analytical purposes. Of course, they do not live out their lives this way. They often encounter life's varied aspects at the same point in time. They may deal with workplace problems and beauty challenges in the same period, or with antago-nistic white women and challenges to their self-esteem from Jezebel images in the mass media. Life tends to weave collective memories, current issues and problems, and discriminatory arenas together. So, we need to keep in mind the holistic terms in which these women experience everyday realities. They experience everyday life as whole human beings confronted by an array of joys, tribulations, and racial barriers. Most of them are able to keep themselves and their families together, and they rarely opt out by committing suicide, because family and children's survival hinges so greatly on them. Suicide may also be an unthinkable option because of women's role as primary keepers of the collective memory of kinship and community. If a suicide occurred, it would enter and stain the collective memory of family and community, and carry with it consequences too painful for their progeny.

In addition, most of these women have strong role models, the foreparents who chose to fight rather than give up. The latter have left marks on the collective memory of the family group, which incite our respondents and other black women to action and encourage them to go on. So, internal strength derives from this knowledge of African American history and culture. As keepers and transmitters of the collective memory, these women pass on the tradition of strength in the face of adversity. The collective memory of resistance against slavery and racism empowers them to challenge their often oppressive social conditions. Suicide is out of character for those engaged intimately in countering daily attempts to make them undesirable if not invisible; such an act would indeed play into the hands of those who want them invisible, in the extreme.

In our interviews black women and black men frequently position families at the center of their lives, speaking of their families in ways that tell us they are both home and refuge. Family represents shelter; closeness to immediate and extended families helps black women reverse the impact of everyday racism. Yet many scholars, such as Daniel P. Moynihan and Charles Murray, have made attacks on the black family, declaring it to be pathological or a special social problem, even as other research shows the presence of strong and viable extended family systems among African Americans. Extended families are important because they give support to individuals and give them back their wholeness that is robbed from them by racism. The presence of an extended family means that African Americans will have this support available to them if they need it. Here is a system where individual members are concerned with and involved in the well-being of other members. This larger family unit is crucial to lifting the burdens of black women and men in their encounters with racism in daily life. The extended family structure contributes to the pool of knowledge so important to coping with present discrimination and to preparing future generations to deal with that reality. Our respondents recognize that this protective role of the African American extended family is not new. Indeed, several historians have shown how the family was the primary place of refuge for those African Americans who were brutally enslaved. That enslaved African Americans were able to maintain some form of family system despite major life-shortening obstacles shows what family has meant to them.

Our respondents acknowledge the contributions of their immediate and extended families to their upbringing and to helping them deal with demanding societal circumstances. They speak highly of mothers and fathers, as well as of grandmothers, aunts, uncles, and other relatives, in protecting and extending the collective memory of the kinship group. They recognize that this is important to maintaining a strong identity and sense of continuity. They worry about black young people who become isolated from good families and thus from their histories and important role models. Such distancing interferes with the development of memories of kinship that are crucial to the development of a strong identity. Where such collective memory is weak, young people can be very vulnerable to negative portrayals of African Americans in the larger society.

Immediate families are central and critical for those black women and men with whom we talked. In spite of lives so often enmeshed in difficult racial realities, black women seek, want, and dream of successful futures for their children. Our respondents express strong goals for themselves and their families, including good health, and happiness, and the higher education that is particularly important for most of them. Moreover, regardless of their goals, African Americans are often concerned with the extended kinship structure becoming weaker or more individualistic. As they see it, these extended families are especially critical to fighting racism and to group survival and prosperity. They are where people acquire the support that they need to go on. As our respondents see it, they must be strengthened and protected.

Motherhood

Dealing with racial images and barriers in the workplace and other areas, black women extract their responses from a pool of knowledge

209

accumulated over time and grounded in kinship and history. Motherhood is generally central to the accumulation and transfer of kinship and community knowledge by virtue of mothers' closeness to children. Our respondents speak highly of their mothers and of their own role as mothers.

Some respondents see one counter to the problem of racism in motherhood because women are primary keepers of the collective memory and have substantial responsibility for the socialization of children. Successful mothering, they also suggest, needs the participation and protection of fathers and other relatives in transmitting the collective memory to children. All have a responsibility to pass on accumulated wisdom, including African American history. Teaching children their history is one way to transmit the sense of identity important to building self-esteem. Children benefit from being told by their mothers about habits and practices that served previous generations, are tested, and are still likely to be relevant in their own lives. Says one woman:

> I'm an activist. I feel very strongly about what I'm doing. I've always felt very, very strong about discrimination and fighting it. And I think I got that from my mother. . . . I often tell the young mothers that when they see the next generation do things different, they won't do things any more differently than their parents are doing it. If their parents are not doing anything, then the children won't do anything either. I look at the struggle of African Americans all over the world, and I relate to them. I look at the apartheid system in South Africa. I also look at the . . . apartheid and the similarities. A lot of blacks are not even able to relate to that. When I say we play such a role in our own oppression, it's . . . [when] we tend to turn our head away from it.

It is a mother who taught this and other respondents how to deal with racism. There is continuity from mother to child. In the same way, the respondent sees ties and linkages in the situations of black people across the world. She may be implying too that parents, in their teachings, ought to emphasize these important global connections and continuities and include them as part of the broader collective knowledge passed along to the next generation.

Because it links a present, a past, and a future through guidance of the young, collective memory can liberate a group. In the United States the accumulated knowledge about how to respond to racism is generally included in the rearing of a black child. Accumulating and transferring this knowledge seems to be a central responsibility for black women. On the ultimate responsibility of women as promoters of change, activist Barbara Omolade writes: "As women of color live and struggle, we increasingly realize that it's time for us to speak for earth and its future. We have heard the voices of white men who speak of earth and its future. When we look at the hunger, despair, and killings around us, we see what white men who speak for earth have done. Their weaponry and visions speak clearly of a future of more and more war."[1] Often, white men speak for the earth and the future, but from their own highly ethnocentric values and memories. From this point of view they have failed to see the other visions of the future and to include the other important values and life experiences. Black women can speak more effectively for the earth and its future by passing on the collective vision to young people, especially their children, and thus building up a collective character. African American women must fight to become their own cultural artists.

What We've Learned

Black women face racial woes that take various forms: workplace and other organizational barriers, attacks on their beauty, misrepresentations by the media, and conflicts and strained relationships with white women. These experiences are often not separated but happen in the same period of time.

The degrading attacks on African American women can be found in many societal sectors, over long periods of time. Take, for example, the degradation of black women in the extraordinarily popular Civil War movie *Gone With the Wind*, which many millions of viewers have seen over nearly six decades since its release in the late 1930s. One early reviewer suggested that this film leaves its audience "with the warm and grateful remembrance of an interesting story beautifully told." He found the movie to have treated Margaret Mitchell's novel "with such an astonishing fidelity [that it] required courage--the courage of a producer's convictions and of his pocketbook."[2] Yet the all-time favorite American movie depicts only what the collective memory of whites wants to see. In this film whites are shown in control of all situations; they are superior and privileged. In these surroundings black people, as slaves, become important only to the extent that they serve and support the superiority and dominance of whites. Enslaved African Americans are portrayed as stereotypes and as devoted to whites to the point that they will even risk their lives for them.

But what about the details of the lives of those who thus served whites? What were their lives really like outside of the presence of whites? How did they cope with such brutal and life-threatening conditions? Did the enslaved black woman, portrayed in stereotyped terms as an obese "mammy," have a spouse? Did she have children or an extended family? What did she do for her spouse and children? From the white-created movie we cannot answer these questions. This personal information did not seem to matter to the movie's white producers then; it does not seem to matter to most whites in the movie industry now. The details of real black lives, what they were and are, seem to mean little for most white Americans. The film *Gone With the Wind* represents a white heritage, a tradition of historical distortions and sincere fictions that most whites want protected. It is a heritage that feeds the mainstream white imagination and shapes the American present and possibly the future. Its consistency with the mainstream imagination and collective memory is doubtless what makes the film still so popular.

In movies like this we see the personal and family sides of African American lives made invisible by whites. Blacks as human beings seem not to have mattered. However, the devoted "mammy" and other black characters in this film—and this era—doubtless had a much different memory of their past and present, and they transferred a different memory to their children. Although largely ignored by whites, they had personal lives that mattered to them and were negatively influenced by white oppression and controlling images. Thus, it is black Americans, women and men, who speak most accurately and effectively about their real lives and families. They speak about what families meant to them in the past, what they mean to them today, and what they want them to be in the future, rather than leaving the past, present, and future in the hands of those for whom black Americans have been invisible as human beings from the beginning. Like black men, black women must and do challenge the whitewashed version of this U.S. history through everyday teachings. They do this through motherhood and grandmotherhood, through involvement with extended families and communities.

"We cannot escape history," said Abraham Lincoln. "No personal significance, or insignificance, can spare one or another of us."[3] But history is experienced and remembered differently depending on one's position in the society, as is well illustrated by the continuing white reaction to the movie *Gone With the Wind*. The character of plantation days will be remembered differently by the white O'Hara family and by the black individuals and families serving them. Linda Brent, an enslaved African American, doubtless remembered a different version of what happened on the slave plantation than that of her white owners precisely because many events like beatings and sexual assaults were interpreted differently or suppressed for the benefit of white privilege. Brent writes:

> Slaveholders pride themselves upon being honorable men; but if you were to hear the enormous lies they tell their slaves, you would have small respect for their veracity. I have spoken plain English. Pardon me. I cannot use a milder term. When they visit the north, and return home, they tell their slaves of the runaways they have seen, and describe them to be in the most deplorable condition. A slaveholder once told me that he had seen a runaway friend of mine in New York, and that she besought him to take her back to her master, for she was literally dying of starvation; that many days she had only one cold potato to eat and, at other times could get nothing at all. He said he refused to take her, because he knew her master would not thank him for bringing such a miserable wretch to his house. He ended by saying to me, "This is the punishment she brought on herself for running away from a kind master."
>
> This whole story was false. I afterwards staid with that friend in New York, and found her in comfortable circumstances. She had never thought of such a thing as wishing to go back to slavery.[4]

Likewise, the narratives of our respondents show that today the collective memory of African Americans inspires and revives them. Black women must constantly fight the myths and fictions of the white memory, the white imagination, and they shape and transmit an African American culture defined not only by its valiant response to white memory but also by a creativity and imagination rooted deeply in many generations of personal, family, and community history. These women can set themselves in opposition to the white memory and white oppression because of their knowledge of the past and of false white assumptions, a knowledge communicated over generations of black families. Although there is often a cost for challenges to white actions and memories, these black women still take countering actions, survive, and even thrive.

President Kennedy's *Profiles in Courage* is about "grace under pressure" and about "stories of the pressures experienced by Senators and the grace with which they endured them—the risks to their careers, the unpopularity of their courses, the defamation of their characters, and sometimes, but sadly only sometimes, the vindication of their reputations and their principles."[5] Kennedy was, of course, speaking of white men. Still, this description of courage applies quite well to those African American women who speak so well in this book.

Notes

Preface

1. John F. Kennedy, *Profiles in Courage* (New York: Harper and Brothers, 1961).

Chapter 1. The Lives of Black Women

1. Philomena Essed, *Understanding Everyday Racism: An Interdisciplinary Theory* (Newbury Park, CA: Sage, 1991), p. 54.

2. See Bart Landry, *The New Black Middle Class* (Berkeley and Los Angeles: University of California Press, 1987), pp. 2–10.

3. Philomena Essed, *Everyday Racism: Reports from Women of Two Cultures* (Claremont, CA: Hunter House, 1990).

4. Kesho Yvonne Scott, *The Habit of Surviving* (New York: Ballantine, 1991).

5. E. Franklin Frazier, *Black Bourgeoisie* (New York: Free Press, 1957), p. 221.

6. Ibid., p. 222.

7. Daniel Patrick Moynihan, *The Negro Family: The Case for National Action* (Washington, DC: Government Printing Office, 1965), p. 29.

8. Patricia Hill Collins, *Black Feminist Thought: Knowledge, Consciousness and the Politics of Empowerment* (Boston: Unwin Hyman, 1990), pp. 67–90; see also Patricia Morton, *Disfigured Images* (New York: Praeger, 1991).

9. Kim Marie Vaz, "Organization of the Anthology," in *Black Women in America,* ed. Kim Marie Vaz (Thousand Oaks, CA: Sage, 1995), pp. xv–xvi.

10. Diane Roberts, *The Myth of Aunt Jemima: Representations of Race and Region* (New York: Routledge, 1994), p. 5.

11. Elizabeth Hadley Freydberg, "Sapphires, Spitfires, Sluts, and Superbitches: Aframericans and Latinas in Contemporary American Film," in *Black Women in America,* ed. Kim Marie Vaz (Thousand Oaks, CA: Sage, 1995), pp. 222-243.

12. Mary E. Young, *Mules and Dragons: Popular Culture Images in the Selected Writings of African-American and Chinese-American Women Writers* (Westport, CT: Greenwood Press, 1993), pp. 19-45.

13. bell hooks, "Save Your Breath, Sisters," *New York Times,* January 7, 1996, p. E19.

14. Quoted in Alice Mayall and Diana H. Russell, "Racism in Pornography," in *Gender, Race and Class in Media,* ed. Gail Dines and Jean M. Humez (Thousand Oaks, CA: Sage, 1995), p. 291.

15. Herbert Lockyer, *The Women of the Bible* (Grand Rapids, MI: Zondervan, 1967), p. 73.

16. Ibid., pp. 73ff.

17. Ibid., p. 152.

18. Ibid., pp. 52–53.

19. Carolyn M. West, "Mammy, Sapphire, and Jezebel: Historical Images of Black Women and Their Implications for Psychotherapy," *Psychotherapy* 32 (fall 1995): 458–466.

20. Joe R. Feagin and Hernán Vera, *White Racism: The Basics* (New York: Routledge, 1995), pp. 6–29.

21. Ruth Frankenberg, *White Women, Race Matters* (Minneapolis: University of Minnesota Press, 1993), pp. 228–229.

22. In George L. Stearns, ed., *The Equality of All Men before the Law Claimed and Defended* (Boston, 1865), p. 38, as quoted in Robert R. Dykstra, *Bright Radical Star* (Cambridge: Harvard University Press, 1993), p. 269.

23. Robert Blauner, *Racial Oppression in America* (New York: Harper and Row, 1972), p. 21.

24. Ralph Ellison, *Invisible Man* (1952; reprint, New York: Vintage Books, 1989), p. 3.

25. Joe R. Feagin, Hernán Vera, and Nikitah Imani, *The Agony of Education: Black Students at White Colleges and Universities* (New York: Routledge, 1996), p. 14.

26. Jessica Benjamin, *The Bonds of Love: Psychoanalysis, Feminism, and the Problem of Domination* (New York: Pantheon, 1988), pp. 12, 15.

27. Feagin, Vera, and Imani, *The Agony of Education,* pp. 14–15.

28. William H. Grier and Price M. Cobbs, *Black Rage* (New York: Basic Books, 1968), p. 210.

29. Stanley Diamond, "The Beautiful and the Ugly Are One Thing, the Sublime Another: A Reflection on Culture," *Cultural Anthropological: Journal of the Society for Cultural Anthropology* 22 (May 1987): 268.

30. Murray Webster, Jr., and James E. Driskell, Jr., "Beauty as Status," *American Journal of Sociology* 89 (July 1983): 140–165.

31. See Camille O. Cosby, *Television's Imageable Influences* (Lanham, MD: University Press of America, 1994).

32. See Feagin, Vera, and Imani, *The Agony of Education;* Anthony R. D'Augelli and Scott L. Hershberger, "African American Undergraduates on a Predominantly White Campus: Academic Factors, Social Networks and Campus Climate," *Journal of Negro Education* 62 (winter 1993): 67–81.

33. See Cosby, *Television's Imageable Influences.*

34. See Mustapha Chelbi, *Culture et mémoire collective au Maghreb* (Paris: Académie Européenne du livre, 1990).

35. Sam Fullwood, III, "Black Women Seen as Reluctant to Claim Harassment," *Los Angeles Times,* October 10, 1991, p. A8.

36. See Michelene Ridley Malson, "Black Women's Sex Roles: The Social Context for a New Ideology," *Journal of Social Issues* 39 (fall 1989): 67–81; Mamie E. Locke, "From Three-Fifths to Zero: Implications of the Constitution for African American Women, 1787–1870," *Women and Politics* 10 (spring 1990): 33–46.

37. Sam Roberts, "Black Women Graduates Outpace Male Counterparts," *New York Times,* October 31, 1994, p. A12.

38. We have kept respondents anonymous and have not used their names or specific place names. Quotes have been punctuated for clarity. A few have also been lightly edited; occasionally we have deleted filler words like "uh" and "you know," eliminated false starts, used common written language for a few pronunciation variations, or (rarely) edited a word for grammatical reasons.

39. Sheila T. Gregory, *Black Women in the Academy: The Secrets to Success and Achievement* (Lanham: University Press of America, 1995).

40. A twofer is "a card or ticket entitling the holder to purchase one or two tickets to a theatrical performance at a reduced price. [from the phrase *two for* (the price of one, a nickel, etc.)]." *Webster's Encyclopedic Unabridged Dictionary of the English Language* (New York: Gramercy, 1989), p. 1531.

41. Roberts, "Black Women Graduates Outpace Male Counterparts"; see also Dorothy J. Gaiter, "The Gender Divide: Black Women's Gains in Corporate America Outstrip Black Men's," *Wall Street Journal,* March 8, 1994, p. A1.

42. Robert Staples and Leanor Boulin Johnson, *Black Families at the Crossroads: Challenges and Prospects* (San Francisco: Jossey-Bass, 1993), p. 70.

43. Elizabeth Fox-Genovese, *Within the Plantation Household* (Chapel Hill: The University of North Carolina Press, 1988).

44. Linda Brent, *Incidents in the Life of a Slave Girl: Written by Herself,* ed. Maria Child (Boston: published for the author, 1861); Vaz, "Organization of the Anthology."

45. On media distortion, see Wahneema Lubiano, "Black Ladies, Welfare Queens, and State Minstrels," in *Race-ing Justice, En-gendering Power,* ed. T. Morrison (New York: Pantheon Books, 1992), pp. 323–363.

46. Pierre Nora, quoted in Jacques le Goff, *Histoire et Mémoire* (Paris: Édition Gallimard, 1988), p. 170, our translation.

47. See, for example, Peggye Dilworth-Anderson, "Extended Kin Networks in Black Families," *Generations* 17 (summer 1992): 29–32.

48. This paragraph draws on Bonnie L. Mitchell and Joe R. Feagin, "America's Racial-Ethnic Cultures: Opposition within a Mythical Melting Pot," in *Toward the Multicultural University,* ed. Benjamin Bowser, Terry Jones, and Gale Auletta-Young (Westport, CT: Praeger, 1995), pp. 65–86.

49. Bernice McNair Barnett, "Black Women's Collectivist Movement Organizations: Their Struggles during the 'Doldrums,' " in *Feminist Organizations: Harvest of the New Women's Movement,* ed. Myra M. Feree and Patricia Y. Martin (Philadelphia: Temple University Press, 1995), p. 100.

50. Beverlyn Lundy Allen, "Black Female Leadership: A Preliminary Step toward an Alternative Theory," unpublished Ph.D. dissertation, Iowa State University, Ames, Iowa, 1995, p. 54. References are omitted.

51. *Statistical Abstract of the United States* (Washington, DC: Government Printing Office, 1994), p. 108. The data are for 1991.

52. Paul Connerton, *How Societies Remember* (Cambridge: Cambridge University Press, 1989), p. 2.

53. Jean F. Brierre, *Les Aieules,* trans. Mercer Cook (Port-au-Prince, Haiti: éditions Henri Deschamps, 1950), p. 13.

54. See Geneviève Fabre and Robert O'Meally, eds., *History and Memory in African American Culture* (New York: Oxford University Press, 1994).

55. See Joe R. Feagin and Melvin P. Sikes, *Living with Racism: The Black Middle-Class Experience* (Boston: Beacon, 1994), pp. 12–20.

56. Scott, *The Habit of Surviving.*

57. Michel-Rolph Trouillot, *Silencing the Past* (Boston: Beacon, 1995).

58. Most were interviewed individually in this research project.

59. There were eleven focus groups. The total number includes two moderator-participants. In all studies we have used, with one exception, black interviewers and moderators.

60. We have taken care to insure that we have a broad group of women (and men) representing various groups in the middle class. We promised respondents that we would keep their names anonymous. In a few places in later chapters we also draw on a small number of interviews with black (and one white female) informants who clarified certain key points for us.

61. See, for example, William J. Wilson, *The Declining Significance of Race* (Chicago: University of Chicago Press, 1978).

62. See Thomas B. Edsall and Mary D. Edsall, "When the Official Subject Is Presidential Politics, Taxes, Welfare, Crime, Rights, or Values—the Real Subject is Race," *Atlantic,* May 1991, 53–55.

63. W.E.B. Du Bois, *The Souls of Black Folk* (1903; reprint, New York: Knopf, 1993).

Chapter 2. Black Women at Work

1. See Joe R. Feagin and Melvin P. Sikes, *Living with Racism: The Black Middle-Class Experience* (Boston: Beacon, 1994), pp. 12–20.

2. See Jacques Ellul, *Déviances et déviants dans notre société intolérante* (Toulouse: Éditions érès, 1992), p. 54.

3. Joy James and Ruth Farmer, eds., *Spirit, Space, and Survival: African American Women in (White) Academe* (New York: Routledge, 1993).

4. Institute for the Study of Social Change, *The Diversity Project: Final Report* (Berkeley and Los Angeles: University of California Press, 1991), p. 40.

5. For examples, see Feagin and Sikes, *Living with Racism,* chapters 4–5.

6. The next two paragraphs draw on Joe R. Feagin and Hernán Vera, *White Racism: The Basics* (New York: Routledge, 1995).

7. Winthrop Jordan, *The White Man's Burden: Historical Origins of Racism in the United States* (New York: Oxford University Press, 1974), p. 80.

8. Feagin and Vera, *White Racism,* pp. 114–124.

9. Norma J. Burgess and Hayward D. Horton, "African American Women and Work: A Socio-Historical Perspective," *Journal of Family History* 18 (January 1993): 53–63.

10. Joan E. Cashin, "Black Families in the Old Northwest," *Journal of the Early Republic* 15 (fall 1995): 468.

11. Ibid., p. 470.

12. Shannon Dortch, "The Earnings Gap in Black and White," *American Demographics* 16 (April 1994): 18-20. See also Melvin E. Thomas, Cedric Herring, and Hayward Derrick Horton, "Discrimination over the Life Course: A Synthetic Cohort Analysis of Earnings Differences between Black and White Males, 1940-1990," *Social Problems* 41 (November 1994): 608-629.

13. Recent research indicates that embracing nontraditional gender roles results in a decrease in the quality of marital life. See Paul R. Amato and Alan Booth, "Changes in Gender Role Attitudes and Perceived Marital Quality," *American Sociological Review* 60 (February 1995): 58–66. For one illustration of the consequence of gender role shifts for women, see Maggie Mahar, "Trading Places," *Working Woman* 17 (July 1992): 56–71.

14. Amato and Booth, "Changes in Gender Role Attitudes," 58.

15. Generally speaking, gender arrangements among enslaved African Americans were not similar to those of whites at the time. Cashin, "Black Families in the Old Northwest," pp. 453–458; Elizabeth Fox-Genovese, *Within the Plantation Household* (Chapel Hill: The University of North Carolina Press, 1988), pp. 29–30.

16. Fox-Genovese, *Within the Plantation Household,* p. 373.

17. See Robert Staples, *Black Women in America* (Chicago: Nelson-Hall, 1973), p. 16.

18. William Julius Wilson, *The Truly Disadvantaged: The Inner City, the Underclass, and Public Policy* (Chicago: University of Chicago Press, 1987), pp. 145–146.

19. Barbara Omolade, *The Rising Song of African American Women* (New York: Routledge, 1994), p. 14.

20. For evidence, see Feagin and Vera, *White Racism.*

21. Daniel Patrick Moynihan, *The Negro Family: The Case for National Action* (Washington, DC: Government Printing Office, 1965), p. 30.

22. See Mary E. Young, *Mules and Dragons: Popular Culture Images in the Selected Writings of African-American and Chinese-American Women Writers* (Westport, CT: Greenwood Press, 1993), pp. 19–45; Burgess and Horton, "African American Women and Work"; Cashin, "Black Families in the Old Northwest," p. 470; Feagin and Vera, *White Racism.*

23. U.S. Senate Committee on the Judiciary, *Nomination of Clarence Thomas to be Associate Justice of the Supreme Court of the United States,* 102d Cong., 1st sess., vol. 4 (Washington, DC: Government Printing Office, 1991), p. 227.

24. Ibid., pp. 431–433; see also Bridget A. Aldaraca, "On the Use of Medical Diagnosis as Name-Calling: Anita F. Hill and the Rediscovery of 'Erotomania', " in *Black Women in America,* ed. Kim Marie Vaz (Thousand Oaks, CA: Sage, 1995), pp. 206–221.

25. Senate Committee, *Nomination of Clarence Thomas,* p. 559.

26. We are indebted to Karyn McKinney for underscoring this point in discussions with us.

Chapter 3. Black Beauty in a Whitewashed World

1. Émile Roumer (1903–1988) is a Haitian poet.

2. Marie-Dominique Le Rumeur, "La femme dans l'univers romanesque de Gérard Étienne," *Francographies* 2 (Annual 1993): 7. There are exceptions to the Caribbean rule of positive representations of darker women. On racist beauty pageants and the apparent preference for light skin in Jamaica, see Natasha B. Barnes, "Face of the Nation: Race, Nationalisms and Identities in Jamaican Beauty Pageants," *Massachusetts Review* 35 (autumn–winter 1994): 471–492.

3. Régine Latortue shows this observation to be true, particularly for women in the working classes. See "Le discours de la nature: la femme noire dans la littérature haïtienne," *Notre Librairie* 73 (January–March 1984): 65–69; Le Rumeur, "La femme dans l'univers romanesque de Gérard Étienne," 7–15.

4. Le Rumeur, "La femme dans l'univers romanesque de Gérard Étienne," 7.

5. Murray Webster, Jr., and James E. Driskell, Jr., "Beauty as Status," *American Journal of Sociology* 89 (July 1983): 140–165; Anthony Synnott, "Truth and Consequences, Mirrors and Masks—Part I: A Sociology of Beauty and the Face," *British Journal of Sociology* 40 (December 1989): 607–636.

6. Webster and Driskell, "Beauty as Status," 162.

7. Iris M. Young, *Justice and the Politics of Difference* (Princeton: Princeton University Press, 1990), p. 128.

8. Ibid., p. 129.

9. bell hooks, *Outlaw Culture* (New York: Routledge, 1994), pp. 173–182.

10. William H. Grier and Price M. Cobbs, *Black Rage* (New York: Basic Books, 1968), p. 210.

11. Anthony Synnott, "Shame and Glory: A Sociology of Hair," *British Jour-*

nal of Sociology 38 (September 1987): 381–413; Synnott, "Truth and Conse-quences."

12. Frantz Fanon, *Peau noire, masques blancs* (Paris: Éditions du Seuil, 1952), p. 8.

13. Grier and Cobbs, *Black Rage,* pp. 42–43.

14. Kenneth B. Clark, *Prejudice and Your Child* (Boston: Beacon), p. 19.

15. Gordon W. Allport, *The Nature of Prejudice* (Cambridge, MA: Addison-Wesley, 1954), p. 302.

16. Ibid., p. 303.

17. Darlene Powell Hopson and Derek S. Hopson, *Different and Wonderful: Raising Black Children in a Race-Conscious Society* (New York: Fireside, 1992), p. xxii; Darlene Powell Hopson and Derek S. Hopson, "Implication of Doll Color Preferences among Black Preschool Children and White Preschool Children," in *African American Psychology,* ed. A. Kathleen Hoard Burlew, W. Curtis Banks, Harriette Pipes McAdoo, and Daudi Ajani ya Azibo (Newbury Park, CA: Sage, 1992), pp. 183–189.

18. One reviewer of this chapter, who works at a day care center, pointed out that white children there sometimes pick black dolls. One white child regularly preferred a black female doll, which she called "baby Jesus."

19. See Webster and Driskell, "Beauty as Status."

20. Naomi Wolf, *The Beauty Myth* (New York: Doubleday, 1991), p. 18.

21. bell hooks, *Ain't I a Woman: Black Women and Feminism* (Boston: South End Press, 1985), p. 40.

22. See Kathy Russell, Midge Wilson, and Ron Hall, *The Color Complex: The Politics of Skin Color among African Americans* (New York: Harcourt, 1992).

23. Sumru Erkut and Fern Marx, "Raising Competent Girls: An Exploratory Study of Diversity in Girls' Views of Liking One's Self," Final Report to the Remmer Family Foundation. Center for Research on Women, Wellesley College, Wellesley, MA, 1995, pp. 8–16.

24. Ibid., p. 10.

25. Philomena Essed, *Everyday Racism: Reports from Women of Two Cultures* (Claremont, CA: Hunter House, 1990), p. 145.

26. Quoted in Wendy Chapkis, *Beauty Secrets: Women and the Politics of Appearance* (Boston: South End Press, 1986), p. 193.

27. We are indebted to Karyn McKinney for this point.

28. Arthur J. Norton and Louisa F. Miller, *Marriage, Divorce and Remarriage in the 1990's* (Washington, DC: U.S. Department of Commerce, 1992), pp. 3–5.

29. Ibid.; see also Robert Joseph Taylor, Linda M. Chatters, M. Belinda Tucker, and Edith Lewis, "Developments in Research on Black Families: A Decade Review," in *Contemporary Families: Looking Forward, Looking Back,* ed. Alan Booth (Minneapolis: National Council on Family Relations, 1991), pp. 275–296.

30. Stanley Diamond, "The Beautiful and the Ugly Are One Thing, the

Sublime Another: A Reflection on Culture," *Cultural Anthropological: Journal of the Society for Cultural Anthropology* 22 (May 1987): 268.

31. Ibid.

32. Webster and Driskell, "Beauty as Status," 162.

33. Survey data showing most whites have great trouble even with the hypothetical idea of a close relative dating or marrying an African American provide support for this point. For other evidence, see Joe R. Feagin and Hernán Vera, *White Racism: The Basics* (New York: Routledge, 1995).

34. Grier and Cobbs, *Black Rage,* p. 46.

Chapter 4. Common Myths and Media Images of Black Women

1. Richard and Judy Dockrey Young, eds., *African-American Folktales* (Little Rock: August House, 1993), p. 11.

2. See also Henry Louis Gates, Jr., *The Signifying Monkey* (New York: Oxford University Press, 1988), pp. 4–5.

3. Not all the childhood stories remembered by black and white Americans have similar meanings. Some childhood stories like the famous Br'er Rabbit account have varying meanings. As captured by white recorders, they may simply be entertaining stories in which a small animal outwits a larger antagonist, albeit with a caricatured African American telling the stories. However, for generations of African Americans these trickster stories—brought originally by enslaved Africans to North America—have had much deeper meanings.

4. Lin Farley, *Sexual Shakedown* (New York: McGraw-Hill, 1978), p. 14.

5. John Dollard, *Caste and Class in a Southern Town* (Thousand Oaks, CA: Doubleday, 1949), p. 143.

6. Ibid., p. 144.

7. bell hooks, *Outlaw Culture* (New York: Routledge, 1994).

8. Robert Staples, "Social Inequality and Black Sexual Pathology: The Essential Relationship," *The Black Scholar* 21 (summer 1979): 29–37.

9. Dollard, *Caste and Class in a Southern Town,* pp. 136–160.

10. On media representations see Stuart Hall, "The Whites of Their Eyes," in *Gender, Race and Class in Media: A Text-Reader,* ed. Gail Dines and Jean M. Humez (Thousand Oaks, CA: Sage, 1995), pp. 18–27; Carol Martindale, "Newspaper Stereotypes of African Americans," in *Images That Injure: Pictorial Stereotypes in the Media,* ed. Paul Martin Lester (Westport, CT: Praeger, 1996), pp. 21–25.

11. For more discussion of this and related issues, see Leslie Inniss and Joe R. Feagin, "The Bill Cosby Television Show: The View from the Black Middle Class," *Journal of Black Studies* 25 (July 1995): 692–711. In this chapter we draw a little on this article.

12. Patricia Hill Collins, *Black Feminist Thought: Knowledge, Consciousness, and the Politics of Empowerment* (Boston: Unwin Hyman, 1990), p. 67.

13. Pictures of nineteenth-century Hawaiians show them to be "thin, healthy women and tall. . . . It was the replacement of native foods with a typical Western diet [when Captain Cook arrived in Hawaii in 1778] that really did [them] in." See "Undoing the Damage: Can We Reverse the Ill Effects of a Lifetime of Eating a Meat-Based Diet?" *Vegetarian Times* 196 (December 1993): 58.

14. A careful search of the literature yielded no significant research on these issues.

15. See Ruth Elizabeth Burks,"Intimations of Invisibility: Black Women and Contemporary Hollywood Cinema," in *Mediated Messages and African American Culture,* ed. Bernice T. Berry and Carmen L. Manning-Miller (Thousand Oaks, CA: Sage, 1996), pp. 24–39.

16. Polly E. McLean, "Mass Communication, Popular Culture, and Racism," in *Racism and Anti-Racism in World Perspective,* ed. Benjamin P. Bowser (Thousand Oaks, CA: Sage, 1995), p. 86.

17. See Joe R. Feagin and Hernán Vera, *White Racism: The Basics* (New York: Routledge, 1995), especially chapters 1 and 7.

18. Sut Jhally and Justin Lewis, *Enlightened Racism* (Boulder, CO: Westview Press, 1992), p. 110.

19. Jan Rhodes, "The Visibility of Race and Media History," in *Gender, Race and Class in Media: A Text Reader,* ed. Gail Dines and Jean M. Humez (Thousand Oaks, CA: Sage, 1995), p. 34.

20. "Scandalous success."

Chapter 5. Distancing White Women

1. See Philomena Essed, *Understanding Everyday Racism* (Newbury Park: Sage, 1991).

2. Joe R. Feagin and Melvin P. Sikes, *Living with Racism: The Black Middle-Class Experience* (Boston: Beacon, 1994).

3. Audre Lorde, "An Open Letter to Mary Daly," in *This Bridge Called My Back: Writings by Radical Women of Color,* ed. Cherríe Moraga and Gloria Anzaldúa (Watertown, MA: Persephone Press, 1981), pp. 94–97.

4. Cited in *Race Relations Reporter,* vol 4, no. 10, December 15, 1996, p. 1.

5. An analysis of historical tensions between black and white women is in Midge Wilson and Kathy Russell, *Divided Sisters: Bridging the Gap Between Black Women and White Women* (New York: Anchor Books, 1996), pp. 12–35; Vron Ware, *Beyond the Pale: White Women, Racism and History* (London: Verso, 1992); see also Thomas Kochman, *Black and White Styles in Conflict* (Chicago: University of Chicago Press, 1981).

6. Elizabeth Fox-Genovese, *Within the Plantation Household* (Chapel Hill: The University of North Carolina Press, 1988), pp. 97, 349.

7. bell hooks, *Ain't I a Woman: Black Women and Feminism* (Boston: South End Press, 1982), pp. 119–158.

8. Judith Rollins, "Employing a Domestic: A Case of Female Parasitism" (paper presented at the annual meetings of the American Sociological Association, August 1984), p. 4. See Judith Rollins, *Between Women* (Philadelphia: Temple University Press, 1985).

9. Anna Maria Chupa, *Anne, the White Woman in Contemporary African-American Fiction: Archetypes, Stereotypes and Characterizations* (New York: Greenwood Press, 1990), p. xiv.

10. Ralph Ellison, *Invisible Man* (1952; reprint, New York: Vintage Books, 1989), p. 3.

11. See Ellis Cose, *The Rage of a Privileged Class* (New York: HarperCollins, 1993); and Joe R. Feagin, Hernán Vera, and Nikitah Imani, *The Agony of Education: Black Students at White Colleges and Universities* (New York: Routledge, 1996).

12. Ruth Frankenberg, *White Women, Race Matters* (Minneapolis: University of Minnesota Press, 1993), pp. 228–229.

13. Vivian V. Gordon, *Black Women: Feminism and Black Liberation* (Chicago: Third World Press, 1987), p. 40.

14. See Sharon F. Griffin, "Double Struggle: Racism and Sexism Can Be Dual Burdens for Many Black Women," *San Diego Union-Tribune,* April 16, 1993, p. E-1.

15. See Edward Ransford and Jon Miller, "Race, Sex and Feminist Outlooks," *American Sociological Review* 48 (February 1983): 51–52; Marjorie R. Hershey, "Racial Difference in Sex-Role Identities and Sex Stereotyping," *Social Science Quarterly* 58 (March 1978): 583–596.

16. See Lynda Dickson, "The Future of Marriage and Family in Black America," *Journal of Black Studies* 23 (June 1993): 472–491; Robert Staples and Leanor Boulin Johnson, *Black Families at the Crossroads: Challenges and Prospects* (San Francisco: Jossey-Bass, 1993).

17. See Betty Friedan, *The Feminine Mystique* (New York: Dell Books, 1963), pp. 11–30.

18. Griffin, "Double Struggle," p. E-1.

19. See also Wilson and Russell, *Divided Sisters;* Ware, *Beyond the Pale.*

20. These quotes are from Tiffany Hogan, "Crossing the Line: The Role of Racial Differences in Black and White Women's Friendships," Ph.D. dissertation, University of Florida, 1997. Used by permission.

21. Barbara Phillips Sullivan, "The Song That Never Ends: New Verses about Affirmative Action," *Southern University Law Review* 23 (winter, 1996): 158–159. Also of interest is Sherry Stone, "Black Women Say NOW Is Irrelevant to Their Concerns," *Philadelphia Tribune,* December 8, 1995, p. 8A.

22. Gordon, *Black Women,* p. 39.

23. Ibid., p. 40.

Chapter 6. Black Families

1. See Joe R. Feagin, "The Kinship Ties of Negro Urbanites," *Social Science Quarterly* 49 (1968): 660–665; Robert Staples and Leanor Boulin Johnson, *Black Families at the Crossroads: Challenges and Prospects* (San Francisco: Jossey-Bass, 1993).

2. Elmer P. Martin and Joanne Mitchell Martin, *The Black Extended Family* (Chicago: University of Chicago Press, 1978), p. 1.

3. Ibid.

4. Harriette Pipes McAdoo, "Ethnic Families: Strengths That Are Found in Diversity," in *Family Ethnicity: Strengths in Diversity,* ed. Harriette Pipes McAdoo (Newbury Park, CA: Sage, 1993), p. 10.

5. Daniel Patrick Moynihan, *The Negro Family: The Case for National Action* (Washington, DC: Government Printing Office, 1965).

6. See Mark Peffley, Jon Hurwitz, and Paul M. Sniderman, "Racial Stereotypes and Whites' Political Views of Blacks in the Context of Welfare and Crime," *American Journal of Political Science* 41 (January 1997): 34–37.

7. Melvin N. Wilson, Christine Greene-Bates, LaMont McKim, Faith Simmons, Tiffany Askew, Judith Curry-El, and Ivora D. Hinton, "African American Family Life: The Dynamics of Interactions, Relationships, and Roles," *New Directions for Child Development* 68 (summer 1995): 5, 6; Shirley J. Hatchett and James S. Jackson, "African American Extended Kin Systems: An Assessment," in *Family Ethnicity: Strengths in Diversity,* ed. Hariette Pipes McAdoo (Newbury Park, CA: Sage, 1993), pp. 90–108.

8. Staples and Johnson, *Black Families at the Crossroads,* pp. 194–195.

9. See Robert Staples, *The Black Family: Essays and Studies* (Belmont, CA: Wadsworth, 1994); William H. Grier and Price M. Cobbs, *Black Rage* (New York: Basic Books, 1968); Sheila M. Littlejohn-Blake and Carol Anderson Darling, "Understanding the Strengths of African American Families," *Journal of Black Studies* 23 (June 1993): 460–471; Robert Joseph Taylor, "Need for Support and Family Involvement among Black Americans," *Journal of Marriage and the Family* 52 (August 1990): 588.

10. See Linda M. Chatters, Robert Joseph Taylor, and Rukmalie Jayakody, "Fictive Kinship Relations in Black Extended Families," *Journal of Comparative Family Studies* 25 (autumn 1994): 297–312.

11. Peggye Dilworth-Anderson, "Extended Kin Networks in Black Families," *Generations* 17 (summer 1992): 29.

12. Taylor, "Need for Support and Family Involvement among Black Americans," p. 588.

13. Chatters, Taylor, and Jayakody, "Fictive Kinship Relations in Black Extended Families."

14. McAdoo, "Ethnic Families," p. 10.

15. For further discussion see Yanick St. Jean and Joe R. Feagin, "The Family Costs of White Racism: The Case of African American Families," *Journal of Comparative Family Studies* 29 (forthcoming, 1998) This brief quote and one other in this chapter also appear there.

16. Herbert G. Gutman, *The Black Family in Slavery and Freedom, 1750–1925* (New York: Vintage Books, 1976); Eugene D. Genovese, *Roll, Jordan, Roll: The World the Slaves Made* (New York: Random House, 1974); James Jackson, *Life in Black America* (Newbury Park, CA: Sage, 1991).

17. John W. Blassingame, *The Slave Community: Plantation Life in the Antebellum South* (New York: Oxford University Press, 1979), p. 151.

18. Staples and Johnson, *Black Families at the Crossroads,* pp. 194–195; Littlejohn-Blake and Darling, "Understanding the Strengths of African American Families"; R. Hill, *Strengths of Black Families* (New York: National Urban League, 1973).

19. Lynda Dickson, "The Future of Marriage and Family in Black America," *Journal of Black Studies* 23 (June 1993): 473.

20. See Dilworth-Anderson, "Extended Kin Networks in Black Families, pp. 29–32.

21. See McAdoo, Introduction, *Family Ethnicity,* p. ix.

22. Joe R. Feagin, Kevin Early, and Karyn D. McKinney, "The Many Costs of Discrimination," University of Florida, unpublished research paper, 1997.

23. In our interviews the questions we asked mostly focused on discrimination and responses to it, which left only modest room in respondents' comments for more general discussions of specific cultural practices. Comments beyond the matters of discrimination were often made, and we have drawn on them, but they are not as extensive as we might have wished.

24. Staples and Johnson, *Black Families at the Crossroads,* pp. 209–210.

25. Philomena Essed, *Everyday Racism: Reports from Women of Two Cultures* (Claremont, CA: Hunter House, 1990).

26. See Loic Wacquant and Pierre Bourdieu, *An Invitation to Reflexive Sociology* (Chicago: University of Chicago Press, 1992).

27. Frederick Douglass, *Narrative of the Life of Frederick Douglass An American Slave* (1845; reprint, ed. Benjamin Quarles, Cambridge, MA: Belknap Press, 1967), p. 67.

28. In *Griggs v. Duke Power Co.* (401 U.S. 424 [1971]) the Supreme Court examined a company's education criteria for employment and found that they disqualified more black than white applicants, even though the educational requirements could not be justified as job related.

29. Only 3.8 percent of all self-employed women were black in 1975, and 3.9 percent in 1990. The figures for white women for the same years were, respectively, 94.2 percent and 91.7 percent. Theresa J. Devine, "Characteris-

tics of Self-Employed Women in the United States," *Monthly Labor Review* 117 (March 1994): 23.

30. See Roy L. Brooks, *Integration or Separation? A Strategy for Racial Equality* (Cambridge: Harvard University Press, 1996).

Chapter 7. Motherhood and Families

1. For a discussion of this issue see Elizabeth Brown-Guillory, *Women of Color: Mother-Daughter Relationships in Twentieth Century Literature* (Austin: University of Texas Press, 1996), pp. 228–242.

2. Maurice Halbwachs, *On Collective Memory* (Chicago: University of Chicago Press, 1992), p. 77.

3. Jacques Le Goff, *Histoire et mémoire* (Paris: Éditions Gallimard, 1988), pp. 161–162. Our translation.

4. Halbwachs, *On Collective Memory,* p. 54.

5. This paragraph is based on the experiences of the senior author, who grew up in Haiti.

6. Joan E. Cashin, "Black Families in the Old Northwest," *Journal of the Early Republic* 15 (fall 1995): 470.

7. See Le Goff, *Histoire et mémoire,* p. 161.

8. St. Clair Drake, *Black Folk Here and There* (Los Angeles: UCLA Center for Afro-American Studies, 1987), p. xv.

9. We are indebted here to discussions with Merlinda Gallegos.

10. See Hariette Pipes McAdoo, "Ethnic Families: Strengths That Are Found in Diversity," in *Family Ethnicity: Strengths in Diversity,* ed. Hariette Pipes McAdoo (Newbury Park, CA: Sage, 1993), pp. 3–14.

11. Le Goff, *Histoire et mémoire,* p. 108. Our translation.

12. Michel-Rolph Trouillot, *Silencing the Past* (Boston: Beacon, 1995).

13. See Robert N. Bellah, Richard Madsen, William M. Sullivan, Ann Swidler, and Steven M. Tipton, *Habits of the Heart* (Berkeley and Los Angeles: University of California Press, 1985), pp. 152–155.

14. See Stanley Lieberson and Kelly S. Mikelson, "Distinctive African American Names: An Experimental, Historical, and Linguistic Analysis of Innovation," *American Sociological Review* 60 (December 1995): 928-946.

15. Le Goff asks whether the involvement of women here represents a feminine function of preservation of remembrance or a conquest of the memory of the group by feminism. *Histoire et mémoire,* p. 162.

Chapter 8. Finale

1. Barbara Omolade, *The Rising Song of African American Women* (New York: Routledge, 1994), p. 203.

2. Frank R. Nugent, "Gone With the Wind," *New York Times,* December 20, 1939, p. 31.

3. Abraham Lincoln, as quoted in John F. Kennedy, *Profiles in Courage* (New York: Harper and Brothers, 1961), p. ix–x.

4. Linda Brent, *Incidents in the Life of a Slave Girl: Written by Herself,* ed. Maria Child (Boston: Published for the author, 1861), p. 69.

5. Kennedy, *Profiles in Courage,* p. 1.

Index

About the Authors

Yanick St. Jean is an Assistant Professor in the Department of Sociology at the University of Nevada, Las Vegas, where she joined the faculty in 1992 after receiving her doctorate in sociology from the University of Texas at Austin. St. Jean has published articles on the experiences of Haitian immigrants and African American women with racism. Born and raised in Haiti, she has lived in the United States for more than twenty-nine years.

Joe R. Feagin is the Graduate Research Professor in the Department of Sociology at the University of Florida. For thirty years he has done extensive research on racial and gender discrimination issues, published (with coauthors) in *Racial and Ethnic Relations* (fifth edition, Prentice-Hall, 1996), *Living with Racism: The Black Middle Class Experience* (Beacon, 1994), *White Racism: The Basics* (Routledge, 1995), and *The Agony of Education: Black Students at White Colleges and Universities* (Routledge, 1996). Feagin has served as Scholar-in-Residence at the U.S. Commission on Civil Rights. An earlier book, *Ghetto Revolts* (Macmillan, 1973), was nominated for a Pulitzer Prize.

5/98

B.C.

BAKER & TAYLOR